SUPER STOKED

HOW PUNK ROCK TAUGHT ME TO STAND OUT IN THE BUSINESS WORLD

BY JAMES SWANSON

ISBN: 978-1-959457-03-9 (paperback)
Library of Congress Control Number: 2025905781

Published in the United States by:
Blue Jay Ink, 451 A East Ojai Ave., Ojai, California 93023

THIS ONE'S FOR CHARLIE.

TABLE OF CONTENTS

FOREWORD

"Hell no, no premonition could have seen this."
- *Tim Armstrong of Rancid, in song*

I cannot emphasize enough that this book should not exist. I could have avoided editing an epic tale of dressing up a 150-foot-tall Statue of Liberty replica with a hockey jersey. I could have skipped who knows how many pages of the jabbing, *How cool is it to be sticking signage all over outfield walls* at my favorite baseball stadiums? Repeatedly. Oh, and don't forget about all the football stadiums and basketball arenas, too. And I wouldn't need my elbow nudged, figuratively, with reminders that my friend James Swanson met Mike Ness of Social Distortion, and other punk rock legends, all *because of his work.*

Writing now, to this day I shake my head at what James pulled off with Screaming Images. I get tired just thinking about all the work it required. It all started on a small bedroom desk and loosely arranged agreements for projects he hoped for with the likes of the Carolina Panthers football team. Nothing at that point was set in stone. With no college degree or previous business management experience – and with no financial assistance or even personal savings – it was super easy to dismiss James and his company early on.

When he sold S.I. two decades later, the company employed 50 people in a 20,000-square-foot print facility that designed, produced, and installed large-format graphics for sports teams, big events, and casinos all over the United States. That fact alone is itself a neat story.

Add the backstory, and you have a thorough, epic tale with a lot of blood, sweat, tears, and hoots 'n' hollers along the way. You see, we're lucky to be alive, James and I. This was no tale of instant riches. The car crashes, the brawls, the numerous near-misses, the police – always, it seemed – the cops everywhere. The arrests. The jail time. Oh, the incarcerations, in different cities and jurisdictions. Calling a parent in the wee hours to pick you up from jail.

Being over 21 with no car, living with a parent. Good times!

If our friend Diana – who introduced us – asked for my impression of James when we first met in the mid-80s in the Valley suburb of Los Angeles, I probably would have shrugged my shoulders and said, *surfer-party dude.* Maybe just *party dude.*

Not *future entrepreneur.* Not *successful business executive.* That's for damn sure.

* * *

Diana was an ex when I called her one Sunday afternoon in June 1985, bored, asking what might be exciting for the evening. My first year of college just ended and I was ready for some fun. "Going to a stupid-fucking softball game," she said. Without hesitation I replied, "I want to go to a stupid-fucking softball game." I was only trying to make her feel better. So off to Lanark Park we went, a short jump over Santa Susana Pass from where we lived in Simi Valley, a suburb northwest of Los Angeles – to the big park in Canoga Park, just to watch a softball game. Involving James, her new boyfriend. That part alone seemed intriguing. I played a lot of softball, and wondered who in the Valley she might be seeing. Who happened to play softball like me.

I honestly can't with words properly describe what I saw upon arrival. The park was familiar – I grew up a few miles down the road and had been to this particular ball diamond many times. The night lights were on, but the field was not chalked, indicating practice or scrimmage, not organized league game. Big grandstand, lots of park lingerers all around like there always seems to be in that low-income neighborhood. Then I met the players. Johnny, who went by "Rotten" in honor of the Sex Pistols' founder, seemed pretty normal and friendly. There was the barrel-chested dude with curly red hair they called "D"; and always nearby was his buddy Tim, the Detroit Tigers fanatic. Those two looked like real ballplayers.

My next memory must be like what Pete Townshend of the Who thought when he first met Keith Moon, the insanely wild, legendary drummer. Here was this really skinny guy, taller and way more tan than I was. He wore cleats, of course, ready for play. But the rest of the uniform, well, let's just say we didn't share the same style. He had this blondish, short spiky hair style, which on its own back then was a red flag on the coolness scale in my mind. This was a period when New Wave music challenged the longtime domination of rock music among us young-uns. (Years later, James would cover the spikes with a do-rag bandana, for that pirate look always popular on ballfields. Haha.)

There were the extremely long and baggy shorts, *years* ahead of their time (to be mainstreamed by grunge in a few years), in an era when nearly all players wore baseball pants. And topping it all off was a T-shirt, customized with cut-off sleeves, displaying what I think was a band, and if it was, I'd never heard of them. And I knew a lot of bands. He had a Miller Lite beer in one hand and a burning cigarette in the other. James Swanson.

Personality-wise, he could be funny and obnoxious in the same sentence of conversations; and usually louder than necessary. Way before I got into coffee and knew what it meant, this guy seemed over-caffeinated, or maybe just super excited about life. And it wasn't like I was a sedated personality myself. I was hyper, but this was next-level energy. In debate, he could interrupt you mid-sentence with a "No way, man!" in that raspy James voice. Eventually, our debates would become mostly about music, and for James in 1985 that meant punk, punk, punk, and more punk, in an era of Rush, Scorpions, Madonna and Springsteen. To this day I remember a post-game beer-swigging session at Lanark, when someone asked for our top three rock bands ever. All of us offered the typical mix of Beatles-Stones-Who, with maybe a Zeppelin or a Doors tossed in. Then James went. "Rolling Stones, Social Distortion, and Black Flag." We laughed. We mocked him. *Social D before the Beatles and even the Who?* Five years later, Social D was making gold records and growing an audience nationwide.

James had this cockiness, some kind of weird swagger I couldn't put my finger on, except that I think I'd seen it before in the punk rockers who hung out in front of the gym at my high school. It was sort of this, *I'm gonna conquer-the-world* confidence, the rest of the world be damned. *Don't tread on me, because I really don't care.* Things like that. We quickly became good friends because of music and baseball. He spoke my language there, except for the punk rock thing – that phase was to come not long after, thanks to him and our teammate Mike J. For the moment, I was into the Who and Scorpions, and hard rock in general. Diana moved on, but James and I did not.

Over the first few years we played a hell of a lot of ball (and won a lot of games), drank substantially, and sometimes crewed together for an evening of mischief. Now and then we got in trouble. Sometimes, maybe we brawled. Other times, we crashed cars (James and I both, separately of course, as did some of our friends). We were not honor students or choir boys, put it that way. Not at all. In 1985, I most definitely did not link the term *future business executive* with James Swanson. We were born to lose, and destined to fail, all of us.

But James didn't fail. Far from it. To this day, I remain impressed. And mystified about how the hell he pulled it off.

***

Fast-forward almost 40 years, and I'm walking through a mall on Maui Island in Hawaii, where I live, and the mobile phone in my pocket buzzes. I peek at the phone display. Swanson.

"Hey man, I got a project for you," he said. I instantly recognized the voice. "Okay. Whatcha got?" I asked in a tone with as little pessimism as I could muster. "I want to write an autobiography."

Oooh-kaay, I thought. His projects are never boring.

"But it won't all be about me," he continued. "I want to include the business philosophy I developed with Screaming Images, and how punk rock was part of it." James explained his vision for the book, and I replied honestly that I liked the concept, and suggested to go and start the process, because writing takes time. A lot of it. He asked me to help edit, which of course I would. Because over many years, James called with "Hey, man" projects, and I never rejected one. As mentioned, I've never had a boring "Hey, man" project.

Upon ending the call, I had two thoughts about how this story would develop. It will end up either a boy-from-single-parent-household-makes-it-big account; or, more likely, a cautionary tale of party-surfer-car-crash-dude-luckily-turns-it-around-before-it's-too-late. Months later, as he emailed me chapter after chapter, and as I read, I realized something. I had it wrong. This isn't a rags-to-riches-like story, and never was envisioned as such. That would be too cookie-cutter for James Swanson.

This is a business book. With a heavy influence of punk rock, which is quite unusual.

Business success and punk are very rarely associated with one another.

I've known the guy for four decades, and I was always impressed with how he ran and grew his own business, because in my household, my wife wouldn't let me near the money, even with a college degree. I couldn't manage a closet adequately. What I learned editing was how James applied principles from punk rock into his life, namely into his business philosophy. And how it always seemed to pay off. When faced with big decisions, he acted as the punkers might. *What would Mike Ness do?* And he did that a lot.

This may not seem overly impressive. Lots of successful business operators find inspiration in any which way, whether through God, from their children, for world peace, or whatever. But I have yet to find a business leader who embraced punk rock on the way to millions in sales. James did, and he wanted to share the how with everyone. He said he hoped to help others in business, to maybe work hard and achieve the same. Fair enough. This is the tale of James Swanson, Screaming Images, and how punk rock can make business super good.

***

Johnny "Rotten" got the band back together, so to speak, in the 1990s in Simi Valley. So I saw James pretty much weekly during our "Rotten's Row" softball games. This went on for quite a few years. We won a few division titles but couldn't quite master the tournament for the overall city title. But we were among the best teams in Simi Valley over that period, for sure.

All during this time, even after sharing hours on the field, as well as at the Treehouse bar after games, I didn't know what James did for work. At all. I also had no idea where he lived. I just knew it was not Simi Valley. Always somewhere "over the hill" meaning toward the big City of Angels. Editing this book, I learned just how far James would drive just to play ball. I'm a fanatic – but would never drive far to play.

* * *

Right after the turn of the century, I found myself working as a communications manager with a trade association in Chatsworth not far from Lanark. One day, James found me on the phone. This was the early stages of improved website design on the internet. He requested some writing for the website for his new signage company. I can't even remember how he briefly explained the business. I just agreed, took the information, and looked up what was there online so far.

I saw big, bright, blue and black logos, and images that seemed familiar. It took a few moments, but then hit: Carolina Panthers! I scrolled to see more images, which showed installation work from the beginning, all the way through the final results. Holy shit! *James was doing work for an NFL team!* I wrote the content, which remained on the site for many years. James knew to use powerful images to drive marketing for his company, a skill he honed to near-perfection in the years to follow.

* * *

Midway into the first decade of the new century, I found myself on the board of directors for the girls' softball league in my hometown, while coaching for my oldest daughter. League officials were always fundraising, with pizza nights and the like, because the league was opening a brand new complex of fields which came with costs like new snack bar refrigerators and field maintenance equipment. Funding talks dominated discussions in most board meetings. We had a lot of shit to do.

One night a friend on the board held up a check and asked aloud where it came from. It was early summer so a lot of us were managing all-star teams, which also demands a lot of money. We all sought donations or sponsorships from businesses; so, during our meetings the league accountant often asked about checks received. Usually, the name of the team it was intended for was written into the memo line.

My colleague assumed the check was to support her team, then the league's top hope for a state or national championship. The whole town knew they were raising funds planning for travel far away deep into the summer. "Who is it from?" I asked. She squinted to read the check. "Screaming Images?" she said, totally puzzled. I just smiled and slowly shook my head.

James, hearing how the league needed funding for the new fields, had mailed in a $500 donation. Not to a team, but for the entire league. For the new fields. Just because.

*　*　*

The years prior to our Maui call, I'd hear from James from time to time, usually with a "Hey, man" project. My favorite was in 2019, when he needed a radio ad script. I told you, never boring. The NFL's Raiders had moved from Oakland to Vegas, and had a brand-new stadium, and James just happened to get the contract for graphics and signage for the entire behemoth of a facility. As part of the deal, he agreed to have S.I. listed as a sponsor, and with that came a free 30-second ad for a local radio station that would be busy promoting the Raiders to Vegas.

"Dude, I've never written an ad script," he said over the phone. By this time, I had moved to Long Beach, a couple of miles from the little bedroom where James had started S.I. long before. I had done a few broadcast ad scripts dating back to my political campaigning days. He connected me with his marketing dude; we had a few rounds of edits and revisions, got the text finalized, and they recorded the ad in the S.I. shop. We tacked on a poll for something to direct listeners to, and when I heard the final version, I could only verbally exclaim in what our old friend Diana would call a "ch," and shake my head. His marketing manager did an exceptional job with the vocal, tone, and timing of the text I wrote. That was impressive, but what I was amused by most was the music they chose for the background. Song by Lars Fredericksen. Punk, of course.

* * *

I last saw James in person at the annual Punk Rock Bowling festival in Vegas, which his company sponsored from its inception around 2000. It was May 2023, and I hadn't attended PRB in 11 years. Boy, what growth. Now there were two stages. Off to the left of the main stage was this big fenced-off area filled with tables topped with umbrellas, with its own bar separate from the general public. It was the VIP section, mainly arranged for friends and family members of the performers. That's where James arranged for me and my friend Karen to sit each night for the biggest acts: Bad Religion, Rancid, Dropkick Murphys, Interrupters, Suicidal Tendencies. He would start with me there but leave early each night because he needed to get up super early the next day to work out and run S.I., just as he had for two decades. James found a routine that worked and stuck with it, even after he'd sold the company. Now, he was working on his new visual arts business, one that wouldn't be limited to static images. I'll leave it at that.

Not too long after I last saw him came our Maui call. What follows is the result. To this day I say with confidence that punk rock changed my life. Without any doubt, I know punk changed the future for James Swanson. It all remains truly unbelievable.

Keith Jajko

AUTHOR'S NOTE

Why am I writing this book? Let's get that out of the way right away. One of my best friends actually said to me, *"Are you really writing a book about yourself?"* I'm writing it because doing so is kind of unorthodox – and I'm totally unorthodox. I'm writing it because there are a lot of things no one knows about – all the crazy shit I did and all the wild things I went through to get to the place where I'm at right now. I've had at least 25 younger people just starting in my industry reach out to me on LinkedIn and ask how I did it. I'm writing to inspire people to go for it – anyone willing to be consistent and determined, and to work super hard can do it. I write because I'm an avid reader, love books, and it's always been on my bucket list to write one. But most of all, I'm writing it because I think it's a pretty fucking cool story.

I tried to have a little fun with the titles of chapters by adding names of punk rock songs I thought were in some sort of way relatable to that chapter. You can just ignore those, or maybe check them out. Your call.

I've read a lot of books – 42 in 2023, as a matter of fact. (I had a lot of free time on my hands last year). In normal years, though, I usually average 16 to 20 books. I've been a reader my whole life. I can remember in elementary school when the "book trailer" came to my school every year and how it was always one of my favorite days. My mother always used to splurge on me when the book trailer came, even though she didn't have a lot of extra money laying around as a single mom. I figure over my lifetime I've probably read close to a thousand books. Mostly I read silly fiction. Lawyers, detectives, gangsters, cowboys and stuff. But I also read a lot of biographies – mostly about music industry folks, but also other types of interesting people.

In writing this book I set out to make it easy to read. My experience with a lot of biographies has been that the first 20% of the books, the part about their childhood, is totally fucking boring and I sometimes barely get past that part. I didn't give a shit about Rob Halford's schoolmates, or Geezer Butler's headmaster – I wanted to know about their bands. I wanted to know how they met each other. I wanted to know how they came up with the name for the band. I wanted to know about the first song they wrote together. Chrissie Hynde is one of my favorite artists of all time, but I almost put her book down because the beginning was so dull. Thank God I didn't, because once she got to where she picked up a guitar and started writing songs, I couldn't put the book down. One of the best biographies I ever read. The reason I always hesitated to just skip past the childhood part in those books was that I was afraid of missing something relevant. Some little piece of information that tied something together later in the book. What they did when they were young that made them tick when they got older.

I did a lot of research before I started the actual writing. All the what-to-do's and what-not-to-do's in writing a memoir. I took them all into consideration – then said *fuck that*. I'm not writing this book to sell a ton of copies or try to make a bunch of money. It was therapeutic.

And a lot of fun. I was super surprised to find out how much information I'd archived from the twenty years I was in business with S.I. I even found the actual invoices from my first couple jobs in Long Beach, Calif., from 2002 to 2003; jobs for NFL teams. I was super stoked taking that trip down memory lane.

Keeping all of this in mind, I realized a lot of people won't care about my childhood and youth. They won't care about my first job as a kid, or my first print industry job, or how punk rock influenced the decisions I was making throughout my printing industry career – so I tried to write this book so you can skip parts that don't interest you. Maybe all you want to read is the Screaming Images stuff, or maybe just the social media stuff. I feel like I gave a lot of information in those sections. Go for it.

If you do decide to read the whole thing, please bear with me, as I do realize I repeated myself a few times. It was all in the interest of keeping the story flowing, and so that the people who do decide to skip some chapters won't miss some of the fun stuff. I had a lot of resources for keeping the dates straight, but maybe not every single one is 100% accurate. A lot of the timelines on the youth parts were based on my memory of what vehicle I was driving, where I was living, or what year an album came out (haha). I did the best I could with the information I had archived. But every story in this book is true and told in my own voice.

Whichever way you decide to do it, I appreciate that you've even gotten this far.

James Swanson

VALUES HERE

What'd you say
When I said we'll be here through tomorrow
In my heart and in my head
Fear of failure
Fear of reprimand
Two big problems I've never had
I never doubted what I had inside... what I have inside

Values here in my heart
And we'll be here through tomorrow
Every day's a brand new start
Fear of failure
Fear of reprimand
Two big problems I've never had
I never doubted what you had inside... what you have inside

Fear of failure
Fear of reprimand
Two big problems I've never had
I never doubted what we had inside... what we have inside

Song by Brian Baker/Dag Nasty

INTRODUCTION
LIBERTY, AT LAST

I stepped out of bed on Tuesday, April 10, 2018, at 10:45 p.m. – earlier than my usual get-up time of 2:30 a.m. Tonight was a big night. I was a mixture of super excited and nervous out of my mind. I kissed my pups goodbye and jumped in my truck to head out into a cold and windy night. The cold was okay. The wind could be a problem.

I arrived at my print shop on S. Decatur Boulevard right at 11:30 p.m. I had my second shift waiting to help load an 800-pound pallet into the back of my GMC long-bed pickup truck. Pallet was ready, we loaded it, and I was on my way. The wind wasn't bad. So far, so good.

Exiting the I-15 freeway, I headed east toward Las Vegas Boulevard, where it was another crazy-busy Las Vegas night despite the hour. I cut through the NYNY casino valet entrance and drove through the parking lot past T-Mobile Arena and turned right at Park MGM, then another right onto the world-famous Las Vegas Strip. The circuitous route was necessary because we had four lanes closed southbound on the boulevard.

As I turned right onto the Strip, I immediately stopped and moved some cones and explained to security who I was and why I was there. I continued down past several huge work trucks, almost to the intersection of Las Vegas Boulevard and Tropicana Avenue. I maneuvered past two massive 210-foot cranes and parked in the second lane from the curb, right in front of the Statue of Liberty outside the NYNY Hotel and Casino. The Vegas Golden Knights jersey had arrived.

All the excitement and hoopla (and nervousness) were because the Golden Knights, in their inaugural season as an expansion team, had made the National Hockey League playoffs – and we were about to help them celebrate by putting this jersey, which we made at our shop on Decatur, onto the Statue of Liberty. This jersey was 85.5 feet wide by 65 feet tall. It weighed approximately 775 lbs.

I was super excited because I'm a big sports fan, and a huge fan of the NHL. It was kind of hard not to jump on the Knights bandwagon when the entire city had been going nutso that they made the playoffs as a brand-new team in a city in the middle of a desert. The hoopla was because any time you close four lanes on the Strip, people notice, especially the media. And my nervousness was because the playoffs started the night after next. And I had no idea if the jersey would even fit the big lady.

It wasn't as if we'd get a chance to try it on beforehand.

I exited my truck and walked down the Strip toward a couple of our badass friends from YESCO who were helping with the logistics of the closures, cranes, and the install. I asked for their thoughts on the wind situation and was met with some grim faces. It didn't look good.

Now, Screaming Images and YESCO are never afraid of a little wind or inclement weather. But there was another little, um, challenge. The cranes were equipped with anemometers at the top – devices that measure wind speed and direction. If the wind reached a certain speed, the cranes would stop working automatically, no matter where we were in the process. So, if the jersey was halfway or even a quarter-way done, and the wind rose above the levels the cranes allowed, they would stop and lower immediately, leaving a 775-lb. mesh jersey flapping around in high wind at the biggest intersection in Las Vegas. Holy shit.

Being who we were, and doing what we always do, we went for it. Each of the cranes carried a fairly heavy-duty four-man basket. The guys going into those baskets were crazy. Six of us took the pallet out of the back of my truck, set it down onto Las Vegas Boulevard, and started unfolding the jersey.

After some spirited debate, we decided to attach the part of the jersey that fit on the arm holding the torch – this would be installed first, with heavy-duty Paracord rope and clips held onto one of the baskets to serve as a temporary hold while we moved around to work elsewhere. The guys then jumped into both baskets, strapped in, and away they went. As soon as they got about 50 feet into the air a big gust of wind came from the west, and the jersey furled out. The entire mammoth garment. It completely covered all southbound lanes on the Strip – quite a sight! It was a miracle it stayed attached to the basket.

At least three news vans had cameras on it, waiting for something disastrous to happen. It didn't. Our friends at YESCO are super-pros. The gusts died down, and our crews continued their ascent. I was standing below on the first lane of Las Vegas Boulevard having a mini heart attack.

It was a momentous sight as the baskets reached the top of the statue, moved in closer to the top of the torch, and began unfolding the jersey more. By this time, besides an additional two news vans, three helicopters now circled above. I noticed some commotion by the base of one of the cranes, so I went to investigate. The anemometer had topped out and was about to shut down the crane. Abort mission. Fuck.

Once the baskets were back safely on the ground, we all convened to make a new plan. Satellite weather reports indicated the wind would die back down in approximately two hours. The problem was the lane closures were only permitted by Clark County from midnight to 8 a.m. If we waited it out, we wouldn't have enough time for the install. There were representatives from MGM and the Golden Knights on the ground with us, and we all agreed we would have to push off until the next night and take our chances with the weather then. We limped back to the shop around 2 a.m., dropped off the jersey, and prayed for good weather the next night.

That night, I repeated the same process, and was feeling hopeful, which is pretty much a requirement if you want to succeed in this business. That, and brass balls. When I arrived at the exact same spot on the Strip at 11 p.m., we unloaded the pallet, unfolded the jersey, and all knuckle-bumped each other for good luck. Tonight was a no-fail situation. The crane operators weren't as optimistic, and pointed out that the satellites were indicating high wind in three hours. We went up anyway.

No drama on this night's ascent. The guys reached the torch about 1:15 a.m. Less than seven hours to get this thing installed. No problem.

The biggest difference about tonight was that now there were six news vans, four helicopters and at least four drones. Who knows where they all came from. News reporters were on the ground hitting up anyone who'd talk. I tried my hardest to avoid them. If this installation failed it pretty much was all on me.

No pressure.

I'd taken some preliminary precautions, which as it turned out were needed immediately. As the guys began mounting the jersey sleeve on the torch arm, it kept sliding down due to the weight. My precaution for this one was the foresight to add grommets every 5 feet around the sleeve's cuff, so the guys could run Paracord through them to secure the cuff. Problem solved.

When that was completed, they began draping the jersey around her shoulders, where it would reach around and attach to itself under the arm on the other side, underneath the tablet. That was the plan anyway. It was a super slow process because of the weight, and the fact that they were trying to manipulate it from two baskets swinging from cranes at 200 feet high with a slight wind. By the time they started doing this I was a little relieved that the arm fit, but was still having a hard time breathing from the anxiety. Adding to this was that my neck hurt from looking up at such an extreme angle for the last two hours. (Try looking nearly straight up for 120 minutes sometime.)

Then things got a lot more uncomfortable. I was tapped on the shoulder and turned to see the Senior Vice President of Operations from MGM Resorts, who then told me he wanted me to meet someone: the President of NYNY Hotel and Casino. Crap.

I knew exactly who she was. Being the president of an MGM casino, or any casino on the Strip for that matter, was a big, big deal. By this time, it was about 3 a.m. She was dressed like she was going to leave any moment for the gym, which I secretly hoped she would, and soon. She ended up the nicest person and made me feel a lot better by telling me all the good things she'd heard about me, and that she understood how crazy this project was, what a big deal it was for her property, and for the whole city of Las Vegas. After about 30 minutes of that I decided to take a walk around to the rear side of the statue to check on the second basket and see how those boys were doing. It was easy to see they were struggling a bit with the weight and the sheer mass of the jersey, but like I said, those YESCO guys are badasses.

By the time they had the jersey wrapped around her it was close to 5 a.m. We had three hours to get it finished or we would have to shut down for the night. I felt like everything would be okay as long as the circumference of the jersey was close to the right size.

Another precaution we took was to add about 20 extra feet of material in case we had speculated wrong on the width, with rows of grommets every 5 feet vertically. I also had taken precautions in case it was too small; I had press operators at the shop on stand-by in case they needed to print and finish an extra panel so we could strap it all together in a giant patchwork operation. After about an hour and half of getting it in place, they were able to start attaching it to itself. It was going to fit.

What a fucking relief.

So now it's 6:30 a.m. We have 90 minutes to get it all attached, then step back and see where we need to tighten. By now I'd walked around the entire base of the statue, while looking up, at least 20 times – probably almost two miles of walking. At least we were almost home.

At this point I felt fairly confident and went looking for the president. She was gone, off to the gym, so I figured she felt fairly confident herself. By now some of the reporters had figured out who I was, and I was feeling better about talking with them as everything looked good. The sun was starting to rise, and the jersey on the statue was an impressive sight, even by Vegas standards.

About 7 a.m., everything was tightened as well as could be, and the baskets began descending.

When they hit the ground and the boys detached and started jumping out of the baskets into the street, we were all jacked up. Big knuckle-bumps everywhere. We had pulled off one of the most impressive graphic projects in the history of the city and had done so in time for the first game of the NHL playoffs. I was exhausted, but can't even imagine how those eight dudes felt after being up in those baskets wrestling with that 775-pound jersey for almost eight hours. Fucking heroes.

It was closer to 9:30 a.m. by the time we cleared the cranes off the boulevard; but I don't think the county cared much. We had just accomplished something incredible, and the entire country was watching. It was on every major news channel.

Once everything was done, and we'd all congratulated each other, I headed to the shop to share pictures with the team and thank them. The news was on every television in the shop, and the atmosphere at little S.I. on S. Decatur Boulevard was electric. After about an hour of sharing installation photos and stories, it was time to go home, hug my pups, and get some sleep. By this time a bunch of my friends and clients from all over the country were blowing me up on calls and texts, and my social media was going berserk; but all I could think about was sleep. I had a hockey game to go to at 7 p.m.

Ho hum, just another day at Screaming Images.

Statue of Liberty

CHAPTER 1
ORIGINS

"Spray Paint the Walls"
- *Black Flag*

I remember a sign in the imaging room at Jordan Horn/Techtron from when I was still an apprentice in the late 1980s. It said: "Quality, Fast Turnaround, Cheap Price – Pick Two." I thought, *Why?* I tucked it into the memory bank and always remembered. It would end up being a solid key to my later success with Screaming Images. If you're capable of doing print work that's quality, and capable of doing it cost-effectively, why can't you do it fast? Because you'd have to work harder? That's some bullshit right there. If you're going to be in business for yourself, the first thing you need to come to grips with is that you will have to work harder – or you won't succeed. Unless you've come up with some idea that no one else has thought of yet. Good luck with that. About 99.9% of the time, when you're going into business for yourself, you're going to have competitors. And the way you win work is to be better than them all the way around.

Pretty relevant to how my career ended up going was the first day I ever worked in sales. I was a prepress operator/designer; it was the late 1990s, and we were still a union trade – but the Mac computers were just coming in and they were bringing in operators at $16 per hour. I was making close to $40 (on third-shift differential) and there were pretty clear signs that the union was breaking. It would no longer be a trade. I had several executives approach and say I should go into sales. They thought I'd have success due to my personality and background in the shop. We quickly struck a deal where I would move to first shift permanently and come in an hour earlier than everyone else on my shift, so I could head upstairs to the sales offices after my seven hours ended (union!) and start learning that angle of the business.

The week before this, I grabbed a girlfriend and headed to the department store (yes, they were still around then) and went shopping for fancy clothes.

My first day in sales, I ran upstairs after my shift, put on my new slacks and shirt and tie, and went into the sales manager's office to start charting out my new career. First thing he said, as soon as I walked into his office was, "What the fuck are you doing?" I asked what he meant and he said, "Why are you dressed like that?" I said I dressed up because that's how all the other sales reps dressed. He said, "No, don't do that. You need to be yourself – stay within your personality. That's what is going to make you successful." That was the best advice I ever got in this industry. It fit perfectly for me. Punk Rock James was on the loose.

I was like a sponge. During the mornings working in design, I would watch the sales people. See how they reacted to things. Watch how they treated the production people. Observe how they handled adversity. Each one of them did things differently, and I quietly decided which ones were better than others with people and situations. In the afternoons upstairs, I would approach the best sales reps and ask if I could hang out with them the rest of the day. They would take me with them to meetings, and I would watch everything. Always soaking every single thing in, always planning.

For the type of printing company I worked for, the main source of work in those days was advertising agencies. Chiat Day, Dailey & Associates, Ogilvy & Mather… They were like whole new worlds for me compared to the boring white walls of the print shop. Visual stimulation everywhere; displays and art on the walls showing off their customers and work; creative spaces for employees for lunch, breaks and recreation; happy people everywhere. I thought to myself, *this is the way it should be done.*

The second company I went to work for (after 11-plus years at the first) was in Hollywood and was my first foray into what would eventually become my main focus: digital printing. The company was actually more like a studio, but a lot smaller; it had a really cool vibe, with a lot of great personalities getting super creative. A few things really stuck with me. First, one of the two owners, Tim. He'd get there crazy early. I'd arrive at 7 a.m., and he would have already been there for two or three hours. I never understood it then – but trust me, I did eventually. Another was that there was a cat living there. It gave it a homey feel. The third was that they had a bar on the premises. It was behind a locked door, and no one went in during business hours; but on special occasions and sometimes weekends they'd open it up and we'd go in and celebrate. It looked like something you would walk into on the Sunset Strip. Total Hollywood vibe. I'd remember this.

It became super clear that creativity was one of the keys. However, I would end up leaving that company as their commitment to quality and customer service was not at the level I wanted, even though I was still new in sales.

My next stop was a large-format print company in Irvine, down in Orange County, Calif., south of Los Angeles. I went there because I was impressed with their facility and equipment, and wanted to expand my capabilities, especially in the sports market. On my first day I arrived early, as usual, and was super surprised by how dead it was. They had a huge, beautiful building with no expenses spared, and at least six grand-format printers that were totally silent. It's early, I thought, and things will pick up late in the morning. But nope. Maybe tomorrow. Nope. Maybe next week. Nope. They were just dead. No work.

I wondered where their money came from. By this point I was getting comfortable cold-calling and brought in a pretty good number of opportunities to bid. I lost almost every one of them because of price. They then signed me up for a weekly "sales class," ostensibly to instruct how to "not sell on price." Okay, I got that, but you can't sell anything with a price that's almost double everyone else's unless you're giving them something the competitors are not, like higher quality or better customer service. Which my company did not. Lesson learned: price does matter. I didn't stay long. One good thing did come out of there, though. There was always a guy in an office who didn't seem to engage with anyone else in sales. So, I asked who he was and what he did. He has his own business, I was told, and he used this company exclusively for all his printing. He had two big accounts. Hmmm. It got me thinking.

My third stop was another big company in Lake Forest. I went there mainly because I really liked the sales manager, who I would end up sharing a decades-long relationship with; he would be a key factor in the early years of Screaming Images. The company had a nice, large building, and a lot of big equipment. At this point in my digital printing career I wasn't very sophisticated about what was good equipment, and what was not. It turned out their printers were mostly outdated and too slow to keep me competitive in a very fast-paced industry. Plus, the customer service was the worst of anywhere I'd been. I thought of the guy in the office at the place in Irvine. It was time to start my own business.

Before getting into this next segment, I want to point out the valuable lessons learned up to this point. Customer service is most important. And this is true in any industry. Quality is right up there with customer service. You have to deliver a product you're proud of, and more importantly, that customers are stoked with. Then, of course, price matters. You can't go into a market you're trying to make headway in with prices that are way above what potential customers are used to paying. And finally, you need to make yourself stand out to get people's attention – being audacious and having a creative space is what will help you get there.

My business was started in my first home office in a small rental house in the Belmont Shores area of Long Beach, Calif., near the southwest corner of Orange County, which I shared with a roommate. I decided on the name Screaming Images and came up with a logo which I thought represented my personality. I had some success straight out of the gate with retaining all my key customers. This was late 2002. I already was getting aggressive with my sales and cold calling and decided I needed some sort of emailable "slick sheet" with my logo and the logos of some of the key folks I was working for, to send to potential new customers.

I also wanted a super basic website (just a landing page, really) in case people started looking me up. One of my first punk rock moves was putting a T.S.O.L. song as the music on my website. This was probably inspired by the fact that MySpace was the current rage and they let you choose and arrange your own music on their platform. Of course, I asked permission for the song on my website. I emailed band leader Jack Grisham himself – no idea how I got his email address. I just said, "Jack, is it okay if I use your song 'Sex Not Violence' on the website for my new graphics business?" He replied almost immediately with, "Of course it is!" I would always remember this, and Jack.

Three years went by rather quickly, and I ended up moving myself and my little business to Henderson, Nevada in September 2005. I bought a house and got a female Labrador puppy I named Scout. The first thing I did was turn my dining room into my home office and get a custom-made desk, set there by a good buddy. I hung banners from jobs I'd already done on every wall in the room to make myself a nice creative space. I had Carolina Panthers banners and prints for Anaheim Angels baseball, Big League Dreams and California Motor Speedway, to name a few. No customers ever saw it, but it was the first thing people who visited my house saw when walking in the front door.

By this time, I was also incorporating skulls and crossbones into my S.I. marketing. The basic reason was that I was just having a lot of fun with it. Shocking people a bit. Drawing attention to myself. Staying within my personality, right? I was starting to have pretty decent success in the sports market, working for several National Football League teams including the Washington Redskins and Carolina Panthers. I was traveling all over the country to stadiums for meetings; McCarran Airport in Vegas was a godsend compared with Los Angeles International and John Wayne Airport in Orange County. I had somehow wrangled an opportunity to bid on the branding and graphics package for the Pittsburgh Steelers at their new stadium, Heinz Field, and arranged a site visit on a morning in early 2006.

The meeting was set for 9 a.m. Early on, I started setting pretty brutal travel schedules for myself. I wanted to be gone from home as little as possible because of Scout. The fact that I was paying for all this travel out of my own pocket now influenced this as well.

My flight to Pittsburgh had a connection in Detroit. My flight leaving Vegas was delayed on the tarmac and put my connection in peril. As it stood, I was to arrive in Pittsburgh after midnight; my hotel was basically just for napping, freshening up and a change of clothes. I arrived in Detroit with 10 minutes to spare for the connection – at a gate at the opposite side of the airport. I hightailed it through the concourses but didn't make it. The airplane pulled away as I arrived at the gate.

The gate told me I could be on a flight the next morning at 10 a.m. for an 11:30 a.m. arrival. No good: my meeting was at 9 a.m. and the flight back home was at 6 p.m. "How far of a drive is it to Pittsburgh?" I asked. Four and a half hours. I got lucky and there was an after-hours car rental place open. I can't remember the name but it wasn't Enterprise, who I had a corporate account with. I secured a car, and they asked when I was going to return it. Tomorrow, I lied. I was driving to Pittsburgh.

By the time I arrived at my hotel it was 6 a.m. and I was about 30 minutes away from the stadium. No time for a nap, so I showered, changed clothes, and went out for breakfast. I was wearing a long-sleeve dress shirt, which I usually did to cover up my arms which are sleeved with tattoos. Something to realize is that, even as late as 2006, tattoos weren't widely accepted.

It was a nice day, but I was super tired. I hadn't slept in over 24 hours. As I was exiting my rental car across the street from Heinz Field, I made a decision: Fuck this. I am who I am, and if they can't see value in the hard work and creativity I can bring to their stadium, screw them. I rolled the sleeves up past my elbows and walked in. Tattoos flying. I was meeting with the Vice President of Stadium Operations, Jimmy, and the Marketing Director, Heidi. When they came out to meet me in the lobby of the front office, Heidi asked with a funny look on her face, "You're James Swanson?" "Yes, I am." I don't think I was what she expected with the tattoos, spiky hair and Converse Chuck

Taylor All Star sneakers.

They escorted me straight to the playing field, where I laid out plans for how I would attach the graphics to the field walls. This was rather new for stadiums then, and I was also bidding to do a dual-field wall system for the Steelers as well as for the University of Pittsburgh Panthers who shared the facility. They seemed satisfied with my structural plan, and I then talked about my ideas for creative, which included skirting some strict NFL rules prohibiting placement of sponsor advertisements on field walls. Specifically, in this case, Rolling Rock beer.

Somehow it hit me: one of the prominent features of Rolling Rock's branding is the number 33, which signified the 33 words in their original pledge of quality, which was printed on every bottle of Rolling Rock. I said, "You can say it's for Frenchy Fuqua," their famous former running back who wore jersey No. 33 and who assisted Franco Harris on the Immaculate Reception – the most famous play in Steelers history. By this time, they didn't even see my tattoos anymore. They loved my ideas. I spent the rest of the day measuring other areas of the stadium while they ran their new creative ideas by Rolling Rock. By 9 p.m. I was back in Henderson with Scout, and by the following week I had the Steelers job. Tattoos and all.

At this point I should fill some gaps. I was working from my home office, in my underpants, doing all the design, project management, and installation coordination myself. I was outsourcing 99% of my printing to a company in Chattanooga, Tenn. called National Posters Digital. I also had backup printers in Denver and Los Angeles for emergencies. I found National Posters through a job we did for one of my (outsourced) installers. I had my hands on a good-sized vinyl banner that had great print, material, and finishing quality. I contacted them and immediately was connected to speak with the company president, which I loved. His name was Tim. After speaking with him for a bit I was very comfortable with both him and his industry experience.

We pretty quickly negotiated basic per-square-foot pricing for the main materials which were vinyl banners, mesh banners, and 3M pressure-sensitive vinyl. The agreed-upon prices fit within what I'd been charging already and allowed for a good profit reselling. As I mentioned earlier, you can't just make up prices and expect to win work. You have to stay within industry standard pricing. Tim understood this and gave me wholesale prices so he could build his relationship with me.

When I started working with National Posters it was probably the beginning of 2003. Right away I scheduled a visit to Chattanooga to check out their facilities and meet the team. I was greeted at the door with a big sign that said, "Welcome James Swanson/Screaming Images," which made me feel really good, like I was important to them. Customer service and relationships are the biggest keys to success – and this gesture, though small, would stay with me and be repeated over and over again with S.I.

Their facility was modern, clean and well laid-out, with current-year model equipment.

The production staff all seemed super knowledgeable and genuinely happy to meet me. However, the biggest impression, for me, was made by the project manager assigned to my account. Her name was Danielle, and I was immediately comfortable with her handling my work.

Customer service and industry knowledge – I can't stress these two things enough and will continue to repeat them. I spent a couple of days in Chattanooga, then hustled back home to Long Beach.

I began sending them work immediately. I had three big accounts at that time which were weekly, sometimes even daily, work: Big League Dreams (sports parks), Free Car Media (vehicle wraps) and KROQ (a top local L.A. radio station). Everything was going great with my new print partner. I had 30-day terms with them, so I just had to make sure things were invoiced in a timely manner to my customers, who were also on 30-day terms. Most of the items were shipped to me in Long Beach, where I would personally deliver them, or take them with me to installations, which I was always present for. Anything going anywhere outside of Los Angeles was blind-shipped directly to the customers from Chattanooga with my S.I. logos plastered all over the boxes. Danielle, National Poster's production team, and I right away settled into a daily scheduling routine that began at 5 a.m. my time (Pacific) and 8 a.m. their time (Eastern). This is the origin of my infamous early starts.

I also had the bigger accounts, which were the NFL teams and the Anaheim Angels of Major League Baseball, which meant bigger jobs but not consistent work. Whenever a big job came through, I would go spend a few days in Chattanooga to help with quality control, labeling, and packaging. It was a great partnership.

My first big job with National Posters was Big League Dreams' brand-new sports park in Redding, Calif. It was about 40,000 square feet of vinyl banners printed and then coated with UV to protect against fading in the sun. I was responsible for every single detail at that park including the dimensions of the three softball stadium facades. My company was doing all the printing and all the installation. I wish I could say everything went perfectly with this job, but I can't. There were some pretty major mistakes made that were on me, and they mostly came from not providing enough detail to National Posters Digital.

No matter, though, because by the time we were finished, the job was perfect – and I have the folks in Chattanooga to thank for that. They worked with me on solutions to the problems, and even ate some of the additional expenses, even though they didn't have to. It was a collaboration between teammates to accomplish a goal, and it taught me the most valuable lesson I had learned to this point about how to work with customers. I used this lesson for the entire 20 years I was in business.

The years flew by, and my relationship with National Posters, and Danielle, grew stronger and stronger. I spent a lot of days in Chattanooga working on jobs for the Panthers, Redskins, Steelers, and the National Basketball

Association (more on that later). As my little home-based business grew, National Posters grew with me. I had intimate knowledge of their shop policies, production procedures, customer service and quality, pricing structures, and accounting methods. When I finally started buying my own printers and equipment, and opened my own first little shop, I modeled almost everything on what I learned from eight years working with National Posters Digital.

Despite appearances, I've always been pretty conservative with business decisions. I took some big risks, but they were all very calculated. I play a long game, and don't push things when they're not ready to happen (*most* of the time). I almost opened my first shop in late 2007. If I had opened a shop then, I probably would have gone out of business. The years 2007 and 2008 saw a major economic downturn for the entire country. At that time the only business I was going after, pretty much, was sports teams and their stadiums. Every cold call I made to the sports market during this time attracted offers to let me do the printing at their stadium *as a trade* for advertising. Meaning, with the stadium. It wasn't going to do me any good to have my name in their game-day programs and flashed on their scoreboards and monitors during games. Printing graphics for an entire stadium wasn't cheap, especially when you don't have your own printers yet and you pay someone else to do it. Plus, you still have to pay the installers. It wouldn't work. I would have to diversify.

Everything in my little catalog of business slowed down drastically. I went from being consistently busy to having not a heck of a lot to do. Really quickly. By this point I'd been in business for four-plus years and had a mortgage and a pup I loved very much, who I was responsible for. I had more overhead than ever. I had been in Vegas for almost two years and didn't have a single local client. I saw all the big building wraps around town, but to me that was only a pipe dream. No way a little guy like me could ever win that kind of work. But as I thought about it more, I started thinking... Why not me? I had a ton of industry knowledge and worked just as hard as everyone else, probably harder. *WHY NOT ME?*

Back in those days social media was new. I had Facebook, but it didn't really connect you with businesses and decision-makers. I had for the past three years used *Sports Business Journal* as a source for leads. It was a yearly subscription, with weekly hard copy magazine issues sent by mail. The subscriptions cost $399 a year, which was a lot of money for me back then. I also purchased a "sports contacts almanac" every year from SBJ for another $999. This provided a list of every single sports and venue executive in the country, as well as their email addresses. I used these subscriptions as just about my only resource for cold calling. I did search for more information via Google once I had a starting point.

Weirdly enough, they didn't have any contact info in the almanac for University of Nevada at Las Vegas Athletics, which at that time had the only sports teams in Las Vegas. I did chase them around a bit in 2005 when I first moved to Henderson, but had no luck and gave up pretty quickly as I was having so much success with the NFL. There was a dude named Daren who from my slick internet sleuthing seemed to be a legend in Las Vegas for sports and events. I couldn't hunt him down back then, but would eventually (remember the long game) and we would become good friends (more on that to come).

One of my best resources for work ideas has always been just driving around. The amount of printed graphics in Las Vegas can be mind-boggling. I still do it to this day. I needed to find something local to go after. Something I saw a lot was "Welcome to Las Vegas" graphics. Touristy stuff. There was a ton of it. A little bit of online information-gathering and I came up with the LVCVA: Las Vegas Convention and Visitors Authority. I started trying to make contact with them directly to convey my capabilities but it was really slow-going.

Cold calling is tough sometimes. If they don't know you or know who you are, they probably won't just start talking with you or handing out information. I was pretty determined and kept at it. If nothing else, I was getting good practice with my approach and methods of getting their attention. I started sending them pictures of things from the sports stadiums I'd worked on. I finally found a really nice woman willing to talk. LVCVA didn't really make those purchasing decisions directly, she told me; they came from their advertising agency, which was called R&R Partners. Ad agency! Going back to my roots as a young and hungry-for-knowledge junior account executive days in L.A.! Now I was cooking with gas.

In 2008, LinkedIn wasn't yet a big thing. I did have an account, but not many people did, and it was not yet a way to meet people. So back to the internet I went. I knew from past experience that it's always important to know where to start position-wise when you're looking for decision-makers, and that advertising agencies usually had a position called Director of Print Production. That was the first thing I searched for about R&R Partners. Research had also told me that LVCVA was R&R's biggest customer, commanding the majority of their business. I found a guy named Pat in the position with that exact same title and started calling. No luck at first, but I was determined. A little spy work and internet searching, and I found out he was a sports fan. I used this to get him to talk. It turned out he's a massive fan of the Premier League (English soccer) and particularly the club Manchester United. I'm also a huge fan of English soccer, but my team is Chelsea. We hit it off anyway.

I wrangled an invitation to visit and tour the agency. Hell yeah. I was super excited. When the meeting day came, I put on my best short-sleeve shirt and headed to the other side of town – they were in Summerlin. I walked in and all my L.A. ad agency memories started flooding back. Super creative décor, huge spaces, and super cool and hip people everywhere. They had examples of their work all over the walls (hmmm… I thought), people playing ping-pong, half-court basketball and lounging and having lunch in the most creative break area I'd ever seen. Pat himself was a super cool dude, and I was more than a little surprised that he had lived in Las Vegas his entire life. Vegas is a transient city; you don't meet too many of those. He had a backstory in print production that was very similar to mine, and we chatted in his office for over an hour. He had a few jobs coming up that he promised I could bid on, and a few wish-list projects he was working on that he went over with me so I could help him brainstorm. Little did I know, he and I would have a decades-long relationship, and that he would eventually give me the biggest job in the history of my little business in Las Vegas. My biggest takeaway from that meeting, however, was the vision of what my future shops would look like.

Now that I had my first local customer, I was hungry for more connections and feeling pretty confident. The next came from a very unexpected source – my love for shoes. The easiest place for me to find my beloved Chuck Taylor All Stars in the size I needed and the colors I liked was online, and the site I used was Zappos. One day, when a new package was delivered to my house, I noticed a Henderson, Nevada return address. Wow. I need to talk to these dudes.

I didn't make any progress via cold phone calls or emails to generic addresses, so I decided to just show up there. The Zappos headquarters was literally five minutes from my home office. I did what I usually do, which is just walk in like I own the place. Wearing my best pair of Chuck's, of course. What I saw when I walked in completely blew me away. It was a creative space like an advertising agency – but different. It was more industrial; an urban playground, punk rock style. I met a couple of people there – everyone was super cool and friendly. Everyone looked like they were having a ton of fun even though they were working. Culture just oozed from that place. It took me a year or so to get work from them, but I was more determined than ever to open my own shop and make it just like that place.

Next up on my local hit list was beer and liquor companies. Every convenience store (and grocery store, for that matter) in Vegas has gaming and slot machines. And a massive amount of advertising for the beverages they sell. I was friends with all the girls at the Speedee Mart around the corner from my house, so I asked if they could get me contacts. They came back and said all the graphics you see on the front of the stores was done by the distributors, and they gave me a couple of names. Back to the internet to do some research. The biggest I found was called Southern Wine & Spirits, so I reached out via a generic email address. I didn't hear back from them for a couple of weeks, and figured I'd have to go knock on their door. But before I could get to that I was called by a girl named Cathy from a company called Crown Imports. She had an opportunity to do a big display for Corona beer, and asked if I could I meet her next week at Imperial Palace. Of course I could! I met her there and she was super nice. A big vinyl wall mural was what she needed. So, we measured; I delivered a quote the next day for print and install, and the quote was approved. I had my third local customer.

Now it was late 2009. I had made good progress on getting work in Las Vegas, and my client list now included Anheuser-Busch and Las Vegas Athletic Clubs (all six locations). I got the Athletic Clubs account by pure perseverance. They had a huge banner on top of the building of the gym I visited every morning, which was the Green Valley location. One morning when I arrived, the banner had ripped and was hanging down on the building, out of its frame. I took photos with my phone. When I arrived at the check-in desk, I showed them the picture and asked who to talk with about it. Got a name, reached out, but didn't get a response that day.

The next morning the banner was still in the same shape, so I showed the front desk the picture again – but this time I said it was a hazard to people and cars in the parking lot. It was a huge banner, probably 60 feet wide. I reached out again to the same lady from marketing – her name was Kim – and said, "Look, I will give you a discount on this one to show you what I'm capable of." She asked for a price for print only and provided the size. I had a quote for her within the hour; she approved it and sent the art.

I sent it to Chattanooga and called in a favor for an expedited delivery. They printed that day and shipped it overnight. LVAC had a contracted, local sign installer called Vision; we worked with them and had the banner up the next day. Everyone was super stoked. You might be wondering about that "discount" I offered. It turned out my regular pricing was lower than what they were used to paying, while I was still making my good profit margin, and I charged them my full, usual price. By the next week I was printing interior stuff for all six of their locations and was quoting on replacing the building banners at four of the six. I also ended up with Vision as a client for printing.

Another big thing was happening in late 2009: my biggest and longest-standing client, Big League Dreams, was opening one of their sports parks in Las Vegas, planned for mid-2010. The laws on graphics installation in Vegas were also getting more stringent, and I would need a contractor's license for this job. BLD was super important to me – one of these new sports park jobs for my little business almost made my whole year. I already did their parks in Redding and Manteca in California, and in Mansfield, Texas. It was crucial to get this license for the Vegas sports park. I signed up for the test, studied my ass off, and passed the first try. The park went up, everything was on schedule, and the graphics all came out perfect. I was so excited that I came out of retirement and started a Screaming Images softball team to play there. More on BLD later, as they were a crucial part of the formation of S.I. A big lesson here was that an important piece of staying ahead of the competition is having all your licenses and proper insurance in order.

One day in mid-2011, I was browsing through my latest edition of *Sport Business Journal* magazine, and something caught my eye. The PAC-10 athletic conference was expanding and changing their name and rebranding to the PAC-12 conference. The article even featured the new logo.

I grew up a huge fan of University of Southern California football, which played in that conference, so this was pretty cool. And even more exciting was that with the new logo and branding I figured there would be a lot of opportunities for swapping out old graphics for new ones. I immediately consulted my SBJ sports contacts almanac and found the V.P. of Marketing and her email address. Her name was Heather. I sent her an email with a bunch of pictures from my past stadium work attached and indicated that I would love to bid on some of her rebranding. She replied very quickly, and said she had a press conference in two days in Las Vegas – and asked if I could help with a big poster board for it. Of course I could! I also said I was so excited to work with her that this first one was on me. What I didn't tell her was that I outsourced my printing, and my partner was in Chattanooga, Tenn. So once again, I had to call my people at National Posters and ask for a rush print shipped out overnight. They of course helped me; the board arrived the next morning, and I delivered it to Heather personally. My little donated board cost me about $250 in total – but would end up paying off in spades. It was the first of many times I would do something like it. What goes around comes around, friends.

I immediately got an opportunity to bid on the entire graphics package for the PAC-12 football championship game. At that time, it was held at the location of the team with the best record – which meant it would be a super-short turnaround because we couldn't "cheat" by starting earlier. We had to be ready with specs for at least four different stadiums; game results would dictate which needed graphics and signage. This type of work was right up my alley, so I put together a very competitive bid. Heather called me to her office just outside of San Francisco. I was given the grand tour, and then told I had placed second in the bidding. I was bummed. To me, second place is just first loser. But she said they *really* liked my bid and promised another opportunity. She said she wanted to tell me in person, which I also really appreciated.

She came through with that next opportunity faster than expected. Toward the end of 2012, she reached out and said the newly expanded PAC-12 conference was moving their March Madness basketball tournament to Las Vegas – specifically, to MGM Grand. She sent me a deck with all the branding opportunities they selected at the property and requested a bid. As far as I knew, I was not bidding against anyone. I went through the deck and priced everything out with the usual pricing structure I used for sports events and stadiums all over the country. She responded within an hour of my submittal with an approval – on every single item in the deck.

She said my prices blew away the vendor MGM had referred her to, which was surprising because I had really good margins on my prices. She set up a meeting at MGM Grand to meet with some of the staff there, in particular, the director of marketing for the property, Dennis. So, we all met there one morning in early January 2013 – me, Heather, and three people from MGM Grand – in the lobby by the lion. Needless to say, I was super excited to be at a meeting in one of the biggest casinos in town. Heather introduced me: "This is James, owner of Screaming Images, and he will be doing all of our printing and installation for the tournament." Dennis immediately spoke up: "No, he won't, you can use our vendor." Tense moment! I thought for a second that all my hopes and dreams had been shot down. But then, Heather fired back: "Yes, he will." WHOA! Major standoff. I was feeling pretty uncomfortable at that point, but it all seemed to end there, at least temporarily, and we carried on with a walk-through of all the graphics locations on the property. They (MGM) asked, and I answered, a ton of questions. At the very least they recognized I knew what I was doing. When the walk-through ended, we went back out to the lobby; when we said our goodbyes, no one from MGM Grand would even look at me. Shit.

I'll be honest, I left there thinking there was no way I was doing this work. However, the very next week I received the first piece of artwork from Heather and a green light. This was for the "diamond wall" on the exterior of the building on Tropicana. This was one of the building wraps I'd seen and dreamt about the last 5 years. The pipe dream was coming true: I was in the building wrap business on the Las Vegas Strip. And I had badass Heather from the PAC-12 to thank for it. That little free poster board the year before had paid off nicely.

The diamond wall went up – there were a few small issues, not our fault – and we had them addressed immediately. More on that in another chapter.

We started receiving artwork the first week of March for the rest of the tournament branding, and I had four installers working all over the casino. I was there every day supervising and supporting. Dennis was there, too, keeping an eye on me. After about three days of installations, Dennis finally approached and asked if I was from the area. Yes. Did I have a shop? Yes. How long had I been in business? Ten years. He said I was doing a great job and asked me to visit him when the current work ended. I was in with the casinos. Dennis and I wound up becoming really good friends, and went to shows and rode Harleys together. A ton more on Dennis later. What I learned from all this was that I could work anywhere, for anyone. Why not me, indeed.

I should again fill in some gaps here. I opened my first shop in November 2012. I had a couple of big jobs from the Washington Redskins and R&R Partners in 2012, and it gave me just enough confidence to once again risk everything to take the next step and spend the majority of my life savings. The shop was 3,200 square feet, and the rent was twice my mortgage. By then Scout and I had added to our little family, and rescued a beautiful black pup from the Henderson Animal Shelter. We named her Ranger.

Inside the shop, we had some walls built and got right to spray-painting everywhere. We hung banners and put punk rock/urban-style décor all over. Our main installer, Chris, was a badass and an old punk rocker himself. He used rattle cans freehand on all the walls. I added a Sonos sound system with speakers all over the shop, hung a huge Screaming Images banner on the outside of the building, and we were in business. Scout and Ranger were super stoked to be getting out of the house and going to the shop every day. But it was a huge change for me. I had worked out of a home office for the first eight years of S.I. and was now responsible for a hell of a lot more. I decided 7 a.m. would be a good start time, and began getting up earlier to hit the gym before heading to the shop. We were busy out of the gate, and 7 a.m. quickly turned to 6 a.m. No more outsourcing my printing, I was a manufacturer now. My life was about to change big-time.

I'd been preparing for this for a long time. I had it all worked out on my expenses/overhead vs. how much the margins would be now that I printed myself rather than outsourcing. Well, most of it anyway. In the beginning I only had one printer that was 64-inches wide, so we still had to outsource big banners. The biggest surprise was how much we spent on material. I went in knowing the per-square-foot prices, but wasn't prepared for how fast we would rip through those boxes. And all the waste and mistakes were on us – which is a really good way to shoot down your profit margins very quickly. We also had to figure out the finishing part. At that time, it was just me and a guy named Matt – a really good guy – doing sales stuff, but also helping some with the production. I was doing all the prepress, ripping, and running of the printer myself. It was a big learning curve, but I'm quite proud of how well we did those first six months.

Sales ramped up quickly – mostly thanks to MGM. Dennis had come through with the opportunities he promised after our success with the PAC-12 tourney. In May 2013, we did our first wall wrap directly for MGM. It was a construction wall wrap; the creative was for UFC 162 featuring a title fight between Anderson Silva and Chris Weidman. I was a massive UFC fan at that time and was super stoked. All my dreams were coming true. Now, by that time, after having the shop open for 6-plus months, I was learning a lot more about the material, which is a heck of a lot easier to do when you're paying for it yourself. We had also cut way down on mistakes and wasting material. Our prices were lower than our competitors at MGM – but my profit margins were higher than ever. The plain truth is, we were just doing it smarter, and the competitors didn't like it.

This was also around the time we started having parties at the shop. The entire reason I decked out the shop was for people to see it. In order for that to happen I had to get people in there. That first shop was located on Boulder Ranch Avenue over by Sam Boyd Stadium. It was a convenient location for me personally, not far from my house, but I learned quickly that no one from the casinos or over by the Strip (which was where all the big fish were) wanted to drive all the way to the other side of town during working hours just to see what my shop looked like. Now, if I had a big party with a bunch of free booze, catered tacos and a UFC pay-per-view fight… that was a different story.

After a few of these parties I started drawing pretty good crowds. About 80% of attendees were my friends and people who worked at the shop. But I would always have four or five people who were customers. They would get to see the shop and equipment, see what we were capable of doing in-house, and it gave them more confidence to trust us with their print work. I would leave little things laying around on tables so they could see the work we were doing for other big-name folks. Plus, they would have fun! It gave them a chance to see me as a regular dude, and not just one of their vendors. The parties were working. If it cost me a grand to throw a big party, it was worth it because I'd get ten grand in work from it. I was taking one step backward to take two steps forward, and it was something I would continue doing. Having those parties was marketing. Plus, my friends always had a really good time – a win-win, as they say.

Sales grew and by early 2014, four of us worked at the shop. I had a really good guy named Lee who took over all design, prepress, and ripping, and was also running the printer most of the time. I bought another 64-inch printer but knew in the back of my mind that if I really wanted to keep growing, I would have to buy a 10-foot-wide printer. It takes money to make money, and it's an agonizing decision to bring yourself to take the risks associated with this sort of business expansion. I did some research and planning, and discovered the monthly payment on this new piece of equipment would double my shop overhead.

After a month of sleepless nights, I pulled the trigger on a 126-inch latex printer. This brought another big portion of my printing in-house, along with the extra profit margin that came with it – as long as we were efficient, not making a lot of mistakes and doing reprints. The only thing outsourced now was what was called "grand format," which was done on 16-foot-wide printers, the biggest printers made for digital print.

The 10-foot printer paid for itself quickly. One of the things that was highest on my wish list was to do the printing package for the Rock in Rio music festival in Vegas. I knew all the decision-makers because I did some ancillary work for them for events at some of the properties I'd been working with, like MGM and the Sahara (it was called SLS at that time). It was pretty scary because all the big local print companies were after it, as well as a handful from out of town that specialized in festivals. I tried to draw confidence from my little mantra – *Why not me?* As decision-time neared, and the field had been narrowed down to three or four of us, the main Rock in Rio producers asked for a tour of my shop.

We set it up for 6 p.m. on a Friday in early 2015. I spent about three hours cleaning and organizing my shop, ensuring everything was just right. Scout and Ranger had dinner at the shop, and we waited for our guests to arrive. I had about a half-hour spiel ready. They arrived and quickly asked to see the shop. I took them in back and started the spiel but they stopped me and said they just wanted to visit to ensure I had a big printer. Once they saw the 10-footer, they awarded me the contract. They also said we had won the work because of our customer service. As I said earlier, and will say throughout this book, customer service is the single most important thing in any business.

By the time April rolled around, we had another huge job come in – the Floyd Mayweather vs. Manny Pacquiao boxing fight. We started working for Mayweather Promotions in late 2013, and did stuff for several of his fights, including some big building wraps on MGM Grand – which, by the way, was officially "The Home of Floyd Mayweather." I guess we did a good job, because they were giving us the graphics package – for the biggest boxing fight in the history of the world to that point. So, this made it a stacked month. The fight was on May 2nd, and Rock in Rio began May 8th. This meant we struck (removed) the graphics for the fight on Saturday night and started install for the festival Sunday morning. Busiest we had ever been. We were doing the two biggest events of the year in Vegas back-to-back. It was putting us on the map. My 50th birthday was April 25, right before we started installing Mayweather, and all my friends had gathered at Lake Havasu, Arizona to celebrate with me. I ended up having to leave early because I just had too many things I was responsible for in Vegas. As it went, I wouldn't take another vacation for 5 years.

May 2015 ended up being our biggest month ever at S.I. – about $250,000 in sales. And I had gotten the attention of just about everyone in the printing industry around the country. My little shop on Boulder Ranch was packed with equipment, and my landlord graciously let us knock down a wall to get us another 100 square feet or so. It was also around this time that people started approaching and inquiring about acquiring Screaming Images. And I was listening.

Screaming Images was on a pretty major upward trajectory at the end of summer 2015. I had some major decisions pending. If we were to keep growing, I needed a bigger shop, and a 16-foot press. I had two companies talking about buying me out, and they both visited the shop several times. I was seriously considering it. But then my best friend – the most successful self-made businessman I know – said I should hold on to it, that he'd make an investment to transition us to the bigger shop and get the equipment needed to continue expanding. I took him up on it and we moved into our new 20,000-square-foot facility in June 2016.

We were super busy then, a team of six. We kept the printers running at the Boulder Ranch shop while we installed three brand new ones at Decatur – including a 196-inch EFI press. No more outsourcing – we were in the big leagues now. The building wraps we were printing at the biggest shop (at the time) in Vegas now came in-house. My life would never be the same.

By late 2016, we had 14 on our team and we added a second shift. In mid-2017, we were awarded our first MGM contract. I used social media not to only attract attention, but also to swing deals with vendors. I quickly realized that if I mentioned material and equipment vendors in posts, I could get discounted prices, and even some free stuff.

Something else happened that also changed the path of my little business in 2017. Right around May, I noticed LinkedIn changed their website to have a timeline-type feature, like Facebook. They may have done it earlier, but I hadn't noticed. I created a profile there in 2008, and was networking, adding connections, looking people up, but there wasn't much else to do there. I had created and used a Facebook Business page for several years, but those were mostly just friends and acquaintances. Sometime in May 2017, I made my first LinkedIn post and attracted about 20,000 impressions. It was working way better than Facebook! I started posting pictures of jobs we'd done on a regular basis and built a pretty big following.

Another group we had the attention of by this time was competitors. About 99% of the times you gain a new customer, you're taking away from someone else. From early 2015 to the end of 2017, we shifted about $3 million dollars' worth of local print business our way. The competitors weren't happy about it. They started saying I had come in as a newbie and undercut all the prices, which wasn't true. I'd been making the margins I sought with the prices I'd used for the 13 years I was in business. I had 30 years of industry experience by the end of 2017 and was just more efficient than them.

With both our processes and materials knowledge, we rarely had to reprint or re-do jobs. We got them right the first time. I was outhustling the competitors and giving customers a way higher level of customer service. I was disruptive for sure and did things in an unconventional way. I wasn't bound by any big corporate burden rates or profit margins. I was outsmarting competitors and leveraging LinkedIn and other social media outlets. And I was getting up earlier and working harder.

When we got big jobs – building wraps and stuff – I thought of the profit margins differently. A lot of people put a number on a margin and stick to that no matter what. Even if it prices them out of a job. Good for you, you stuck to your guns... but you didn't get the job – your presses aren't running. I look at it like this: I have a job that I'm billing $80,000 for, and the material costs me $30,000. No matter what happens, if I do the job or not, I'll have to pay rent on the building, the lease on the printers, and pay the employees for at least 40 hours. (Real quick: my policy on the 40 hours was that if we were slow, it was my fault, not the employees'. I would never cut their hours; I would find other things for them to do around the shop like clean and organize. They had families to support.) So why wouldn't I do a job with a $50,000 difference between what I charged and what I paid for material? That money went a long way toward my rent and lease payments. Unorthodox maybe, but it worked.

In any market there are prices customers are used to paying. With all my industry experience, I knew a lot about it. I also knew who I was bidding against most of the time, and how they quoted jobs. We all had the same equipment, basically, and bought our material from the same three local vendors. I guess I was just the least greedy.

The point of this chapter is to provide insight into why I did business the way I did, and convey what I learned and used as I progressed – which, in a nutshell, is this: Customer service is No. 1, the most important element by a very large margin. You must respond to customers right away and work very hard for them, so they know they're important to you. You have to do quality work and stand behind it. Price matters. And you have to work very, very hard. But the most fun one of all is this: to separate yourself from competitors, you must be loud and get noticed. You can't be afraid to be different. And you have to have the guts to take chances. These last three things are what being a punk rock kid taught me, which I transferred to the business world.

At S.I. We are not perfect. But we will own it every time. We had an imperfection in the main building wrap we did yesterday. We would NEVER patch or bandaid it; wouldn't do that to one of our customers. So we reprinted and reinstalled it. Quality and customer service are our main goals, always. #screamingimages #thegoodguys #delivered

Customers Always Come First - The Good Guys

CHAPTER 2
YOUNG JAMES

"White Trash (2nd Generation)"
- Bad Religion

*R*ight before I closed the deal to sell my company of 20 years, I met up with my old punk rock buddy 220, aka Jim Quinn, down at the Cosmopolitan on the Las Vegas Strip to see Billy Idol. We connected in the lounge downstairs for a quick beer before hitting the venue. We were just chatting about life in general, and he all of a sudden said, "Back in the day, none of us would have ever thought you'd pull off all of the shit you've pulled off." I wasn't sure if it was a compliment or not. Maybe this chapter will provide some understanding of why he said that.

* * *

My very first memory was when I was maybe 2 or 3 years old. I remember being in a crib-type bed, looking out a bedroom door and hearing my parents in the front room laughing and talking loudly. They had friends over at their home in Highland Park, Calif.

I remember bits and pieces of that apartment off Figueroa Boulevard, even the outside. And I remember it was at the bottom of a hill and that they had a friend who lived at the top.

I remember more clearly the day we moved into our house in Eagle Rock, Calif., on Avoca Street. My parents purchased a home – it was probably 1968 or 1969. Incidentally, I own that house as of this writing.

Around this time, I started attending a preschool back in Highland Park. I don't remember the inside of the school, but I remember the outside, and my mom being with me.

I was born in Frankfurt, West Germany in 1965. My dad was in the United States Army, and I was born on the base. Dad was from Kansas. He met my mom, who was from London, while stationed there; she was on holiday in Germany with her girlfriends when they met. Jerry and Elaine.

My brother David was born in the house on Avoca when I was around 4½. I was super stoked to have a little brother.

My elementary school was right around the corner, maybe a five-minute walk. Rockdale Elementary. My kindergarten teacher, Ms. Gin, made us take naps. And I wasn't into naps. I remember playtime during kindergarten and that we had wooden toys and plastic hats that represented different jobs in the community – I always wanted to be the fireman. Nothing else was acceptable other than being the fireman.

That school, especially its playground, was a big part of growing up. I walked to school and back by myself from a very early age – maybe even starting in kindergarten. Different times. My folks didn't do anything wrong; that's just how it was back then. Every day after school I begged Mom to let me go back to the playground. They had caroms, four-square, handball, tetherball. I was super competitive from an early age.

* * *

Dad worked at Lockheed on the loading dock, on a second shift. Mom eventually went to work at the local Sav-on Drugs (like today's CVS) down the street, in the bookkeeping department.

I remember they had friends over all the time, and my dad and his buddies would play ping-pong and drink beers in the garage. They were just kids themselves, in their mid-20s. Dad had a green 1966 Ford Mustang with mag wheels and big, loud black pipes going down the sides. It was his pride and joy. He and I used to sit in it on weekends and listen to 8-track tapes. All country music stuff. I was into music from a very early age.

Music and sports were my favorites – especially baseball. Dad had a big record player "cabinet" and I had the freedom to play his records whenever I wanted. I was on the playground and in the street in front of our house playing baseball or football with my friends every day until I joined my first organized sports team – T-ball baseball. I was 7 and played for the Cardinals. The first day of practice the coach said to me, "You're left-handed, you play first base." I ended up playing first base into my 50s.

The next big thing was my first bike. It was green and Dad helped me rake the handlebars way forward and slant the seat real low in the back. That was a big thing for boys back then. As soon as I could ride, I started looking for anything I could find to jump off.

By the time I was 8 years old I had joined Cub Scouts – another fun thing to do after school, and I liked wearing the uniform. I made a bunch of friends right away in Den 199, and a couple of them are still my friends to this day. One of them was Efren, and I remember being super stoked when I discovered he was on my next T-ball team, the Giants. We played at Yosemite Park in Eagle Rock. He's been one of my best friends my whole life – 50-plus years.

The next year we both started Little League again, but went separate ways on teams. It was always fun playing against him, though. By this time, I'd been exposed to a lot of new things and people, between the playground, T-ball, Little League, Scouting, and just the parks in general. We all rode bicycles and skateboards and were always trying to outdo each other with crazy stunts. There was another development around that time I was starting to pay a lot of attention to as well: girls.

Little League was also at Yosemite Park. We had what we thought was a pretty nice field, until we reached All-Stars play and traveled to other leagues' fields. One thing we had at Yosemite, though, was a sort of amphitheater in the back, behind the community pool. There was always something going on back there. Every once in a while, there'd be a band practicing, and we'd walk back and check them out after our games. There was one band we really liked – two brothers and a kind of chubby guy. They played some really hard tunes. Turns out it was early Van Halen (minus David Lee Roth). We were 10 or 11.

***

To back up a little, my parents got divorced when I was 7. I remember lying in bed at night hearing them argue. Mom was pregnant, and my little brother Chris was born right after they separated. They were still young; early 30s. I didn't really understand it all back then; just thought it was what happened to everyone. Dad got an apartment nearby in Eagle Rock, and we saw him every other weekend.

My teachers were all very nice at Rockdale, and school was pretty easy. I couldn't wait for recess and lunch, and the games and competition. Kickball and handball were favorites. After school on the playground, it was always football, and I loved playing with the older kids. Being at the playground after school also kept me supervised until Mom got home from work.

Two weird things I remember that were super important to me back then were my shoes (blue Vans) and my lunchbox. The lunchboxes were awesome, and almost like a competition. There were lunchboxes for just about every classic television show – Starsky & Hutch, Brady Bunch, Partridge Family. Mine featured two dirt bikes racing. I loved my lunchbox.

By the time 4th grade rolled around, girls were important, too. There was one I was especially fond of. Rockdale didn't have a traditional schoolhouse set up – it was all bungalows. And each bungalow had two concrete stair structures that I could easily get into, then sit down and not be seen. Her and I used to sit in the stairs and hold hands and say we liked each other. It was super exciting. Especially since she was a grade higher.

She lived close to my neighborhood, and when we weren't on the playground, I'd ride my bike over to her house. She had a younger sister, one grade below me, and an older brother that was two years older than her. I used to go there, and the brother and his friends would all be sneaking around behind their garage, and there was this funny smell. I asked her what he was doing, and she said he was smoking "pot." I'd never heard of it, but was definitely curious, since he was older and a pretty cool type of guy.

Around 5th grade, I was still wearing Vans sneakers. The boys wore the blue ones, and the girls wore red ones. I used to think, *Why?* I talked Mom into getting me a red pair, and everyone was shocked the first day I wore them to school. By the end of the year a few of the other boys were wearing red Vans, too.

* * *

My first couple of best friends were John and Doug, and I met them around the neighborhood riding bikes and skateboards. They were both a year older. We'd build little jumps out of bricks and plywood and fly off them, not only on our bikes, but also skateboards, and sometimes even just skates.

I had a skateboard in those days that literally had metal wheels. John's little sister had skates, also with metal wheels, that we'd, uh, borrow. I lived at the bottom of a really big hill, and we'd race down it on anything that had wheels – or even if it didn't have wheels – as long as we could go fast.

John moved away when I was in 6th grade; and then it was just Doug and me. We upgraded our bikes and skateboards – we now had Webco frames and Black Knights with clay wheels. Another activity we wanted to add to our repertoire was smoking pot. We both were super curious. The first pot we ever got our hands on was a roach, the butt end of a joint. I don't remember where we got it, but we smoked it at Doug's house in his garage.

* * *

I'd been playing baseball and flag football since I was 7. Doug wasn't really into sports, so I had another group of friends for that arena. The last flag football team I played on was the Steelers; we had orange mesh jerseys which I thought were super cool. I was the quarterback, and we were coached by a couple of older kids who were on the football team at Eagle Rock High School. I was 11. Toward the end of the season, they told me they were going to start a tackle football team the next year, and that I should join. The organization was Jr. All-American Football, and the division for me would be Jr. Pee Wees. It went by weight and age.

I begged Mom to let me play. She was against it – but not for the reasons you'd think. She knew I was a little roughneck, and she wasn't afraid of injuries. It just was expensive. She was a single mother. Plus, we'd have practice three days a week in Glassell Park, a pretty far drive for a mother of three, three evenings a week. Two of my buddies from the Steelers who also wanted to play had the same issue at home. So, we devised a plan where the three moms would each drive to practice and back one time a week – and it worked! We were now Northeast Eagles.

The practices were pretty brutal for 12-year-olds. We had to run up and down hills, do timed laps around the park, and then had hitting drills with pads and helmets. I remember the first week of practice, there were a lot of kids there and we were informed that not everyone would make the team. I was nervous; most of these kids were almost a year older and a lot bigger. After the first week they announced the cut, and I made it. After three weeks of practice, they announced all the starting positions. I was named starting quarterback.

We played eight games a season and our home games were at Eagle Rock High School. We also played four games on the road against teams that were basically junior versions of the high schools, like we were. I remember playing Garfield, Roosevelt, Arcadia, Diamond Bar, Glendale, Temple City, and two teams from Pasadena.

We had a weigh-in before every game, in full pads, and the coaches would always switch equipment around on us before weigh-ins. The bigger guys got helmets with smaller face masks, and us little guys got the linebacker's helmets because they were heavier. I was super skinny, and the coaches used to make me drink water before weigh-ins and hold it until I thought I'd piss my pants. I remember sitting in the front of the bus with them on the way to road games, while they fed me bananas the whole way. I barely made weight every time.

* * *

My activities at this point, from getting up to going to bed, were pretty much split between sports, bikes, and skateboards. We never stopped. I was never inside. Up through elementary school, I was at the playground until it closed at 4:30 p.m., then home to play football and ride bikes and skateboards on my street. My neighborhood housed a lot of kids, so we had some pretty good pickup games in the street. We would all call out the names of our favorite players and say that was who we were. I always played quarterback, and called out that I was Kenny Stabler, from the Raiders, since we were both left-handed. He was by far my favorite player. If I ever switched over to receiver in pickup games, I'd call out that I was Fred Biletnikoff or Cliff Branch, on the same great Raiders team. Sometimes, if no other kids were out, I'd build jumps and have my little brothers lay down on the sidewalk so I could jump over them. Mom caught me a few times and was not stoked. We stayed out every evening until it was too dark to see.

Summers were different. Until I was 12, I would go to the YMCA day camps while Mom worked. It was fun, and I didn't know any different. There were tons of kids, including girls, and we did a ton of activities. Mom would retrieve me after work, and I'd be back to my street and all its action.

Once I was 12, I was allowed to stay home, under the "supervision" of a neighbor, Mrs. Howell. One thing Doug and I did every day in the summer was go to the community pool. It was huge; had two big, high-dive boards, and cost just 25 cents to use. Plus, there were girls everywhere. Doug and I were each other's wingmen. We picked up on different girls every week.

Another thing I liked in summertime was hitting the beach. A couple times a week, Mrs. Howell let the neighborhood kids all jump in her van with our boogie boards and fins, and she'd drive us to El Segundo so we could hit some waves for the day. Another way I got there, sometimes, was to take RTD buses. Three buses, via downtown Los Angeles – land in Manhattan Beach three hours later.

* * *

When 7th grade came around, I left Rockdale for Eagle Rock Junior/ Senior High School. There were a lot of kids from other schools who I already knew through sports, which was pretty cool. But the biggest thing was the girls. They were everywhere. And it wasn't just at school either. By this time, we had girls coming to all our baseball and football games. And our parents, still in their 30s for the most part, always had parties at their houses after games. And the girls would come. It was heaven. I was obsessed with girls.

By this time Doug and I were pretty much smoking pot every day. And his mom would even leave us a couple of beers when she went to work (she was a really cool mom). We would always invite girls over to Doug's. He attended Catholic school, just like some other friends, Efren being one of them. I would ditch school and ride my bike to St. Dominic's school with my other buddies, and the girls would crowd around the fence to talk with us as soon as we rode up. God bless Catholic school girls.

I was still playing baseball and football. After Little League, we moved away from Yosemite Park up to Eagle Rock Park, and the juniors league. My schedule was so busy! I'd leave Doug's house high as a kite from bong hits at 4 p.m. so I could get up to baseball practice by 4:30 p.m.

My group of friends and I also ramped up our bike-riding adventures. Saturdays were spent riding bikes all day (unless I had a baseball or football game). Sometimes we'd ride down into Glendale and hit all the record shops, stereo stores, and dirt bike dealers on the way there and back. We'd ride 20 miles in one trip. Other times we would head over to some of our dirt lot spots where big jumps were built – the Gulley, 57, and the Fire Road were a few of our favorite spots. What we did on our bikes wouldn't be a big deal nowadays, but they were back then. We were launching off big hills and flying some 100 feet down the sides of mountains. It was super crazy.

They knew my mom well at the emergency room at the Kaiser hospital in Hollywood. I was kind of a regular. One evening on our street, for some reason, I was riding my little brother's bike, jumping off curbs and stuff. I went off one of the bigger ones, and I guess the front wheel fell off while in mid-air. All I remember is, when I came to, I lifted my head off the street and could feel my face sticking to the asphalt. And when I looked up there was an ambulance there. Off to Kaiser we go.

I had 12 stitches over my left eye, a broken cheekbone, three chipped teeth, and had skinned the whole left side of my face. They brought in a plastic surgeon because the entire side of my face was one big abrasion, and Mom was worried about scarring. He said, "No problem.

Come in once a week and we'll strap your head to a chair, peel off all the scabs, and put ointment on it." It sure was no fun. But it worked.

Days after the accident, on a Saturday, I had a baseball game. I was playing on the Pirates up at Eagle Rock Park. I woke up in the morning and put on my uniform, and Mom sees and says, "No way!" I said I was just going to watch, and somehow she let me out the door, gear and all. Just watching – yeah, right. It was the left side of my face, and I was left-handed. My left eye was swollen almost shut, but I didn't need it. My right eye was facing the pitcher. Of course I played, and even got a couple of hits. My teammates were tripping out and gave me the nickname "Swami."

Mom put up with a lot. She let me get away with most everything because I got good grades and stayed involved with sports and Scouts. Plus, I had always been involved with something called "Special Class" in elementary school, which upon reaching 7th grade was known as "AE" (academically enriched). This is how it was explained to me:

A specialized learning opportunity designed for students who have mastered the basic curriculum or who quickly grasp new concepts.

In addition, the Jr. All-American football league gave me what they called a "Scholarship Award" for having the best grades in the league. The combination of these things gave me some grace with Mom regarding the shenanigans I pulled.

One of those times was when she caught me sneaking out the bathroom window at night, which I actually did pretty often – out the window, sneak my bike out of the yard, and off into the night. This time, I decided to go up to Eagle Rock Lanes and play some arcade games. I was right in the middle of a grueling game of Pole Position when I got a tap on the shoulder and turned around to see my furious mom. She followed me home; me on my bike, she in her car with the brights on me the whole way. I was totally busted. Grounded for a month.

Although I didn't realize it at the time, she was still really young. And single. It must have been difficult with three kids. She was a good mother, and we had healthy meals cooked for us just about every night. She did go out on the weekends with her girlfriends sometimes, and I had babysitters up until I was 13. I did have one favorite sitter I always hoped for, because she used to make out with me and let me touch her boobs. She was only two or three years older.

***

Mom was also always good for giving me an "allowance" in exchange for some chores around the house. I got $5 a week and always went straight to Camp Records on Eagle Rock Boulevard. The owner was a cool dude. Most of the records actually cost five bucks and change, but he always let me slide, probably because he knew I'd be back with five more bucks the following Friday.

Dad was good, too. He always saw us every other weekend, made big deals out of birthdays and Christmas, and took us on fishing trips with his buddies. Music was always a central theme. We'd sit in his Mustang singing along to his 8-track tapes of George Jones and Kenny Rogers – our favorites. Once I reached 12 or 13 years old, I started venturing off on my own with the music. My first two bands were KISS and Alice Cooper. My dad was crushed.

Doug and I continued to share adventures chasing girls, and we weren't having any problems. Besides the community pool, a couple of other hot spots were the Eagle Rock Plaza (local mall) and the Moonlight Roller Rink in Glendale. The roller rink was my favorite – girls everywhere. I remember they had this session called "Kissing Couples" and we always saved our favorite girls to ask to skate just for this one. Everyone would pair up, and then we'd hold hands with the girl and skate in the circle until the music stopped. Then you'd "kiss your partner." They turned the lights off and everything – full-on five-minute makeout sessions. And it was being sanctioned by adults running the rink. Good times! One of the girls I met there I ended up having my first sexual experience with. Guess I should just say, the first time I ever got laid. I was 14.

Another fun thing around that time was the Eagle Theater. Every Friday at midnight they showed rock 'n' roll movies – Led Zeppelin's "The Song Remains the Same," Alice Cooper's "Welcome to My Nightmare," "Live in Concert" with the Rolling Stones, and others. It was at one of these shows that I took acid (LSD) for the first time.

It was just a continuation of the pot. We always took it in groups, and usually it involved a lot of laughing hysterically. Sometimes when it was better stuff we'd see "trails," and things seemed a bit trippy. We never just sat around taking it. That wasn't our style. We'd take it and go on adventures. One night we decided, after we were already tripping, to ride our bikes down to our school, throw our bikes over the fence, and ride around campus, launching ourselves off the big staircases all over campus. In the dark. It was super fun. We never hurt ourselves, or anyone else.

Another first when I was 14 was my first real concert – Jeff Beck at the Greek Theater. Doug had an older brother, Greg, who always let us tag along; he took us to the show. Mom kicked me down some cash for a concert T-shirt, and for a year after that show I wore it to school three days a week.

* * *

When I was about to turn 15, a big decision approached: whether or not to keep playing football. Because my school was grades 7 to 12, we were eligible to play junior varsity in 9th grade. But, one other thing loomed. I really wanted a car. Which meant I'd have to get a job.

My second year of Jr. All-American hadn't gone well. When I showed up for the first practice, I told the coaches I wanted to play defense; specifically, cornerback. They told me the same thing as the year before – if you play quarterback, we can't let you play defense. You'll get hurt. I was still super skinny. I told them I'd give up quarterback to play defense, so they agreed to let me play both. The first play of the first game on defense I took a facemask to my left hand on a tackle and broke it. Out for most of the season. The guys who coached the J.A.A. team were all seniors at my school, and still wanted me to play junior varsity in 9th grade. I decided to get a job instead.

Mom landed Doug and I jobs at Sav-on shagging shopping carts when we were 15. We couldn't legally start employment until we were 16. I saved my money and started working on an old car Mom had in the garage that didn't run and was super beat up. It was a 1974 Chevy Impala.

Doug was 10 months older and when he turned 16, he went to work on the store floor. When I reached 16, I was promoted into the ice cream department. I made people ice cream cones all day. It was an okay gig. The only thing I hated was having to wear a funny little hat that messed up my hair. One of the ladies who worked with my mom, who I'd known since I was a kid, was named Beverly – she had a son that was close in age named Johnny, and he started working there around then, too. We became good friends.

I got my driver's license the day I turned 16 (everyone did back then, unlike today), and the Impala was all fixed up and ready. It fit six of us comfortably. Five of my friends would ride their bikes 5 miles to my house every morning, then hop in and ride 2 miles to school in my new car. We'd get there early to do donuts in the back turnaround of our school in my Impala.

When I turned 17, I was still working in the ice cream department. The fact that my mom worked there wasn't getting me any favoritism. Not for Doug or Johnny, either. My "uncle" John was manager at the Sav-on store in North Hollywood, which was about a 20-minute drive. He wasn't an actual uncle, but one of my dad's buddies. As a matter of fact, I was named after his older brother Jim, who was my dad's best friend. I was making $3.35 per hour (minimum wage) at that point at the Sav-on in Eagle Rock, but John offered me $4.05 per hour if I would work 28 hours a week, including a 7 a.m. to 4 p.m. shift Sundays. Let me tell you, 7 a.m. on a Sunday was super early for me, and 28 hours a week was way more than I had been working. But I agreed, because back in those days that $0.70 extra per hour was a lot of money.

From that point on, I'd leave school around 2:30 p.m. to head home, and then sat out in front of my neighbor's house on their wall smoking pot until 4 p.m. Then I'd change into my work clothes and head to North Hollywood. I'd be stoned out of my mind when I got there, and no one knew except for a younger guy named Joe. He'd look at me and say with great exaggeration, "Ooooh!! You're stooooooooned!" Another guy I met at that job was Scott. He was around my age and looked like a surfer. We became friends pretty fast. I still had long hair and was basically a stoner-rocker guy. He, on the other hand, was into punk rock. I was curious. This guy would end up changing my life.

Around the time I was in 11th grade, Mom briefly was re-married, and we moved to this dude's house in Burbank. I was okay with it because he had a nice house with a pool, I got a really good bedroom, and I was closer to work in North Hollywood. I decided to stay at Eagle Rock High since 11th grade was almost over, and I could finish there the next year. Mom decided my little brothers David and Chris would go to school in Burbank.

Working at Sav-on in North Hollywood was totally fun. I became super good friends with Scott, and he started taking me along to surf, and to nightclubs in the San Fernando Valley that were packed with girls. When Johnny heard about how much fun we were having, he joined us.

Now all my friends also had cars, and we would do some crazy shit in them. We had a bunch of dirt roads and empty lots to race up and down and do donuts in. All while drinking Moosehead beer, which had become the consensus favorite. A couple of my friends had 4x4 pickups that could get us to spots high up in the San Gabriel Mountains, where we would just hang out, drink beer, and smoke pot.

Mom was pretty cool about letting me go wherever I wanted in my car. In October of 1981, where I wanted to go was to see the Rolling Stones at the Los Angeles Coliseum. I had just turned 17, and she gave the green light. So, me and the gang all piled in the Impala and headed over the evening before. It was all general admission seating, so we wanted to get in the gates early to get a good spot. And we wanted to party. Upon arrival, there was already a huge crowd, lining up to get in the gates when they opened in the morning. We each had two hits of acid, so we had to space them out. And my buddy Chuck brought an empty Marlboro cigarettes box filled with hand-rolled joints. We were set.

We stayed up all night, no sleep, and got a pretty good spot in the stands on the Coliseum's south side. There were three opening bands: J. Geils Band, George Thorogood, and some guy called Prince who no one knew. Well, we all thought Prince sucked, and we weren't alone. He was wearing a short coat and garter belts and opened with a song that had the lyrics "jack you off." He was booed off the stage after two songs. I may or may not have hit him in the head with an empty Coke cup. But the Stones jammed, we all had a great time, and we made it back to Eagle Rock safely.

* * *

In 1982, 11th grade, I talked Mom into letting me buy a brand-new Toyota pickup truck. I was doing well at Sav-on, so she agreed and co-signed. I wanted a Toyota because Efren and my other buddy Sean had them – except theirs were 4x4s. All I could afford was a stock model. Mom and I went to the dealer one day after school, and I picked out a shiny white one. It had a four-cylinder engine, was bone stock, with manual transmission. I'd had my license for over a year but had never driven a stick shift. I'd practiced shifting gears in my friends' parents' cars while they were parked in driveways – that was it. After we signed the papers and I was stepping in, Mom asked if I was sure I knew how to drive it. "Yeah, for sure I do!" And off I went. I made it around the corner and out of her sight before I started stalling it and causing a traffic jam. It took me about an hour to learn how to drive it, and by the time I got home around midnight I had it all figured out. Mom was pissed. I put a Black Flag sticker in the back window the next morning.

In 1982, I was pretty much all-in on punk rock. I hung out a lot with Scott, surfing on weekends and hitting nightclubs in the Valley and Hollywood, chasing girls around. I still hung around with Efren, Chuck, and my Eagle Rock crew, but they weren't into the punk stuff. And that was okay.

The Who played the L.A. Coliseum in October 1982, so we all went. One huge bonus for me was that The Clash opened for them. I got the best of both worlds.

Also that year, I started going to punk rock shows. I still hadn't cut off my hair, so I had to stand in the back for the first handful of shows. The very first show I saw was my friend Vic's band, S.V.D.B., at The Vex in East Los Angeles. It was dangerous, dark and loud. And I loved every minute of it.

1983 came quickly, and it was time to graduate high school. I was way ahead on my credits and only had to check in at school a couple of hours a day the last semester. I'd spend the rest of the day at the beach and then be at the North Hollywood Sav-on by 5 p.m.

Another thing I did around then for the first time was cocaine. I didn't really do a lot, because it was expensive, and I couldn't really afford it. We'd get into it on special occasions. Senior prom and stuff like that.

My plan for continuing my education was to enroll at Pierce College in Woodland Hills. Then called a *junior* college, it was in the northwest corner of the Valley. I chose Pierce because that's where Scott went. I had to choose some sort of direction, so I chose architecture. I had a pretty half-assed schedule and spent most of my time during the days at the beach.

* * *

I'd developed a new trick at this point: drinking and driving. Moosehead beers did not have twist-off caps, and in no time, I figured out there was something shaped kind of like a bottle opener in the doorjamb of my Toyota

– which I'd use, even while driving, to pop tops off. One Saturday I left work at 4 p.m., picked up a six-pack (I had a fake ID, created in graphic arts class) and went home to shower. I got in my truck to head over to Eagle Rock and opened my first Moosehead right around the corner from my house. I must have done a California rolling stop at the next intersection, because I was pulled over by a Burbank cop. I tried shoving the full bottle under my seat, but it was just spilling out on the floor. So, there was that, and the paper sack sitting on the passenger seat containing the six-pack holder with five full bottles. I was busted, so I just admitted it. It was easy for him to see the five in the bag and that a full one was spilled – so he knew I wasn't drunk. I was super lucky, and he just made me pour out all the beers and gave me a warning.

Next day, I did the same thing after work. Six-pack in the passenger seat, one open between my legs, headed to Eagle Rock, and saw the same cop as the day before. He pulled up beside my truck, rolled his window down, and said, "Hey Swanson, you don't have a six-pack of Moosehead on your passenger seat, right?" I said, "Nope." And he let me go. So lucky.

* * *

Let's back up a bit here. Dad moved to Simi Valley, Calif. in the late 1970s. It was a newer, suburbia-type city in the southeast part of Ventura County, immediately north of L.A. County adjacent to the Valley. He was still picking us up and having us over every other weekend. Well, his live-in partner Darlene would pick us up, as he was still working second shift. I always brought my bike and skateboard and made friends out there fast. There were a lot of kids in the neighborhood, and more importantly for me, a lot of girls. I'd bring joints, too, and sneak around the corner to the park with the neighbor girl to smoke them. I always looked forward to trips to Simi Valley.

My every-other-weekend visits to Dad's ended once I got a car and a job. Unfortunately, when I stopped going, so did my brothers David and Chris. I started going out there on my own after I started surfing, as Simi Valley was just a skip over Malibu Canyon or Kanan Road from the beach. Things were going okay at Pierce College, but I wasn't really applying myself, and didn't know anyone besides Scott. I made a big decision when I was 19 to move out to Simi, live with Dad, and switch to Moorpark College (Moorpark is immediately west of Simi Valley) which is what they now call a community college, equal to Pierce. I said switch instead of transfer, because I didn't have anything to transfer. I hadn't completed any classes.

My first day at Moorpark I had a placement class, and I was determined to make some friends. The classroom was packed, tons of cute girls. Even better, they were all beach girls. I was the only kid in the whole class with spiked hair, and I was getting a lot of looks. A minute before class started, a guy walks in and everyone yells out his name. He was slapping hands all the way down the aisle. Blonde surfer-looking guy, all the girls smiling huge at him. I knew I had to make friends with this guy. When he walked by, he high-fived me and said, "Nice Taco Surf T-shirt," so I figured he'd surfed K-38 in Mexico too. Then right as the teacher was standing up to start, another surfer-looking guy walks in – same thing. Girls smiling and blushing at him. He had a darker complexion, also with his hair spiked. He sat next to the other blonde guy from earlier – they were buddies. These two guys were Chuck and Kevin, and that day would be the first day of lifelong friendships among us. Kevin, in particular, would become instrumental in the accounting and financials of Screaming Images 35-plus years later, as my outsourced CFO.

As I turned 20, the hard partying continued. I was drinking and driving everywhere I went. By this time, though, I had stopped smoking pot, as I realized it wasn't really doing anything for me. Acid and mushrooms were still fun but weren't quite fitting in with my current activities and hobbies, so that was curtailed a bit. Not stopped, just curtailed.

Summer of 1985, I planned a surf trip to Mexico with one of my punk rock buddies named Brian, who I met through Scott. We were planning on driving my Toyota pickup a little more than halfway down Baja California. I made a plywood cover for the bed of my truck, painted it bright green with the names of punk bands spray-painted in red. This was our attempt to keep our boards and wetsuits safe while down there. We would be gone for 10 days.

The trip was rad. We didn't get as far as we hoped, only down to Guerrero Negro, but hit some good spots including Punta Santa Rosalita. We'd go into towns where no one spoke English, and we struggled to buy simple things like ice. It probably didn't help that we both had bleached hair, mine all spiked out. The local folks seemed scared of us – I'm sure they'd never seen punk rockers before. We drove through towns with only dirt roads that had Mexican soldiers with machine guns, down roads to the coast that were lined with old shacks and cemeteries. We bought fish off local fishermen to cook on our grill, almost totaled my truck on a cow in the middle of nowhere – and even spent a really dark night at the edge of a cliff we didn't know was there.

About a week after we returned from Mexico, I was out partying with Scott and Brian in the San Fernando Valley. Phases and Hot Traxx were a couple of our favorite clubs. We were drinking pretty heavily, and when the night came to an end, instead of heading home to Simi Valley, I headed to Burbank, maybe going to Mom's house, I don't remember. On Interstate 5, around 2:30 a.m., near the Sunland Boulevard exit, I flew off the freeway and hit a tree. I don't remember it. I remember coming to, the steering wheel hanging in broken threads across my lap, and the entire passenger side of the truck caved in, so much so that I couldn't even see the floor. My first thought and reaction was that Brian was still with me, and trapped under there. I climbed out of the truck, stumbled to the side of the highway to a Call Box, and contacted the cops. They sure did come. And they arrested me on the spot. I don't remember much, but I do remember the cops were super angry and shaking their heads at me. They handcuffed me, put me in the back of the California Highway Patrol car, and took me to L.A. County Jail.

When I woke up the next morning, I was in the hospital wing of the jail and had been arrested for drunk driving. Mom was there, crying, and everything on me hurt. I had a broken hand, three broken ribs, and a separated shoulder. I had stitches in my face and head, and a severe concussion. By this point, even though I didn't remember it, I had already been processed and once the doctor arrived and cleared me to go, Mom could take me home.

Once we left the jail, we had to go to the impound yard in Burbank to sign a release on my truck – it was a total loss. When we walked in a guy met us at the gate. I saw my truck sitting across the yard, pointed, and said that one's mine. First thing he said was, "You're still alive? We thought you were dead for sure – there was blood everywhere." I was still trying to piece together what happened. I wasn't sure if I'd blacked out, fell asleep; I had no idea. To try and jog my memory I walked over to the truck and hit eject on the cassette player to see what I'd been listening to. It was T.S.O.L., "Dance with Me." Still nothing.

Needless to say, both my parents were pissed. And I didn't have a vehicle. We were waiting to hear about the insurance payout on the truck, but Mom wasn't in a hurry for me to have another ride. I had moved back to her house at this point and was bumming rides to work in North Hollywood.

The payout came through, and it covered the balance owed on the '83 Toyota. My credit was a little better by then, thanks to the fact that Mom had been handling my finances and ensuring payments were made. By now I had a Visa credit card, too, which I wasn't being very responsible with. I got a credit union to approve a vehicle loan with no down payment and bought a brand new 1986 Toyota pickup truck that was pretty much exactly like the other one, just a newer model.

At this point I was about to turn 21 and was driving a ton. To North Hollywood for work, to Simi Valley to see my friends, to the beach every day, out every night – and I was still drinking and driving everywhere I went.

Another thing I'd started doing on a pretty regular basis was cocaine. It wasn't a lot, because it was expensive – and it wasn't really an addiction, either. The primary reason I did it, really, was because it helped me drink more. Mostly just on weekends.

* * *

We loved going to Mexico to surf and party. Just easy two-day trips to Rosarito and Ensenada. We could drive right across the border and back – you didn't need passports. We'd surf during the day at K-38, La Fonda, and San Miguel, and party at night in Rosarito.

You always had to beware of the Federales and keep some cash in your pocket. They'd stop you for anything, and $20 in U.S. bills usually assuaged them.

One night after partying at Papas and Beer nightclub, I had taken it a little too far. For some reason I was down by the beach wearing nothing but flip-flops, board shorts, and a trench coat. The inside pockets of the coat were all filled with full bottles of Corona – I had at least a 12-pack in there. I was shit-faced, the Federales grabbed me, and threw me in the back of their van – and I didn't have any more money. I was going to a Mexican jail.

Then suddenly I heard a girl outside the van yelling my name. Two minutes later the van doors opened and the Federales pulled me out and threw me into the dirt street. I looked up and it was a girl I knew from Eagle Rock. She saw me get thrown in the van and had bailed me out! Funny thing was, this girl didn't even like me. I had been going back and forth between two of her friends for the past couple years. But she was from Eagle Rock, and that's what we did over there. Thank you, Michelle!

* * *

I'd never stopped playing ball in organized leagues, from age 7 on. In the west Valley, we had a team called Irish Creamers that started playing A-League softball at Lanark Park in Canoga Park. We were really good. It was mostly set up by my friend (and store manager) Tim from Sav-on in North Hollywood. We played Sunday nights and drank the whole time. Before, during, and after games.

By the time we were all 21, and could go to any bar or club, we went out almost every night. I think the only nights I ever stayed home were Mondays, only because there was nowhere to go. Another thing that started happening around this time was we were getting into a lot of fights at clubs. We never started them – but always finished. There was always a group of us, and I guess everyone thought because we just looked like skinny surfer guys, we couldn't defend ourselves. And I never had to worry anyways, because I had Jeff "The Brawler" on my side.

I was really missing Simi Valley and all my friends. Plus, all the girls out there. I was driving there and back three or four nights a week, so I just decided to move back. Three of my friends and I decided to all rent a house together, and found one on the west side. It was owned by a nice family, and I still can't believe they agreed to rent it to us. Around this time also, there was some tension on the Creamers. The guy running the team wanted to bring in a new pitcher to replace the one we'd had since the beginning. That to-be-replaced pitcher was a very good friend of mine. Four of us on the Creamers secretly decided to leave and start our own team, with some of our friends from Simi. We had just won another A-League championship (undefeated, by the way), and we waited until our celebration party to announce it.

We called our new team the Shindiggers. It had four of us from the Creamers and then a bunch of our surfer buddies from Simi. Here's where we got the team name: every weekend after we were done at the beach and got out of the water, everyone would ask, "Where's the shindig tonight?" It was the perfect name for us.

We decided to play our first season in Simi Valley, in a shortened summer B-League, to see what we had. And we actually had a pretty good team. Simi was a small town back then, and word spread quickly about us, and who was on the team. We got a local muffler shop owned by the older brother of one of the guys on the team to sponsor us, so we had uniforms. Our first game, we had a crowd of about 50 people cheering us on. It might not sound like much, but other teams were lucky to have a handful of fans in the stands. We drew a crowd. Afterward, we invited everyone back to our rented house to party. We played Tuesday nights.

The next game we had about 100 people in the crowd, and the next week even more. It was hilarious. Coming to our games was the hottest thing to do in town, and I have to admit, it was a lot of fun. We were 3-0 at the time, too (on the way to a second-place finish). On my way to the park for our third game I stopped at Dad's to grab something, and my little stepbrother John looked like he was getting ready to go somewhere, so I asked where. He said he was going to watch some softball game, and it was supposed to be crazy and super fun. I said, "Yeah, I'm on the team." He just laughed and said, "Figures." That night, after I had just hit a triple and was standing on third base with the crowd all wild and screaming, the third baseman asked me, "*Who the hell are you guys?*" (haha). The bigger the crowds at the game, the bigger the party at our house afterward. By now everyone in town was calling our house "The City," which was coined by my best friend, teammate, and roommate Kevin (the one I met at Moorpark College, with Chuck). It was every Tuesday night, and the neighbors were not stoked.

Fun at The City didn't last long. I'd been working full-time at Sav-on, now in the receiving department, and wasn't happy with how it was going. So I quit, without considering my next move. I had been living paycheck to paycheck, so I could no longer pay my rent, and I had to move out. It was pretty embarrassing. I was so irresponsible.

And it got worse. I had to move back into Mom's house, and she wasn't stoked. I tried several jobs but couldn't make anything stick. It had been about 90 days since I quit Sav-on. I was broke, unemployed, and living with my mother. One morning I woke up, got off the couch, and looked outside. My truck was gone. Repossessed.

It was the lowest point of my life.

* * *

I felt completely worthless. I really needed a job. I already had an interview lined up for a paid intern position at an architecture company, when my buddy Sean stopped by and said the company he worked for was hiring. He took me to the company picnic that weekend; I set up an interview, and accepted a job as the shipping clerk. This is exactly where my printing career began.

I still didn't have a vehicle, so between Sean and his cousin Richard, who also worked there, they got me to and from work the first couple months. After 60 days or so, I struck a deal with the company's vice president, Gavin (who really liked me) and bought an old company vehicle from them. Payments were taken out of my paycheck. It was an old Oldsmobile Cutlass that leaked oil really badly and didn't have much of a future.

So now that I had some money and a car, I was back to going out again. I'd hang with my Eagle Rock buddies during the week, and then head out to Simi Valley on the weekends.

Still drinking and driving.

By this time, '86 to '87, real punk rock shows were becoming more scarce. The scene had kind of died out. It's funny, because I had been having so much fun going to those shows that I was always kind of worried it would end. It was also a shame because, for some reason, I never drank myself to oblivion at those shows. The energy was enough of a high.

* * *

I was doing well at Techtron/Jordan & Horn and liked working there. Everyone kept saying I had room to grow. The Cutlass finally died, and I used my income tax refund to buy an old Volkswagen Bug. I had to push start it, and it had no brakes, so I used the emergency brake to stop. It got me back and forth to work.

One day at work around this time, an old punk rock guy who worked with me named Henry said he heard a rumor Social Distortion was recording a video in a warehouse in Downtown L.A., pretty close to the shop. He didn't have an address but knew the general area. I asked my boss to leave early, and he approved, as the shop was slow. I went off in search of that warehouse – and found it. It was pretty easy to sneak in, and I sat there for about two hours watching my favorite band record the video for the song "Ball and Chain" (which would eventually be played consistently by a local radio station I later did print and sign work for). I stayed to the very end, and even got a picture with band leader Mike Ness outside, next to his car. I do not know, to this day, how I just so happened to have a camera in my pocket that day. In those days if you wanted to take pictures, you had to have a camera. There were no nifty mobile phones.

By this point I'd moved to La Crescenta, out near Pasadena, to share a rental house with my buddy Chris, who I'd been friends with since Little League. It was a cool house with a pool, and we had big parties all the time. One weekend we went to a bar in the San Fernando Valley we'd heard about. We'd both been drinking heavily, and Chris was driver. We had his older brother's truck (I can't remember why). When we were walking out, I saw Chris stumbling, and told him to give me the keys. He obliged, I hopped in, fired up the engine, and got pulled over as soon as we pulled away from the parking lot. Drunk driving arrest No. 2.

Since it was a Friday, I wasn't going to see a judge until Monday, and I had no bail money or anyone to help. On Monday morning I was informed that I had a warrant (an old seatbelt ticket unpaid) and had to clear that one first. By the time I went to court for the DUI and was released I had spent four nights in jail.

So that Tuesday night I was at home, bored, and decided to go over to my buddy Chuck's house to hang out. I told myself I'd only have a couple of beers but ended up staying there past midnight. And drove home drunk. One night out of jail. I got lucky and didn't get caught – but I was for sure not learning any lessons.

Chris and I hung out a lot. There weren't really any punk rock shows anymore, but we still went out to Hollywood. Chris was a metal guy anyway. One weekend night we went down to the Rainbow Bar & Grill on the Sunset

Strip. There wasn't anything particular going on; just went to hang out and have drinks. Once again, I was wasted and caused a little bit of a ruckus. Chris had to pull me out of a back room, where the bouncers had me. I was "politely asked to leave," so Chris and I headed outside, where he had his car parked with the valet. Now, Chris had a *really* nice car. An IROC Camaro convertible, cherry red, chrome-dipped rims – the whole bit.

As they pulled the car up and we were getting in, a couple of Hollywood kids started heckling Chris, saying he was "driving his daddy's car," which was absolutely untrue. Even in our mid-twenties, Chris was already a super-successful guy. They kept carrying on, so I asked if they wanted to go around the corner and talk about it. They said yes, so we went out, turned right on the Strip, and right onto the first street. They walked up, and we hopped out of the car. I went up to the taller guy and asked if he was ready. He said "yeah" and put up his hands. I popped him with a straight left, between his hands, and he hit the sidewalk. I asked him if he wanted more, and he said no and took off running. I looked across the street to see how Chris was doing, and he had the other dude by the back of the collar and was giving him continuous kicks in the ass – it was hilarious. He finally let go, and the second kid took off running. Don't underestimate the skinny guys! Just another night in Hollywood.

Later that year Chris bought a house in Simi Valley. I went with him and rented a room. Right around this time I got moved to second shift at my job, which was 3 to 10:30 p.m., which meant I was missing out on a lot of the activities with my friends on Friday nights. But it was better for me – less time for drinking at night.

After a couple of years in Simi I drifted back to L.A. and Eagle Rock. For a while I stayed on the couch at Mom's, and then I rented an apartment in Glendale, next to Burbank. While still at Mom's, I went out one night with my friend Johnny to a place in La Crescenta called Lady Jane's. We were drinking beers and playing pool for three or four hours, and when we left, for some reason, I ended up driving his car.

Once again, right out of the parking lot, I was pulled over. I was drunk and thought: here comes another DUI. The Glendale cop asked me for my driver's license and went to his car to run it. When he came back, he asked me to get out of the car, and I thought, oh boy, here we go again. I was being arrested – but it was for outstanding warrants. I had three unpaid tickets for not wearing a seatbelt, and one unpaid speeding ticket. I was transported to the La Crescenta police department and put in a holding cell for the weekend. It was a Friday night, and I couldn't see the judge until Monday morning. But I was lucky: I didn't get a third drunk driving charge.

I saw the judge Monday morning, and he immediately sent me to L.A. County Jail. I was told that all the warrants were from different cities and courts, and I would be taken to one every morning to see the presiding judge in each court. I was processed into County on Monday afternoon, and the biggest thing on my mind was that I was going to miss my softball game Tuesday night. I had my personal clothes and property taken away, and I was given the L.A. County Jail blues. I was wearing my Doc Marten boots; they let me keep those on. I was housed in a huge open dormitory with hundreds of other dudes and everywhere I went the other inmates kept asking me, "Are those Docs?" I took them off every night and slept with them under my pillow thinking I'd have to fight to keep them.

Tuesday morning, I started going to a different court every morning, by the L.A. County Sheriff's bus. I remember riding in the bus on the freeway, looking through the bars in the windows at everyone driving their own cars, and being free. It was an awful feeling. The same thing happened at every court for every warrant. I'd walk in, and the judge would say, "Time served," and the warrant was cleared. Friday afternoon, after the fourth court visit, I heard my number being called for release. They took me from the dorm and put me in a very long hallway with hundreds of other dudes awaiting release. I had no idea what time it was. After what seemed like forever, my number was called and I was brought into another cell and given my clothes and personal items back, to change for release. The only problem was my leather jacket was missing. I told one of the deputies watching the cell that my jacket was missing, and he immediately said: "Do you want to go home or not?" One of those deputies had himself a nice punk rock leather jacket.

When I finally exited and stepped into the night, it was about 2 a.m. and freezing cold. I was in downtown L.A. without any money, so I did the only thing I could. I called Mom to pick me up. I had been in jail for a week.

The biggest thing about all this was my job. I got one phone call every day and used it to call my boss Jim with updates. I just told him the truth about what was happening; it was really all I could do. I thought for sure when I got out and back to work, I'd be fired. But Jim just gave me a written warning, and a heavy-duty talk. He said I was super talented, that all the bosses liked me. But I needed to get my shit together, because there were no more chances. He seemed like he was genuinely concerned for me, and that he really cared, and I always remembered that. And I used it during my 20 years of owning Screaming Images with a couple of guys who I felt were super talented and just needed a little more time to grow up. Pay it forward.

I moved back to the apartment in Glendale after that – Mom needed a break from me and my shenanigans. It was a crappy place, and I had two roommates. I was just working and keeping my head low. While living there, I started hanging around with a girl named Staci, and she ended up being my girlfriend. I actually had known her since 9th grade, and we'd gone out a little when we were kids. After about six months she decided we needed to live together, so we got an apartment in South Pasadena.

Things were super fun for a while. My friends came over all the time, and I was pretty mellow. Everyone was tripping out on me. After another six months or so she started posting around the house pictures of engagement rings. On the fridge, on the cork board, sitting on the dining room table. I wasn't ready for it, but I wasn't saying no, either. Our personalities were almost exactly the same – we were both stubborn and both alphas, and after a while, things started coming to a head. I was still a punker, and she wanted me to be more of a preppy guy, and that wasn't going to happen. We began to fight, and I knew it wouldn't last. She finally suggested maybe we should just not live together any longer but keep dating. She would stay, and I would get a place nearby. Maybe the space would do us good. I didn't see it that way but agreed to try. One day she asked if I'd gotten a place yet, and I said yes – in Newport Beach. I was out of there.

By this time, Chris, Efren, and Chuck were all living down there, so it was a no-brainer.

Plus, I always loved Newport. Maybe I'd start surfing again, which I really missed.

Staci was still coming around when I first moved down there. I was rotating between first, second, and third shift at work. One weekend while on second shift, my roommates and the Brazilian guys downstairs decided to have a party. I got home from work around 11 p.m. and the party was still raging. I'd been home for about 15 minutes when the cops came busting through the door. My roommates all ran out the back door, and I was left just standing there. The cops asked if I lived there, I said yes, and they cuffed me. I hadn't even had a beer yet.

The Newport Beach jail was the nicest I'd ever visited. In the morning, they gave us McDonald's for breakfast, and even dropped off the sports section from the *Orange County Register*. They cited me for disturbing the peace and told me my girlfriend was waiting outside. Staci gave me a ride back to the pad, and as soon as I got there, I cracked a beer. It wasn't 11 a.m. yet.

I was having the time of my life in Newport. I lived right across the street from the ocean; my front yard was sand. Chuck got me on his company softball team in Costa Mesa, so I was playing two nights a week (along with still playing in L.A.). Around this time, also, I was invited to join a baseball team in L.A. Real baseball, not slow-pitch softball. It was pretty competitive, and I loved it. I ended up playing hardball until I was almost 40.

After my first summer, Chris and Chuck both met the girls they would eventually marry and moved away. Efren also had a girl and moved up to Huntington Beach. I was having way too much fun, so stayed and made a whole new set of friends, which included Jason.

We were partying hard. Mostly booze and cocaine. I was staying as responsible as I could, and my job was still going really well. But weekends were crazy. Jason and I became inseparable.

In 1995 there was a show called Lollapalooza at Irvine Meadows Amphitheatre down in south county. It fell on a weekday, so I asked well in advance for the afternoon off. Around noon I headed home to Newport, met Jason, and away we went. It was a killer show featuring Hole, Elastica, Sonic Youth, and Pavement. We hit the beers as soon as we walked into the venue and surprisingly had really good seats in front. One thing led to another, and we both ended up buying and taking something they were calling "Herbal Ecstasy." It was legal; they were selling it from a booth at the show, but damn! That stuff kicked our asses. Toward the end of the night, for some reason, Jason got into it with security, and I ran over to defend him. We both got detained and taken to a backstage area. They said they'd only keep us until the end of the show. The show ended, and they told Jason he could go. Not me. They had found an old warrant in Orange County. I was off to Orange County Jail.

The warrant was like 10 years old for something I had done on a day trip down there with Efren. They didn't find it when I got busted in L.A., because it was Orange County (and they weren't as sophisticated back then). They released me in the morning, and I caught a taxi to Irvine Meadows. My truck was the only vehicle in the massive parking lot. I had no idea how Jason got home – again, no cell phones.

I knew Jim would be pissed. I just went straight to the shop, dirty clothes and all, and arrived around noon. I apologized profusely, but he just told me to get to work. The shop was completely buried with a new ad campaign, and he needed me. I was lucky again. I ended up working 16 hours that day to make up for it.

After about 5 years of Newport, I was feeling homesick for Simi again. I went back for two years, but then missed Newport. It was a long haul to Burbank (where the shop was now located) from Newport, so I moved to Belmont Shores in Long Beach, just over the L.A.-Orange County line. I shared a pad with Jason.

I was in my mid-30s, and you'd think I would be grown up by then, but it wasn't the case. We were still doing all the same old shit. Unfortunately, I wouldn't grow up completely until I moved to Las Vegas in 2005, and more importantly, brought a blonde Labrador named Scout into my life.

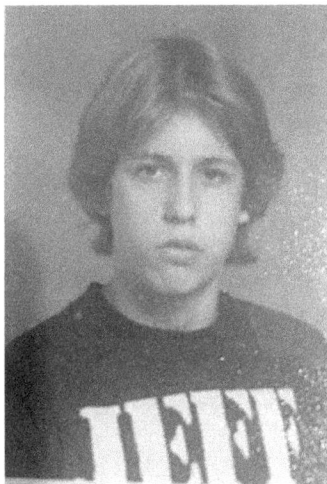

Jeff Beck Concert T-shirt
14 years old

Mexico surf trip 1985

US-Mexico border
returning from
surf trip 20 years old

Outside LA
warehouse with
Mike Ness from
Social Distortion

CHAPTER 3
PUNK ROCK

"Sound & Fury"

- *Youth Brigade*

*O*n *a hot night in August 1984, we all met at Mom's house in Eagle Rock to hit a show in downtown L.A. We had a pretty good group – all the usuals, Scott, Johnny, Chuck and I, plus Diana and Andrea, a couple of girls who hung around with us. I warned the girls that this probably wasn't a show they would enjoy, but they were gung-ho to participate. Also along for the ride were my little brother David and a couple of his friends, so we had my truck and another car. There were several reasons I warned the girls. First, the headlining band; secondly, the venue; and third, the fact that it was right at the end of the Summer Olympics, and I knew L.A. cops would be out in force. Scott jumped in my truck, David and his two friends jumped in the bed in the rear (back when they let us do that), and off we went.*

When we arrived at Olympic Auditorium, the parking lot was already packed with punk rockers drinking and doing who knows what else outside their cars. There were cops around on the streets, but I didn't see any in the parking lot. The atmosphere was super tense. We found two parking spots pretty close to each other in the back and got out. I gave the girls some rules: Stay close to us. If you get separated go to the lobby and wait for us. If you have to use the restroom, take one of us with you. Do NOT go anywhere near the pit. Then I gave one rule to my brother and his friends, same as always, as they tagged along with us to a lot of shows: If you want a ride home you need to be in the back of my truck by 30 minutes after the show ends.

We walked to the front of the Olympic, and noticed at the entrance three ambulances, rear-end parked, doors wide open and ready. It put a pretty good scare into the girls, but it didn't surprise me. The Dead Kennedys were playing

– just six bucks to get in. I loved going to shows at the Olympic because it was a pretty big venue, but rumors were that it was condemned, which didn't surprise me either. Punks loitering in the lobby, kegs up against the back wall, the smell of stale beer and who knows what else, and the massive sound of thrash coming from the main room. I'd already lost David.

We all walked into the main ballroom and the first thing I saw was my little brother making out with some punk rock lady. I walked up to her and said, "Hey, that's my little brother, and he's only 14." She shrieked and pushed him off, and then David ran off into the crowd and jumped into the main pit. About an hour later Dead Kennedys came out and their singer, Jello Biafra, said, "This one is for our friends outside," and they busted into their opening song, "Police Truck." The place went fucking nuts, and the only thing I could think of was, it would be a bitch getting home.

Our main group stayed intact, and we all walked out together after the show. The girls had stayed very close to us (no surprise there, haha). No sign of David and his friends. As soon as we walked outside there were cops everywhere, helicopters hovering above, people running all over the parking lot, and hooligans tossing bottles at RTD buses. It was pretty much a riot. In my opinion it was the cops who usually provoked these situations. On the other hand, there also usually was a fair amount of people at punk rock shows looking for trouble. And it was easy to find.

We reached our vehicles, and David had about 10 more minutes before I was out of there. After that period ended and no David, I started up my truck and said, "Let's go." The girls asked if I was really leaving them, and I said, "Yep." As I cruised through the parking lot, I felt a big thump in the bed of the truck and looked back – one of the youngsters had just jumped in.

Another 100 feet or so I felt another thump – there's two. And right as I was pulling out of the parking lot, David came running up from out of nowhere and did a barrel-roll into the back of my moving truck. Got 'em all. To be fair here, and I didn't mention this to the girls because it was kind of fun, this was how our exits always went. I would never have left my little brother behind in the middle of a riot.

＊＊＊

Without punk rock there likely wouldn't have been a Screaming Images.

What punk taught me was that it was okay to be different. It showed me how to stand out in a crowd. It ingrained into me the "do it yourself" work ethic. It gave me the guts to take chances.

The bands back then were doing the same things that I did when I started Screaming Images – they were doing everything themselves. DIY. They were starting from scratch. They were using new ideas instead of conforming to what society and precedents told them they ought to do. They were learning as they went. They were being creative, breaking new ground. They were taking risks.

Another thing back then was that there were no barriers between the crowd and the band. About 90% of the places to see shows had no stage. There were no bouncers or security guards. When you got fired up about a song the band was playing, you just joined them. It took the whole participation thing to an entirely different and highly exciting level. There were no rock stars – you were one of them. When the bands finished playing the members just simply walked out into the crowd. You could actually talk to the people in your favorite bands. This might be why I was always so front facing with my customers. I was always 100% available. I wasn't just doing their jobs; I was participating in them.

＊＊＊

Everyone has different opinions about what punk rock is (or, for some, was), and I won't try to say anyone is wrong or right. People have their own interpretations and get their own things out of it.

What attracted me to punk was that it was authentic. The bands played aggressive, high- energy, fast-paced music, and I liked that. It got my adrenaline going. I guess it was a natural evolution into punk rock from the music

I listened to as a kid. It was always the harder-edged stuff. I was always a rebel, and when I saw that a couple kids at my school cut off all their hair and started wearing altered/homemade clothes with handwritten slogans on them, with rips, tears, and straps, it set off all my insurgent instincts. They stood out. They were doing something different, and I had always liked being different. I wanted in.

In 10th grade, 1981, I had science class first period, and for some strange reason all the teacher did was show Star Trek episodes. Yeah, weird. I always met my friend Vic in the park before class and we'd smoke a joint before heading in. Vic was like me – stoner, long hair, surfer clothes, baseball player. One morning when we met before class, he said he was going punk rock. His older brother was going to shave his head when he got home from school and he would join his brother's band as the singer, along with another of our buddies named Pat playing drums. This was exciting news. There were only two other "punks" at our school at the time, and they were taking a lot of shit for being different. Back in those days, shaving your head was a really big deal. Vic would get a lot of crap from people for that alone. He came in the next morning and, sure as shit, he'd shaved his head and bleached it. His new band was called S.V.D.B.

This was around the time I met Scott. I was 16 and working at Sav-on Drugs as a cashier out in North Hollywood. He started about a week after I did. We were around the same age, and way younger than everyone working there, so we became friends quickly. He was a total surfer- looking guy. I loved the beach but had only ridden skateboards and boogie boards. We of course started talking music, and he said he was into punk rock. I was super curious now. Scott and Vic were both a couple of the coolest guys I knew, and they were both punk rockers. I didn't have a lot of experience with the music. I knew and liked the Ramones and had heard of the Sex Pistols, so I asked a bunch of questions. His response was to just loan me a cassette tape. On that tape was a compilation album titled, *Someone Got Their Head Kicked in!* from

BYO Records. The album had songs by Youth Brigade, Social Distortion, Agression, Bad Religion, and a few others. Also on that cassette was an EP (extended play) by a band called 7 Seconds: Skins, Brains and Guts. I was hooked. It was all I listened to.

My life was about to change big-time. Scott started taking me surfing with him, and to a few nightclubs, and we became super good friends. We still are to this day.

The majority of guys I met at the beach with Scott were punks as well. They didn't dress like some of the other punk rockers I'd seen so far – with bondage pants, suspenders, engineer boots, etc. They all had real short hair, though not mohawks or spikes like I'd also seen. But they definitely had an edge. Being on the fringes of this little scene was exhilarating. And I was 100% sucked in on the music. The more I heard the more I liked.

For me, the music is what brought me in. There was definitely a fashion-type edge to it, but that wasn't what mattered most. I still had pretty long hair, but I started dressing a little differently. I dropped the OP/Hang Ten surfer shit and just started wearing jeans and flannels. "Wino" shoes were a cheaper alternative to Doc Martens and engineer boots, so I did that. It wasn't really much of a change, but my group of childhood friends noticed and made comments. They didn't know a lot about the music but were definitely vocal about the fact that they didn't like it. And that was okay with me. They were still my friends. I was on my own little mission.

The punk rockers at my school were kind of split down the middle on the dressing part of it as well. One guy was wearing plaid pants and straps, a leather jacket with band buttons and band patches. Slogans hand spray-painted on his clothes. Another was dressing more like my friends from the beach. His name was Steve, a grade older. I clearly remember him explaining to me in graphic arts class that you couldn't like both Black Flag and Adam and the Ants. Haha.

Scott then turned me on to an album called The Decline of Western

Civilization, from a documentary film released in 1981, and this is the one that cemented it for me. I loved all the tunes on there – but those three Black Flag songs were exactly what I wanted out of music. The energy in those songs was firing me up. I was all-in.

* * *

Back in those days society wasn't ready for punk rock. It was radical and definitely different. I witnessed a lot of unnecessary hostility to guys because of how they dressed. And I figured, once I cut off all my hair the same would happen to me. But that wasn't going to deter me.

Punk rock shows were kind of dangerous. I liked that as well. It was pretty easy to get yourself into a really bad situation if you did something stupid. There were gangs that could get pretty violent. The slam pits could get pretty intense. There were people jumping off stages and speaker stacks and you had to keep your eyes wide open and head on a swivel. And the clubs and warehouses that hosted the shows weren't always in the best neighborhoods.

* * *

I remember one day I had five of my childhood friends, my regular group, in my '74 Chevy Impala on our way up to the Angeles Crest in the San Gabriel Mountains. This was probably early 1982 and we were in 11th grade. We'd ditched school to go up and party at Wickiup in the Los Angeles Crest. Beers, joints, and who knows what else. As always, we were listening to music full blast. Probably Judas Priest or something similar. After one tape ended, I told my friends, "Check this out" and put in my 7 Seconds mixtape. My friend Jeff, who I'd known since Cub Scouts, immediately ejected it and threw it out the window. This is how it was going to go with this across the board.

Early in 12th grade, I cut off a lot of my hair. Above my ears. That sounds pretty trivial but back in '82 things were different, and I got a lot of shit from people at school. By this time, I was going to clubs in Hollywood with Scott – there were girls everywhere. I had upgraded to a brand-new, totally stock, lowest-end Toyota pickup truck, thanks to hard work at Sav-on. I was going to the beach after school and every weekend.

I was a little bit of a hellion when I was a kid, but Mom never sweated it because I got good grades, played sports, and had a job. She had recently, though, made comments about how I was dressing, and my hair. She kept alluding to the fact that graduation was coming up and I knew it was a big deal for her, so I let my hair grow back a bit.

Vic's band, S.V.D.B., was kicking ass. He gave me a practice tape, and I played it until it wore out. They had three songs released on punk rock compilation albums called *Destroy LA* and *We Got Power*. I bought both right away, and those records turned me on to a lot of other bands. We Got Power had 40 songs on it. Punk rock songs were notoriously short with no solos, which I loved.

When the principal of our school discovered Vic and Pat were in a band that had made real records, he invited them to play the quad. One of the things I remember the most was Vic standing up on a school bench, pointing at all of the jocks, singing, "It won't be long until all of you become one of us…" Haha. He was just playing it up – we were friends with all those dudes from baseball. But then I looked over toward Yosemite Drive and there were about a hundred punk rockers from Hollywood (which was not far away) hopping the fence by the softball fields and running across campus to come watch the band play. The principal shut down the band after only two songs. Mini-riot at Eagle Rock High School. By this time, I was ready for my first real show.

I had turned Scott on to S.V.D.B. and he loved them. They were playing a show at The Vex in a really bad area of East L.A., and we were going. I couldn't wait to introduce Vic and Scott. We met up outside and they both said since my hair was still kind of long, I should stand in the back so I wouldn't get any shit. I remember the feeling when I walked into that first show – the loud and raw songs of the opening band, the smell of stale beer and smoke – a tiny decrepit, beat-up venue full of punk rockers. I felt at home. I stood in the back most of the show but couldn't help myself from moving up closer a few times. S.V.D.B. absolutely killed it, and I also loved another band that played, Battalion of Saints. I was fucking thrilled.

I waited until after graduation, and then cut off all my hair. I was using egg whites to spike it and keep it standing up. I'll never forget the first time I came home like that. Mom literally screamed. Then kicked me out of the house. But she got over it pretty quickly, and I slept at home that night. And after that she never blinked at anything I did – hair, clothes, tattoos – everything.

* * *

I mentioned earlier that one of the big things that attracted me to punk rock was the authenticity. It seems to me that a lot of trends and fashions come and go, then circle back around a few decades later… but no one had ever done anything like punk rock. The clothes, the hair, the attitude, the music. It wasn't just new and different; it was, in a way, confrontational. There was a pretty common misconception that punk rockers were outcasts – but that couldn't be further from the truth. The earliest kids into punk rock were the cutting-edge kids – surfers, skateboarders, artists. They were the types that were the alpha's, the leaders of their social scenes, and they weren't afraid to take chances or be different. And they certainly didn't care what other people thought about it. Punk rockers were unique, authentic – the elite. And the music went hand in hand with the surf and skate scenes – it was all aggressive.

* * *

Something to remember about back then is we didn't have Hot Topic for T-shirts, and crazy color for your hair. We just made our own. Scott and I used to have a lot of fun with our dads' old work shirts, spray paint, and magic markers. Or old shirts we'd buy from Aardvarks and War Babies down on Melrose in Hollywood. We'd buy pants from big barrels full of them in the thrift stores, and then use paper clips and safety pins for modifications. We had to wear shirts and ties at work at Sav-on, and we'd buy the oldest, ugliest ties we could find out of huge boxes in Retail Slut, also on Melrose. For our hair we'd use peroxide and Sun-In. I'd put on these little rubber caps, make holes, and pull the tops of my hair out, and bleach them. Sun-In we bought at Sav-on, and we'd just spray it on our hair right before we went surfing.

One thing I enjoyed most about punk rock from day one was the notoriety. The shock value. People would notice you the second you walked into any room because of your hair and how you dressed. Sometimes they'd be shocked, sometimes offended – and 100% of the time they'd underestimate you. And I'd make that work to my advantage with Screaming Images decades later, big time.

We had a few really cool managers at Sav-on the first couple of years. Then they brought in a gay female manager, Ms. Ramsey. Before she arrived, we were warned she was super- corporate, and as soon as she walked in the store, she was all over me. My hair was spiked and bleached, I wore thrift store clothes and ties, had a big hanging cross earring, and had punk rock buttons all over the little blue Sav-On vest we had to wear over our clothes.

She called me into her office and the first thing she said was, "That earring, take it off." I asked why and she said it was against dress standards. "Girls wear them," I said. Then she went on to my clothes, which were thrift store stuff but clean. She didn't have anything there either. She had me a bit on the buttons with the band names – but I was able to argue and salvage one. The Black Flag button. We sold ant spray with the same name on aisle 26.

Work wasn't the only place I'd get hassled. One night coming home from my girlfriend's house in Sunland (I lived in Burbank at the time, age 18), a couple of big cowboy-looking guys in a full-sized truck started yelling at me at a red light. I had a bunch of punk rock stickers on the back window of my pickup, and I guess they took offense. They started yelling stupid stuff like "punk is bunk." Pretty pathetic.

I was just ignoring them, and I guess this made them even more mad. They followed me for several miles, honking and yelling, and finally I pulled into a parking lot to see what they wanted. It was really late at night, no one else was around, and I was outnumbered. They got out and came over to my truck and were making a sign for me to roll my window down. I did, and one of them punched me in the face. I usually would have been up for a fight, but they were two big, old, drunk guys, and who knows what else they had going on, so I just peeled out and left them standing there.

On the other hand, though, if you were ever out anywhere in public, and you saw another punk rocker, you would approach and talk with them, no matter what. It wasn't a common occurrence. We'd chat about what bands we liked, albums we'd bought, shows we'd been to, shows coming up. It wasn't just good bonding but also good street information on what was going on. Bands and shows we maybe didn't know about; this was vital since there was no internet or cell phones back then. Punk rock was always good for camaraderie.

Speaking of camaraderie, I think slam pits have evolved over the years into just a contest to see who's the toughest. It wasn't always like that. Slamming (and please do not call it moshing) was a way to release intense energy at shows. Sure, there were always a handful of guys trying to prove how macho they were, but for the most part people would help each other. If someone falls in front of you, pick them up and send them back into the circle. We were comrades. It was actually a lot of fun most of the time. Stagediving was the same. If you were on the floor and someone dived in near you, catch them. Unwritten rules.

Speaking of stage diving. One night in 1984 our whole gang went to the Roxy in Hollywood to see the Vandals. They'd just released a new album, When in Rome, Do as the Vandals. They opened with the first song on the album, "Lady Killer." On the album, the song featured a "scratch" sound, like a DJ uses on dance floors. When the singer Stevo came out he had an old-school record player strapped onto his side – to scratch, just like on the record. It was so rad! They were killing it, and there was a good slam pit going right in front of the stage. I saw an opening and jumped up on stage to do a dive. When I got up there, I was standing right next to Stevo with only the microphone between us. He kind of gave me a look, then looked at the microphone, so I grabbed it and belted out a couple lines of "Urban Struggle" before I dove off headfirst. When I finally got back to my feet, I realized I only had one shoe on. I looked up and Stevo had my other red Vans sneaker in his hand. He saw me, threw it at me, and everyone carried on.

It didn't always go that way, though. Like I've said already, for the most part, the shows had a lot of camaraderie and everyone looked out for each other. There are always shitty people in every crowd and punk rock was no different. Shows could be dangerous; you could always find trouble if you wanted. My friends and I were mostly there for the bands and the scene. You could stay out of the trouble if you were smart about it.

I'm not trying to be a punk rock historian or anything, but punk had different eras. We just didn't realize it then. By the time we started going to shows in 1982, the music had gotten faster and the crowds had gotten more physical. The Hardcore Era. People on the outside looking in could only see the violence; consequently, this was how punk rock was portrayed in the media. The LAPD were also encountering this new era. The people going to the shows were more physical and athletic than the previous ones. And when the cops came out in force on horses and with billy clubs, the crowds were fighting back.

There were several big gangs that always showed up to the gigs, but they were easy to spot. We just stayed clear. One particular night we were at Cathay de Grande on Selma in Hollywood, kind of by the Palladium. It was a super small, little old dive bar-restaurant and bands played downstairs in the basement. We were there that night to see 7 Seconds. As usual, there was a big pit in a little room, and I noticed some Suicidals walk in. They were a gang that followed the band Suicidal Tendencies, a hardcore band out of Venice.

I was standing on the edge of the pit and there was a girl who'd been in there a while, and she was holding her own. A couple Suicidals jumped in, and one of them was being really rough with the girl; totally uncalled-for.

As they came by the part of the circle where I was standing, at the edge, one started going after the girl again, so I reached in and pushed him out of her way. Almost immediately I had six Suicidals on me. It hadn't gone on for more than a few seconds when I felt two hands grab me and yank me away. I looked, and it's my friend Johnny pulling me up out of there. Usually, it wouldn't just stop there with those guys, but for some reason they backed off. I was lucky. And thank God for Johnny.

Cathay de Grande was maybe my favorite place for shows. It was such a dive, and I loved Hollywood. Tuesday nights were $1 to get in for six bands and you never knew who would show up. Don Bolles from the Germs played drums in the house band. One night we headed there to see a band called Ill Repute from Oxnard. I had heard them on Rodney on the Roq, on KROQ, the city's most popular alternative music radio station. Rodney did his show late on Sunday nights and it was all punk rock. I loved Ill Repute's song, "Clean Cut American Kid," so I went down to Vinyl Fetish record store to see what else they had and found their 7-inch EP called *Land of No Toilets*. I grabbed it, stoked.

A lot of punk rock bands released their music this way. The songs were so short they could put seven or eight songs on a 45, and you just played it at 33 rpm speed. My friends up in Canyon Country and I all loved the Ill Repute record, and they just happened to be playing that weekend at Cathay. We got there early so we could see all the bands. There weren't many people there yet, so we sat at a folding table with four other dudes and said, "What's up?" They asked who we were there to see, and we said Ill Repute. "That's us!" they said. So, we were able to hang out with them the whole night until they played.

I told my girlfriend the next day that we had met the guys from Ill Repute and hung out with them the whole night, and she didn't believe me. She was a cute little new wave girl I had met at a nightclub in the Valley. Duran Duran all over the walls of her bedroom. I had corrupted her and got her into punk rock and her mother wasn't happy with me for it. She bleached the front of her dark brown hair and started wearing studs and straps. About a month after the Cathay show, I took her, along with all my friends, to a show at Perkin's Palace in Pasadena. Might have been GBH, might have been Toy Dolls, I can't remember. There was a big line to get in, and we were walking down it toward the back. We saw the Ill Repute guys in line, and she said, "There's your friends," still not believing I'd hung out with them. As we walked up, Tony, the guitar player, jumped out of the line and said, "JAMES!" Ha. She believed me now. I'm still friends with Tony to this day.

Youth Brigade were among the favorite bands for Scott and me. The Stern brothers, Mark and Shawn, promoted their own shows, had their own club for shows, put out records on their own label, and were huge supporters of youth and punk rock in general. We were super stoked when we found out they had video-recorded their 1982 tour with Social Distortion, including connecting with Minor Threat on the East Coast, and made it into a documentary called "Another State of Mind." They were debuting the movie in Hollywood, and Scott and I were getting in no matter what.

We picked up a bunch of beers and wine coolers and headed to Hollywood. We parked and finished off what we hadn't drank on the way down there. Scott was buzzed, but I was still doing pretty good. It was super crowded in front of the venue and my plan was to sneak past the door guy when he was distracted. I went first and got in easy. Scott went next and easily got caught. Shit! So, I went back out, told him what to do and gave him a pep talk, and went first again. In, no problem. Scott went – easily caught again. The door guy asked him what the hell he was doing, and Scott replied, "I'm Mike Van Ness." For those who don't get this, the name of the singer/guitarist of Social D. is Mike Ness. I have no idea where Scott came up with the "Van" part, but he was super drunk and delivered it with a completely straight face. The door guy and I both started laughing hysterically and he then said to Scott, "Just go ahead," and let him in. Hilarious memory. I don't think Scott realized what was so funny. The documentary was killer. I absolutely loved it. I became really good friends with Mark and Shawn decades later, with Screaming Images becoming a big sponsor of their Punk Rock Bowling music festival in Vegas. I always have a good time telling them how I snuck into the premiere of their movie – twice the same night. And FYI: I had a 100% success rate sneaking into shows and venues; and Scott, almost 100% on the failure side.

* * *

A lot of people back then had the perception that punk rockers hated the cops and the government, and it was semi-accurate. Again, this is just my opinion, but I saw a lot of incidents in L.A. and Hollywood that were clearly instigated by the police. They would come in with billy clubs swinging and it was hard to avoid them. The Daryl Gates-led LAPD clearly had something against punk rockers, and in particular Black Flag and TSOL. Black Flag responded by writing and recording the song, "Police Story" on the Damaged album. That didn't make the situation any better.

As far as the government, most of the music was aimed at Ronald Reagan. Albums like "Reagan's In" by Wasted Youth, the song "Hey Ronnie" by Government Issue, "Fuck You, Ronnie" by D.O.A., the band Reagan Youth from New York City, the Dead Kennedys song "We've Got a Bigger Problem Now," for a few examples. My perception was just that they saw him as a threat to art, aesthetics, and creativity. I had never been much of a politics guy, and mostly stayed out of it. I just liked the music.

Regarding the LAPD, the first time I ever saw the Ramones was Sept. 13, 1986, at the Hollywood Palladium. Social Distortion opened, and they were my favorite band. They hadn't put out an album since Mommy's Little Monster in 1983 but had been playing songs from what would become the Prison Bound album for the last couple years. (It would finally be released in 1988). We already knew and loved all the songs. As far as the Ramones go, it was kind of a rare show, as they had "Richie" Ramone playing drums.

I headed there from Eagle Rock with my little brother David, and his buddy Troy. Troy and I were friends, too, as he was also a surfer. We packed into my pickup, headed to Hollywood, and parked in the lot across the street from the Palladium, on Selma. The show was sold out with a huge crowd outside. The atmosphere was like a high-tension wire. We got inside just in time to catch Social D's full set. They played a killer show, and the place was going fucking nuts. Then the Ramones came out, and it was everything I hoped for. They sounded amazing, and they played for what seemed like two hours.

The high tension continued while exiting the Palladium, and as we approached the doors, we heard a bunch of yelling and screaming coming from the street. As soon as we cleared the doors, we saw cops on horses in riot gear storming up and down Selma. David and Troy were only 15 and 16, and my only thought was to get them to my truck and out of there, pronto. Being the punk rock kids they were, they were yelling and screaming at the cops, and it was a feat just getting them to cross the street. We got to my truck and stepped in and locked the doors but couldn't go anywhere because of all the commotion in the parking lot. Punk rock kids running in every direction with cops on horses chasing them down and smashing them with billy clubs and batons. It was crazy.

Dave and Troy were shaking the truck trying to get out and into the fray, but that wasn't happening. I had promised Mom I'd get them home safely. After about a half hour the parking cleared up enough for us to sneak out and head back to Eagle Rock. I wasn't ever able to find out what happened before we got outside, but I can tell you that I didn't see the crowd do anything wrong. The only thing I could think of was: retaliation for the last time the Ramones played there. With Black Flag.

There were a lot of crazy venues we went to for shows, but one of the craziest might have been Fender's Ballroom in downtown Long Beach. There were always big slam pits, and fights inside and outside. Like I said earlier, it was just part of the scene, and easy to get into if you wanted, and easy to stay out if you played it smart. We were always in the pit at every show and every venue, but we never started fights at punk rock shows. One funny thing that sticks out in my mind is that it was always so fucking hot in there that I always brought spare clothes, like jeans and a T-shirt, to change into afterward because we always came out of there soaking from sweat. Another thing that always sticks out in my memory of Fender's is my little brother swinging from the plumbing on the ceiling right over the pit. Good times.

* * *

As I've said before, if I never got into punk rock, I might never have had the guts to start Screaming Images. There are a lot of comparisons. Punk rock was DIY (do it yourself) almost across the board. A lot of kids who started bands back in those days either weren't very good at playing their instruments, or didn't know how to play at all. They got by on sheer ambition and determination. They *became* good at it. And a lot of it was perception. Punk rock wasn't polished or overproduced music, which maybe they could have done if they wanted. They just didn't want to. They were sounding rough intentionally. Underdogs. Diamonds in the rough. Punk rockers as individuals stood out in a crowd just about everywhere they went. It was easy to notice them. They looked and did things differently than everyone else. Punk rock kids never conformed to any type of thing that society was telling them they should. They were thinking outside the box, doing things their own way, and owning it. Any of that sound familiar when it comes to my little printing company?

CHAPTER 4
JORDAN & HORN / TECHTRON

"New Day Rising"

- *Husker Du*

In August 1987, I took a leap of faith and started in a new direction: the printing industry. I'd just turned 22 years old.

I had been kicking around junior college for several years taking architecture classes, but it hadn't really grabbed me. I was sleeping on my Mom's couch and didn't have a job. I wasn't doing a heck of a lot besides partying, surfing and playing baseball, and Mom wasn't happy about it.

I'd secured an interview at an architecture company for a paid internship. A week before the interview, my childhood buddy Sean said the company he worked for was hiring, and I should go check it out. It was a "graphic arts" company in downtown Los Angeles. There was some sort of company picnic that weekend, and Sean said they were playing softball, so I tagged along. I was always up to play some baseball or softball. I met a bunch of nice folks, including some of the bosses, and set up an interview for the following Monday. I didn't even know what the position was for; I was just going to go check it all out.

The shop was at 1220 S. Maple Avenue in downtown L.A. in the garment district. I was instructed to park in the small lot directly across the street. It was all sports cars, a couple Cadillacs, and a really nice Corvette. I'd borrowed my friend Kevin's truck to get there. I walked in the building and up the stairs and Sean greeted me. He promptly took me to the office of one of the vice presidents, Robert. It was decided that before the interview I'd be given a tour – which was great because I didn't really understand what all they did.

They walked me through a few departments with names like "dot etching," "proofing," and "stripping." Sean worked in the proofing department and was making something they called "Chromaline's." It was all pretty interesting stuff. They then took me through a room called "Scanning," and then upstairs to the press rooms. I'd seen printing presses before – but nothing this big. They were called "Heidelberg's." Everyone in all the departments seemed busy and generally happy. They looked like cool folks. I was then told we were going to go check out the "ECI" department, and Robert and Sean both had shit-eating grins.

I was told enroute that ECI stood for "Electronic Color Imaging." I had no idea what that meant. They opened the door, and I followed into a very modern-looking, darkish room. There was a big device in the center that looked kind of like an oversized television – think of the first big-screen televisions, the really boxy ones. There were three guys sitting at a table in front of it working with what looked like some kind of video game controls. Remember, computers weren't yet commonplace, and I'd never even seen one, really. The three guys sitting in front of the huge monitor were very cool, stylish-looking guys, slicked-back hair and all that, and I immediately thought of the sports cars and the Corvette outside. As I moved closer, I could see an image of a car on the screen, and they were manipulating the vehicle's color using the controls. It was very cool; I was very impressed. I was then told they were working on an ad for a magazine – that was the main line of what the company did, building advertisements.

After a bit more of me gawking, we left the room, and Sean split off. We ended up back in Robert's office, and he asked me what I thought. What I thought was that I was going to apply for any job they had open. This all looked super-futuristic, and I was excited. I was informed the job was for shipping clerk, and the starting pay was $8 per hour. I filled out an application while Robert asked a bunch of questions. I headed out and went home with my fingers crossed. The next day Robert called and offered the job, and I accepted. I was now employed in the "graphic arts" industry. Hell yes.

Little did I know, I'd spend the rest of my career working with graphic designs.

* * *

I started the same week. Luckily between Sean picking me up and Kevin loaning me his truck I was able to get to work and back. It was a trip working in downtown L.A. – a lot went on there! My main duty as shipping clerk was dispersing "proofs and progs," printed sets of color sheets, and "final film," which was a set of four pieces of film, the cyan, magenta, yellow and black layers all separated into four sheets of film. Sometimes these got shipped out of state, but mostly they were couriered to local advertising agencies. What this meant was, I would call a delivery company, or "courier," and they'd come pick it up, and then deliver it. I coordinated mostly with the salespeople, or "account executives" handling the account for whatever job it was I was sending out. It kept me busy. The sales guys were all older, and super dressed up with suits and ties. They carried pagers because cell phones weren't even close to being a thing then.

I became acclimated pretty quickly. I was using couriers I'd inherited for the local deliveries, and Federal Express for deliveries outside the Los Angeles area. I began getting sales calls from other courier companies, and quickly learned there were a lot of them out there. I started checking prices and was able to find a few companies that delivered for less, so I gave them some test deliveries. A couple of them worked out, so I ended up switching to them and keeping the old ones the previous guy had used as backups.

Three months into my new job, I had the shipping department running on all cylinders. My new couriers were kicking ass and saving us money at the same time. I hustled all over the shop and all my new teammates noticed. There was a computer that had been sitting on a desk in my little shipping area the whole time I had been there and had never been turned on. I had zero experience with computers, but one day decided to fire it up and see what it did. As soon as I turned it on, an airplane flew across the front of the screen and then a big logo: Airborne Express. I guessed it was placed there by that company with hopes of winning some business from Techtron. I continued fiddling with it, with no idea what I was doing, and eventually got to a page where we could set up shipments. Cool, I thought, I was figuring it out. I stopped there and didn't think about it the rest of the day.

The next day a super cute blonde walks into my shipping office wearing an Airborne Express polo shirt. Wow! I guess she was prompted when I turned on the computer and got it to the shipments page. So, of course, I gave her a shot and started alternating shipments between her and FedEx. Airborne had the advantage because all the shipments could be set up and tracked on that little computer. The shipping department had lots of options on all platforms now, and the bosses and salespeople were noticing. Everyone was calling me Wozniak (haha!).

For guys like Sean and I, the goal to shoot for at Jordan & Horn/Techtron – and in the printing business in Los Angeles in general –was to get an apprenticeship. When that happened, you were taught a specific area of the trade, joined the union, and had four years until you became a journeyman. Once you were in the union you were set. Then you had 35-hour workweeks and anything over that you were paid time-and-a-half, and anything past two hours overtime in a day was double-time. The journeymen in all the departments made really good money – which is why on my first day I saw a parking lot full of sports cars. The printing industry was a legitimate trade back then. All this gave me goals and made me work even harder to get that coveted apprenticeship.

All my hard work paid off, because after six months as shipping clerk I was offered to move up to the press room for a new position as a general worker – which was a fast track to getting an apprenticeship as a press operator. I came in an hour earlier than my previous shift hours and was starting at 6 a.m. with the press guys. My main duty was cleaning the "blankets" on the presses, which were rubber covers on the rollers that the sheets passed through, sandwiched between the blankets and the plates with the artwork. After every run was finished, the plates for that job were removed, and the blankets still had ink on them with impressions of the art from that job. I wiped them all off, on all presses, after every run. Besides that, I kept all the solution containers filled and folded and I stacked the clean rags and towels and kept them stocked for the journeymen. It was a good gig, and I was happy. There were six press operators, and they were all super cool and treated me well. But it wouldn't last long...

* * *

After about 90 days in the press room, I was offered a different general worker position. They had just purchased a new proofing machine called a Kodak Signature, which would replace the Chromaline proofing system, and they wanted me to run it. This position would move me back downstairs, and my apprenticeship could go into several different departments from there. I would be working directly for the people in ECI, scanning and stripping.

I took the position, of course. I trained with Kodak on the new proofing machine as soon as it was installed. I would then train someone else from our shop to work second shift on the machine. It would be one of the busiest departments in the shop, and I was told if I took the position, I would be expected to work 6 a.m. to 6 p.m. Monday through Saturday. By now I was making $11 an hour, and with all that overtime, I would make more money than ever in my life. However, the schedule would be brutal. I figured they were testing me, to see what I was made of, before they offered me that apprenticeship I wanted so badly.

To work 6 a.m. to 6 p.m. Monday to Saturday is a gnarly schedule. I should mention here that I was 22 years old, had a hot girlfriend, a lot of buddies, and a ton of things to do. I was routinely out after midnight. I was playing high-level softball two nights a week and Sundays. I stayed at my girlfriend Michelle's apartment a lot in those days because she would make sure I got up to get to work on time. By now I had a beater car to get me back and forth to the shop, so at least I didn't have to depend on her for rides. I was busting my ass every day, hangover and all, and everyone saw my hustle. I also loved the job. It felt cutting edge and important. I was proud of what I was doing.

The two departments I worked with the most were ECI and scanning. What the Signature proofing machine did was basically verify color and get approval on the images for the ads. The guys would bring me a set of color separations and I would lay them all on top of each other, in register on clear sheets, and combine them into one color proof, printed onto the paper type needed for whichever publications the ads were destined for. Sometimes it was glossy, sometimes it was matte. There were also different thicknesses of paper such as 80-pound (80#) or 100-pound (100#).

I had the department humming along at a very high pace. I had a super cool dude working in the department with me on second shift, named Ban. We got along great, and both worked our butts off. After a little over a year in the Signature department and on 12-hour shifts, I finally got offered that apprenticeship – but it wasn't in any of the departments I expected.

In the beginning of 1989, I was given an apprenticeship as a four-color table stripper. Fun name, but not what it sounds like. Basically, the stripping department built the ads on a light table using exposure/lights and by cutting film and then applying rubylith (a process using colored masking film) and pasting and taping it all together in the four color layers of black, cyan (blue), magenta, and yellow. It was a complex process, which I'll try to explain in more detail later.

The first step in my apprenticeship was joining the union, which back then was called Local 404/Graphics Communications Union. I then had to sign paperwork to go to a school called The Printing Industry Institute, which was for seven semesters, and indentured me to the state of California for four years. Classes were two nights a week, for two hours, and started after my seven-and-a-half-hour day shift. The school was right at the intersection of Normandie and Florence, famous as the location where Reginald Denny was beaten in retaliation for the Rodney King police beating incident in 1992. Needless to say, not a great area, and after everyone had arrived for classes in the evenings, the gates were locked behind our cars.

I enjoyed the classes. They were all over the place sometimes but helped me understand the basics of four-color table stripping. The guy running the school was named Ray, and for some reason he had it out for me. Yeah, I was a punk rock kid, and he probably wasn't used to that, but I was always there, on time, and did well in the classes. Every week at work the journeymen would ask me about the classes, what we were doing, and the instructors. I always made fun (lightheartedly) of Ray from the school because he gave me such a hard time. It took me about a year to figure out that one of the journeymen in my department, named Bill, was Ray's son-in-law; and Bill was relaying to him every story I told. No wonder Ray didn't like me!

The way the apprenticeship worked pay scale-wise was, once I signed my life away to the state of California and started at the school, my hourly rate was bumped up to 55% of the journeyman's scale – a significant raise for me. From there on, upon successful completion of semesters at the school every six months, I had a 5% raise added to my hourly pay, and it went like this until my four-year apprenticeship ended. I then became a fully-paid journeyman.

Things were humming along during my first year, and I was super fortunate to be placed under the wing of a guy who would become my biggest mentor, Gene. He was supervisor of the stripping department, and a tall and skinny biker guy, which I guess gave him some affinity for a skinny punk rock kid like me. He taught me more in those first four years than I would ever learn from anyone else in the printing industry. I keep in contact with him to this day. He did constantly make me do menial tasks, but I guess it was like the Karate Kid movie with the "wax on, wax off" thing. One thing he always did that sticks with me was he made me take the gradation sheets used for exposures, rub them on the floor to get dust on them, then dupe the film and then make me stipple out the dirt spots between the dots on 70%

and 80% dot patterns. Haha… I always did everything he asked, and Gene would end up having my back for decades. I learned a lot from him besides just the graphics trade.

I'll try my best to describe how table stripping worked. It truly was a trade, and the journeymen were paid well:

The advertising agencies created an artboard and sent it to us. It basically was a cut-and-pasted board with the typeface, logos, and images on it, with a slipcover over the top with handwritten instructions for colors, etc. After job orders were written up, the artboard would go to our "camera" department, and a photo would literally be taken of it with an old-school camera set-up. They'd then make a negative and that was what we used for type, logos, and position. The agencies would also send over the images that went in the ad, and those would go to scanning and then ECI for color separation and corrections. By the time the job bag got to the stripping department it would have the instructions as well as the negative from the camera department and the four-color separations for each image. So, say the ad had two Ford trucks in front of mountains or some other backdrop, we would get separations for each, the truck and the mountains. It was our job to build the ad, and then make four-color (cyan, magenta, yellow, and black) "final film" via exposures to the film. Each color of film would have whatever was in that color on the final film. So, each color would obviously have that color layer of the image, and the logos, if they had different colors. So, if it was a Ford logo that had certain percentages of blue and red in it, that would be exposed into the final film for those specific colors. For example, if the logo consisted of 80% cyan (blue) and 20% magenta (red) we would hold gradation sheets of those percentages over the top of the logos as we burned them into the film.

If it sounds complicated, it kind of was – and it's even harder to explain. Around each image in the ad (the trucks), we'd have to hand cut a mask around it to expose it onto the film. If it was a dark image going onto a light background, we'd have to make a "shrink" mask so the images blended together perfectly without hard edges; and if it was a light image going into a darker background, we would have to make it a "spread" mask. In addition, moving backward a bit here, everything had to be lined up to match the artboard, and the images had to be aligned on top of each other precisely on each separation, on optically clear sheets using tape. This process featured using a magnifying glass, or "loop." Over the top of the clear sheets on which we aligned all of the critical pieces, we cut loose masks out of light-blocking paper. So, let's say the ad has two trucks, mountains, a logo that has two colors (cyan and magenta), and black copy. Each sheet of final film would have the following amount of exposures: Yellow: three exposures, one for each image; Magenta: four exposures, one for each image, plus one exposure at 20% of the logo; Cyan: four exposures, one for each image, plus one exposure at 80% of the logo; and Black: four exposures, one for each image, and one exposure for the black type. To get to these final four pieces of film you probably have a stack of "working materials" two or three inches thick. These all need to be labeled very clearly and precisely, because the job is likely to be picked up and redone down the line with revised copy or images. To build and process a full- page ad from start to final film generally took an entire 7.5-hour shift – and that's for a simple one like that described above.

It's all a lot to process, I know, but if you are still curious you can Google "four-color table stripping for print" and it might explain better. No wonder we had seven semesters of school and a four-year apprenticeship for this.

Once again, I picked up on this new department very quickly. Within six months they were letting me do simple jobs on my own. I was getting a lot of moral support from Gene, and also from the general manager of the shop, Jim, who was relatively new to L.A., coming from our shop in Chicago. Right as I was really getting rolling, we got some big news – we were moving. If memory serves, this was early 1991. I guess it was the right time, as the company was growing; we were getting new big accounts thanks to a rad salesperson named Rita, and it seemed like the area of our location in downtown Los Angeles (garment district) was getting worse and worse. That parking lot right across the street where I admired all the sports cars that first day was gone. We were parking in a lot two blocks down from Maple, on 12th Street. I was on second shift by this time, and we had to be walked down to our cars after our shift ended by an armed guard. Literally.

So off to Burbank we went, to a big new shop in a nicer area, pretty close to the Burbank airport. I was living in Silver Lake at the time, so this worked out well for me. Not to mention it was pretty close to Mom in Eagle Rock. I can remember it being quite the transition with trying to set up presses in the new building while keeping a couple running in the old building so we wouldn't skip a beat with the customers, as we were very busy. I learned a lot during this move and would end up using these lessons when I had to move my own shop to a bigger location some 26 years later. Another thing around this time that stands out in my mind was something Jim said as I was personally moving to the new building. He told me I had "carte blanche on overtime" which was, essentially, a golden ticket to make money. And a sign of his confidence in my abilities.

Eight months rolled by quickly. My skill levels were growing very fast and by this time I was two years into my apprenticeship and on a daily basis was given the hardest jobs on second shift. It even got to the point where I was building jobs, and then turning them over to one of the journeymen for him to burn/expose the films. We had a new 2nd shift stripping boss at this time, and his name was Dan. He was a cool guy, and we got along pretty good – except for one thing. He made me turn off my radio. I didn't see how it was a big deal, since I only listened to Dodgers games and KROQ. We went back and forth over this for a long time – and he finally relented. I was the top stripper on the shift by then, even though I was still an apprentice.

More big news came to the shop toward the middle of 1991: we were getting a Scitex Assembler. This was basically a computer that could do table stripping. It was a pretty big deal, and they were very expensive, so we were only getting one. They would pick two people, one each from first and second shift, to train to be the operators. Gene was chosen for first shift, of course, and he would still carry on with managing all of the stripping department as well.

The pick for second shift operator surprised everyone: it was me. I was the only apprentice in stripping, and only a little more than halfway through my apprenticeship, and there were at least seven journeymen strippers in our department. Needless to say, this didn't go over well with them. But the decision was made by Jim the general manager, and the stripping supervisor, Gene, so there wasn't a lot they could say. And besides, they all knew deep down it was the right call; and in the end it all ended up good with them. They were super cool dudes.

I was excited. Especially since the new Assembler would be set up in the ECI room, at that time a super high-tech space. I didn't get any more money for this promotion since I was still under apprenticeship rules, but I was okay with it. I was moving forward.

The color correction computers in ECI were also made by Scitex. Side note: interestingly, Scitex ended up producing some of the earliest model digital printers and was eventually bought out by EFI, whose printers I ended up using to print millions of square feet in Vegas. Anyway, our process for uploading data was the same as ECI. Everything was delivered and stored on magnetic tapes. Picture a big film reel like you used to see when you watched movies in the old days. They were 10½" in diameter and literally were like tape or film. We'd get the one that was correlated to our current job, attach it to our server, and download the data onto the Assembler, then start building the ad. It really was a pretty simple process to do the actual work, way easier than on the table. Once Gene and I had the new department cooking with gas, Gene brought in a journeyman named Eddie to be our third team member. Eddie took over second shift, and I moved to third, which was all right with me. On third shift I could play softball before work.

After six months or so, the Assembler was doing 50 to 60% of the stripping department's work. Gene, Eddie, and I were a killer team. It was now toward the end of 1991, and I had started hearing rumblings about the "interweb." By now, also, the company had been bought and went through a name change and we were called Wace Imaging. They were based out of England, and from what they were saying we were one of the biggest printing companies in the world, network-wise. They brought in a guy named Mark who was an internet specialist and also worked with Macintosh computers. Coincidentally, around this time, the Assembler was upgraded with an interface to work with Macs and was rebranded as the "Scitex Star." One of those machines was brought in, and we kept the same assembler team working on it. It was the first time I was able to work with Photoshop, even though I'm not sure it was called that back then.

1992 rolled around and my apprenticeship was coming to an end. By then it didn't matter workwise, but it sure did pay-wise. I was about to get a big bump in pay. They also paid a shift differential to keep people on second and third shift happy, so I was at the highest pay level. Once I became a journeyman, and on third shift, I was making close to $40 per hour. God bless the union. But once again, there were rumblings that we were ditching the Scitex Star, and all of table stripping, and were going to start doing all the work on Mac computers with software called Photoshop, Illustrator, and Quark. Another rumor going around was that they were trying to break the union and bring Mac operators in at $16 per hour.

* * *

In 1993 I was living with a girlfriend in South Pasadena. It was a fairly short commute to work in Burbank. We ended up needing a break from each other, so I decided to move out, and she suggested I stay close. I moved down to Newport Beach instead. Even though it was a super long commute, it ended up being one of the best personal decisions I ever made. I lived right across the street from the sand on 40th and Seashore. I was still working third shift, so I had all day at the beach every day. I'd usually get home from work around 7:30 a.m., sleep until 10:30 a.m., then get up and then hit the beach.

Around 7 p.m. I'd take a two-and-a-half-hour nap, shower up, and head to Burbank for my shift. None of my neighbors down there even knew I had a job. I was living my best life.

I wasn't super worried about the union breaking and them bringing in low-paid Mac operators. The people they were talking about bringing in could probably run the shit out of a Mac, but they would know nothing about prepress for the printing industry. If this was going to happen, it would take a while. Once they actually started bringing in the Macintosh computers, it took them 90 days just to set them up and get all the cable and optics set. As soon as they were set up, everyone was trained on them. They kept a table stripping apprentice at night in a smaller room to do easier tasks like duping film for shippers, etc. Of course, I picked up on the Macs pretty quickly because of my experience with the Scitex Assembler and Star; but some of the older guys struggled. They'd been building ads by doing prepress on light tables for decades.

By this time, we also had a new general manager named John. I was super bummed Jim left, but John seemed like a cool dude. He was a printing industry veteran and had come from a company called Southern California Graphics that I definitely had heard of. It took him a couple of weeks to settle in, and then he sought me out and said the magic word: "Softball." He wanted to start a company team to play in the "Advertising League." All the league's teams were basically advertising agencies. It was co-ed, and I wasn't really used to that, but I was all-in. We played in West Los Angeles, so it was a haul from Newport Beach. I would stick around after work, hang out, maybe work some overtime, until game time, and then go to the fields. John had moved me from third shift to first shift so I could play. It was fun! I met a lot of cool people, and two guys from another team in the league would end up becoming one of my biggest customers in about 22 years: Kawasaki.

I have a fun story from the advertising league. We always, after every game, met up at this one bar for some post-game beers. I wish I remembered the name of it. It was in West L.A. By this time, I had a big white Chevy truck, and always had a hard time finding parking for this bar, so I was usually the last one inside the establishment. One of those nights, as I had just found a parking spot on a side street that was pretty close, I got out and started walking in. A car pulled up to me and rolled the window down, and the driver said he wanted to ask me a favor. I heard him out, and he asked if he could have my spot, because he had Patrick Swayze with him in the car, and Patrick had a broken leg from a movie stunt gone bad. They were going into the same bar. He asked to pay for my spot. I walked up to the car and sure as shit Patrick Swayze was sitting in the passenger seat. I said, "Tell you what: I'll give you the spot. Once I get into the bar and sit down with my teammates, I want Patrick to bring a pitcher of beer over to our table and say to me, "Hey James! Long time no see!" They both said "deal," so I moved my truck. It took me a while to find another spot, but once I got inside and sat down, Patrick walked right up to our table, where I was sitting with six or seven teammates, and kept his end of the deal. Haha! My teammates' jaws dropped.

After he walked away, they all asked me how the hell I knew Patrick Swayze. I said we were old friends and left it at that for a while. After a couple beers, it was too much fun not to fill them in on what really happened. We all had a good laugh. I left the bar earlier than everyone else because I had a long drive home, and when I went out the back door Patrick was sitting outside on a bench. He started laughing and said our prank seemed like it went well. I sat down and had a cigarette with him, and we chatted for about 10 minutes or so. He told me he had broken his leg falling off a horse filming a movie. What a super cool dude. RIP, Patrick.

* * *

We were mainly using Quark, Illustrator, and Photoshop to build ads on the Macs. There was another small computer that was used by everyone in the department – and it was used to make "traps," which basically replaced the shrinks and spreads we used to make on the masks for the images via exposures and diffusion sheets. It was easy work. I could kind of understand why they didn't want to pay us so much money anymore.

One thing I'd been doing the entire time I was with Jordan & Horn/ Techtron/Wace Imaging was watching salespeople. I knew for a fact that the good ones were making over six figures a year (a lot back then), and I always had it in the back of my mind that I might try to go down that path one day. I didn't have to initiate it on my own. I was called into John's office one morning in 1998, and when I got there, a guy named Rick, who was the sales manager, was also in there. Uh-oh. They talked about the whole situation with the Macs coming in, and the operators being paid less, and the possible breaking of the union. They told me they thought I would make a great account executive/ salesperson because of my personality and industry background. I agreed. My salesperson job just fell into my lap.

We made a deal that I would come in for my prepress job an hour early every day, and then head upstairs to the sales offices to start training and building sales skills. The reason is, the salespeople were paid on a draw and commission basis, and I wouldn't be able to walk right into that because I had no clients yet. I told the story earlier about my first day in sales and walking into Rick's office all dressed up and how he reacted, so I won't repeat it. But I will say again that the advice he gave me that day was the single best piece of sales advice I ever got. Still to this day.

I hit the phones right away. Email wasn't a big thing yet back then. First thing I went after was the record companies – a lot of those are in L.A. and Hollywood. My thought was album and compact disc covers, and lots of them. The first cold call was to Warner Brothers, and I made some progress pretty quickly which was surprising because I was so nervous and had no idea what I was doing. But they gave me some stuff to quote on. I was working/ training with a female salesperson (who I ended up having a lot of other fun with) and she helped me get the opportunity into estimating. It took a couple days to get a quote out, which surprised me, but what astonished me more was her reaction when we finally got it back. I saw the quote and didn't think it looked like a lot of money – but she said it was really high. I was thinking, damn! How many jobs do I have to sell at this low amount to earn six figures a year? It turns out maybe record companies weren't the best sector to go after if I wanted to make the big bucks. Shit.

Another thing happened while training with Raquel: new materials popped up that I'd never heard of before. Lambdas, duratrans, pressure-sensitive vinyl, and light jet prints to mention a few. There was a new type of printing starting to develop, and apparently Seven WW (as we were now called) had purchased a small company that did it. They were calling it "Photo," eventually to be called digital printing.

One weekend, our company advertising league softball team played in a tournament in Palm Springs at a sports park called Big League Dreams. The outfield walls had bleachers built that looked like Major League Baseball stadiums and had graphics of crowds in the bleachers. It was a lot of printing, and it looked really, really bad. It was peeling and cracking everywhere. I started going into the sports office in between games, trying to find out who to speak with about these graphics. I was finally pointed toward a guy who it turns out was the managing partner of the ballpark. His name was Jeff.

I asked if he'd be interested in talking to me if I could find him a better solution for his outfield graphics, and he said yes. I talk about Big League Dreams a lot later in the book but it's important to outline it here, as it was a huge learning experience going through this process of finding a better solution for a client.

We projected it was around 30,000 square feet of printing. Installation wasn't even mentioned or discussed, which indicates I still had no clue what I was doing. We took a ton of pictures of the bad spots and brought back some samples of the vinyl we had pulled off the wall. I was told it was some sort of 3M pressure sensitive vinyl, so they called in the 3M representative. Her name was Michele, and she went back out to Palms Springs with me to see it all for herself. She ended up becoming a really good friend who I still talk with to this day.

We all agreed the reason the current graphics were peeling and cracking was because a laminate wasn't used. Additionally, the plywood the bleachers were made of had warped sheets, and the 4-by-8-foot panels were lifting between the seams and breaking the pressure-sensitive vinyl. I was informed the best solution was to print the 3M vinyl, add the laminate, and wrap it around the 4-by-8 sheets of Masonite, with 4-inch bleed on all four sides, and wrapped around the back. We even made a couple of samples I could take back and show them.

They liked the samples and asked for a quote for all three fields. The quote turned out to be astronomically high, and they said absolutely no chance. I didn't have enough experience to come up with a better, more economical solution myself, so this one got punted to the back. I'd eventually figure it out for Big League Dreams, but it would be several years down the line, after I had learned a lot more about my trade and could figure things out myself.

Time flew by while in my dual role. John was being super fair by not making me work a lot of overtime in the shop, and I was getting a ton of help and training from Rick upstairs in sales. I was also getting mentored by two other sales guys, Michael and Ricky, who were on the company softball team. But toward the end of 1998, it was announced that the company was being sold to Applied Graphics Technologies – a competitor. Everyone was in shock.

Everything happened really quickly, and the AGT executives came to our shop to interview everyone to see who they'd keep. The rumor was they would lay off half the staff. When it came time for my interview, they seemed a little confused by my dual role. I explained that I was transitioning into sales, and that was the direction I wanted to keep going. I even talked to an AGT executive named Mike who used to be an account executive for Techtron. He remembered me from my general worker days, before my apprenticeship started. He was now the Vice President of Sales for AGT. I thought this maybe gave me a chance to stay in my sales role.

It took about a week for them to come back with their list of who was staying and going. They laid off a little more than 50% of the staff from our shop. They had a special meeting with me, and said they wanted to keep me, but wanted me to go back to prepress and design. No more sales.

They moved everyone over to their shop in Glassell Park at the end of 1998. I reluctantly went and moved back to the Mac's full time. It wasn't what I wanted to do any longer.

My old friend Sean who landed me the job at Jordan & Horn/Techtron had moved on from that company in the mid-1990s to work for a company in Hollywood that was doing "digital printing." He once again scored me an interview and tour, and I went and checked it out. The company was called Imagic.

I had worked in prepress/design at the AGT plant in Glassell Park for about 30 days and was miserable. The only good thing about it was Glassell Park was right next to Eagle Rock, and I could pop over and visit Mom after work most days. I was back to living in Simi Valley by that point. I decided to take a run at the V.P. of Sales one more time about heading in that direction. He told me straight up that wasn't their vision for me. I gave my two weeks' notice on the spot, then went home and called Imagic and accepted their job offer as a full-time salesperson/account executive. Hollywood, here I come.

.

CHAPTER 5
IMAGIC / HOLLYWOOD

"Hollywood Babylon"
- *Misfits*

I fucking love Hollywood.

A city where dreams are both made and destroyed daily. A fusion of glitz and grit. A mixed bag of stars, strippers, and misfits. Neon lights and dark, dirty alleyways. Violence amid opulence. My favorite city in the world.

Hollywood was where I was heading for the next step in my career, after I left Jordan & Horn/Techtron/Wace, where I'd worked for almost 12 years.

I was still six years away from moving to Vegas (which was in no way at all on my radar at this point), but I was about to make the biggest gamble of my life. On myself.

***

As I said in the previous chapter, the graphics industry was changing. It was no longer a trade. The union had been broken, and prepress, as it was in those days, was about to become a commodity. No more $40-plus per hour, 35 hours a week jobs. They were now using Macintosh computers and getting paid $16 per hour. I had been enamored with the salespeople since my days in the shipping department. They came and went – not tied to a desk or workstation all day. They made their money on commission, which was basically a performance basis. Their earnings had no ceiling. The more you sold, the more money you made. This was what I wanted to do.

The gamble I was making was the fact that I was leaving a job where I was making $75,000 a year, to take another job where I would make only $40,000. Now that was a base salary, and I would get commission on whatever I sold, but the problem was I had no customers, and they weren't going to just hand me anything. So, I had to hustle – with Hollywood as my backdrop.

It was still the printing industry, just a different kind of printing. I came from a litho printing background. Digital printing was brand new, and I was betting on it. I was going to use my background of shipping, design, running presses, running proprietary hi-tech prepress software, and running Mac computers. I was going to take everything I learned from watching the salespeople at Jordan & Horn. I would let my personality shine – and I was going to sell a shit-ton of printing.

Imagic was a totally different world than where I'd been. The first couple weeks, it was weird coming to work to a bunch of people I didn't know. I was 35 years old, and I'd only had two jobs my whole life – Sav-on, starting when I was 14, to Jordan & Horn when I was 22. Not only all that, but now I was in sales only. I had to start calling people I didn't know and asking them to give me work.

I'll be honest, I was not comfortable at all making cold calls. The sales manager at Imagic, Tom, was a super cool guy and gave me a few leads on who to call. But it didn't make it easier. I figured I'd go with what I knew from Jordan & Horn and hit all of the L.A. advertising agencies. The internet was a few years old, but for me it was brand new. Emails were fairly new, too, and I'd just gotten my first email address, so had to figure that out. The way the guys at Jordan & Horn taught me was to just call them and ask for work. But first I had to figure out who to call.

The guys downstairs in prepress at Imagic taught me how to look things up using a "search engine," which at this time was Yahoo! So, I started using it to look up phone numbers for agencies. I was so green at sales, I didn't even know to look people up by their positions and hit them up directly. I just asked questions to whoever was answering the phone, who was a gatekeeper for the right people, and I was just saying dumb shit. I was getting nowhere.

Another thing I did was get my very first cell phone. It was huge, like a walkie-talkie. I still have the same phone number issued to me back in 1999 with that first phone, and that is the origin of my (323) area code phone number for any of you who wondered. I can remember the very first time it rang in my truck while driving on the freeway. It scared the shit out of me. It was my buddy Michael, and he was just calling to shoot the shit. Weird how I remember that.

I did love working in Hollywood. Back in those days I was still going out at night a lot, so there were hangovers probably three or four mornings a week. I played softball two nights a week, and we always went to bars after games, and then other random stuff. The shop was off Wilcox right between Hollywood and Sunset boulevards, so I had a couple good places to get greasy breakfast burritos and try to pull out of my head spins in the morning.

There were two owners at Imagic, and it was a super cool and creative space. It was three floors in a super old Hollywood building. I guess the backstory was they both had design studios in the early 1990s and decided to join forces. Paul was one of the owners; he sat on the second floor with all the other designers. Tim was the other; he had an office up on the third floor, totally secluded from everyone else. Up there by Tim was where they put me, with a little desk by a window overlooking Wilcox Avenue. I was getting there (what I thought was) early, around 8 a.m., and Tim was always already there. I'd go say hello to him when I arrived, and eventually started asking what time he got there. He'd say 4 a.m., and I'd trip. Years later when I was an owner and doing the same thing, I understood Tim better.

After about a month at Imagic, I had made no sales progress. I got a call down to Paul's office one morning, and he was in there with Tim and a guy named Clay. I guess Clay had been running the prepress department and wanted to get out of there to be a designer. Paul asked if I would take over managing prepress for a while until they found someone else to do it. I could tell by the vibe of the room that it was Paul's idea, and that Tim was against it. I guess I didn't have to say yes, but to be honest again, I was really uncomfortable with the cold calling. I agreed to do it on a temporary basis. So, what had happened here was I went from making $75,000 as a prepress operator, to being a prepress manager for $40,000 a year. Way less money. Not good.

So down to an office in the basement with the prepress guys I went. They were all totally cool and didn't really need a lot of managing. I took it as an opportunity to learn about some of the equipment. They were printing vinyl banners using a dye-sublimation process. I now know that is super weird, but back then I had no clue. And it went only 48 inches or so wide. They'd print banners on paper and then transfer them to vinyl banner material. They also had an old light jet type of machine that made duratrans and other film/type of prints. This was all totally new to me; I didn't have a clue.

I decided to keep trying the cold calls thing from down in my prepress office. I was just randomly picking places to call, and one day called KROQ, the radio station. I left my number with a gatekeeper and didn't expect anything to come of it. I was on my way home one evening and my cell phone rang – it was a guy named Hutch from KROQ. He had a Rage Against the Machine show in three days and needed a ton of vinyl banners. I told him for sure! So, he asked for my email address to send me logos. To be honest here again, I didn't even know logos could be emailed.

Another thing I didn't know was if it was even possible to print 25-plus banners in three days. I called Tim on his cell phone and asked, and he said we could do it. When I got to the shop the next morning, super stoked about my first sales win, I found out that not everyone else felt the same way as Tim about the turnaround time. But he squashed all that and pushed it through. Thank God I had called him, and not Paul.

We pulled off the KROQ job for Hutch and he was stoked. He said his old vendor had been screwing up and he was going to use me from now on. I had my first account. And I am still friends with Hutch and his wife Suzan to this day.

This gave me some confidence. I wanted to get more accounts. One of Imagic's biggest accounts was the Los Angeles Dodgers. They did the graphics on the outfield walls, and I knew of this, as I was a huge Dodgers fan and attended a ton of games. I started asking questions regarding how it was done, how they contacted them, what they said, how much it cost, how long it took, etc. It didn't seem all that complicated. So I asked why they didn't have any other sports accounts. Paul just shrugged his shoulders like he didn't know. I would look into this.

Also – I want to give Imagic some props here – they were the first company I knew of that put printed images of players on field walls at a sports stadium.

First thing I did after this was call the Anaheim Angels and ask if they'd seen the Dodgers' walls. I found a gatekeeper, but soon afterward was called by a guy named Kevin, Vice President of Operations at the "Big A" stadium in Anaheim.

Unbeknownst to me, there was another guy who noticed the Dodgers' walls and had the same plan. Tim Horan worked for a company called American Athletic, which was a manufacturer of the outfield wall pads. He was based out of Pennsylvania. He was also new to sales and was ready to hustle like me. He also was calling the Angels.

What he eventually did was call the Dodgers to ask who did the graphics on the outfield walls. Imagic in Hollywood, they told him, so he gave a cold call to the shop, and was transferred to me. It would become a huge moment for us both.

His enthusiasm completely invigorated me. He was new to sales, too, but had more experience. We were both huge sports fans. We started having conversations every day about strategies to get more work at sports stadiums as a team. Since he was in Westchester, Penn., he was three hours ahead in time. If I didn't start working til 9 a.m., it meant he didn't get to talk to me until noon, his time. That wasn't cool. I would be wasting half his day.

I made a big decision at this point: I would start getting up and working earlier. My living would depend on how hard I worked. Before I started with Imagic I'd been going to the gym after work with my buddy Wolfie. I was back living in Simi Valley and was getting my ass kicked in traffic every morning. So, I found a nice gym in Hollywood and joined, and started getting up at 4:45 a.m. every morning to beat the traffic, and I'd call Tim H. on my way in. I'd shower at the gym after my work out and be at the shop by 7 a.m. Another thing this did for me was cut my drinking nights during the week.

Around this time, Hutch at KROQ called. They were having their annual "Almost Acoustic Christmas" concert at the Shrine Auditorium in downtown L.A. They had some killer bands lined up: Blink 182, Hole, Depeche Mode and 311, to name a few. Hutch explained that the station had another vendor but he was going to give me some smaller stuff and try to work me in.

They gave me a bunch of wayfinding and directional signage, a few banners – and one big backdrop for a photo opportunity. The problem was, they didn't have art for this big backdrop. So, I took it upon myself to create it for them. I was still managing the prepress department at that time but had my own office with a Mac that had all the design programs. And I had the skills. Let's just do this ourselves.

So, I put art together. It took me maybe half a day. I sent it over, and they were thrilled. Not just with the design, but also about the fact that I just ran with it and did it myself. They said none of their other printers had ever done anything like that. I threw that information into the memory banks for later use.

Right before the show, after all the work had been printed and delivered, I got a call from Hutch and his boss offering me tickets and backstage passes for the show. Another lesson noted here: take care of your folks and they will take care of you. I took my buddy Jason to his first of many future KROQ shows.

* * *

By now Tim Horan and I were on a roll. We got the job wrapping the Angels' outfield wall with player images – this was 1999. I was still in disbelief that Imagic had done the Dodgers three years running and had no other sports accounts. Once word spread through the shop that I had landed the Angels account, one of the sales reps named David approached and asked, "You really solicited the Angels?" He was pissed. I guess he had tried, unsuccessfully, for three years. The owners knew I was going after it, though. And it wouldn't be the last time I tangled with David.

Since Imagic was also a design studio, we sold those services to the Angels, too. Tim (one of the owners) would be doing it personally.

Tim Horan flew out from Pennsylvania, and we went down to the stadium to survey the outfield walls. Besides the walls, we also got a bunch of player banners in the concourses.

The job went super smoothly. They loved the designs – except for one thing. We had put only current Angels players on the walls. They were owned by Disney back then, and Disney always deferred to Gene Autry's (the original owner of the original California Angels) widow, Jackie. Gene died the year before, and she sold the team to Disney. She asked if we could do a tribute to Gene on the outfield wall mural, and the answer was yes, of course we could.

The Angels gave me tickets to opening night, right behind the first-base dugout. I was super stoked to go and see reactions of fans as they came in and saw the outfield wall murals. I was really surprised that it got mixed reviews. The people who were for it absolutely loved it. The people who weren't kept saying it looked super cool, but the Angels were giving up space that could be generating revenue instead. Our killer mural only lasted one year, giving way to paid sponsors the following year (Dodgers did the same). But out of that one year I got a million miles of marketing value.

* * *

The National Football League has different rules than Major League Baseball. They did not allow teams to put sponsor logos on the playing field walls. With this in mind, I started hitting NFL teams hard. I was using the internet to search for who was in charge of operations for stadiums; I learned that from the Angels – contacting them and sending them pictures of the

Angels' walls. "Did you see this on TV last night?" I'd ask. They all loved it, and Tim Horan and I got immediate opportunities from the Washington Redskins and Carolina Panthers.

In December 1999 I got another call from Hutch. This year's Acoustic Christmas concert was moved to Universal Amphitheatre in Studio City, in the southeast corner of the Valley. He wanted me to come and measure some areas for him. I met him there and we walked to the back. We met with an operations guy from the venue. Hutch introduced me as "his banner guy." This was weird for me, and I didn't really like it. I had always referred to and thought of myself as a "graphics" guy, and being called a banner guy seemed a little denigrating. Looking back after 20 years, I was being totally silly. I was selling millions of dollars' worth of banners.

We got the entire sign package for the show this time. They mentioned several times that they remembered me designing the backdrop the year before by myself, on my own initiative. And I was taking it! KROQ was actually my favorite radio station, so I was having a total blast doing all this work.

Everything went perfectly, and once again they hooked me up with tickets and backstage passes. And once again I took my buddy Jason. It was a killer lineup, featuring Rob Zombie, Foo Fighters and Oasis.

A pretty fun story about this KROQ show: Jason and I were hanging out backstage and I saw a kid wearing a Black Flag T-shirt. I had downed a few beers, and as I always did when I saw someone wearing one of these shirts, I approached and asked who was his favorite singer from Black Flag? Without hesitation the kid said Keith Morris, which was one of two acceptable answers for me. Immediately this huge guy rushed up to defend the kid. It was Fletcher, the guitarist from Pennywise. His band was obviously heavily influenced by Black Flag. The kid told him we were cool, and we all started chatting. Turned out Fletcher liked Jason and I very much and ended up hanging around with us the rest of the night. Pretty cool, as we both loved Pennywise. Fletcher was having a good time himself, and kept asking us, "Did I ever tell you about the time I beat up Kid Rock?" We kept telling him, "NO!" And he probably told us the story 10 times. Haha. Great night, and what a cool dude. And for the record, my favorite singer from Black Flag was Keith Morris, too, though I also loved Dez Cadena.

By 2000, I had a little bit of sales going, and with some pretty big names. I was now wrapping vehicles for KROQ as well as doing banners, so I started sending pictures to potential clients saying, "Have you seen this?" Vehicle wraps were then a new thing. I'd never given up on my dreams of printing for record labels, which started when I first went into part-time sales at Jordan & Horn. Now working in Hollywood, I figured maybe my chances were better. I got back at it.

I had no luck with any of the big labels, but got some interest from a smaller one, Death Row Records: home of Snoop Dogg, Tupac, and Suge Knight. They had a Cadillac Escalade they wanted wrapped; it was Suge Knight's personal ride. I went to their offices in West L.A. on Wilshire Boulevard. I brought a tape and said I'd measure it – but they said, no, just take it with you. I had my truck there, so I drove back to the shop and got a ride back to West L.A. by Greg, who ran operations for Imagic. They threw me the keys, I hopped in, fired it up and took off down Wilshire Boulevard in Suge Knight's Cadillac.

When I returned to the shop we measured it right away, and Tim created a template. I sent it to Death Row, and they responded with just a bunch of images and logos and asked us to put it all together. We revised the quote with design added, they approved it, and Imagic's design team got on it.

Everyone was tripping out on what they wanted. They had sent the Death Row Records logos, a bunch of pictures of scantily clad girls who appeared to be dancing, and the typeface "stripper bitches." We designed it up, they approved a proof, and we sent it off to print.

This kind of verbiage on a vehicle wrap wouldn't fly today – and probably shouldn't have then. But it was 2000, and Imagic didn't care, so why should I? I was just trying to sell stuff. The real fun came when it was done, and I had to drive it back to West L.A. from Hollywood. I got a lot of honks that day. Too bad there was no social media back then. It would have made for a hell of a LinkedIn post.

In mid-2000, Tim Horan and I flew to Charlotte, N.C. to meet with the NFL's Panthers. We met a guy, Scott, who then was the stadium operations manager for the Panthers and Ericsson Stadium. They were interested in wrapping the end zone pads with banner vinyl like we did for the Angels baseball team. I asked if they had a design in mind, and they said they had no ideas.

I thought about this on the flight home and came up with an idea: cat's eyes. I sat down with Tim (the owner) and together we worked on a basic mockup using photos I'd taken on my stadium visit. We both thought it looked pretty cool, and we sent it to Scott from the Panthers. He responded right away that they loved it, except for one thing. They had to run it by their kicker, who at the time was John Kasay, to ensure it wouldn't mess him up on field goal attempts. His response was that he thought it was great – and would actually help him aim kicks better. *Perfect!*

The "Cat's Eyes" became iconic in Charlotte, and they even made T-shirts to sell in the stadium's team merchandise store.

Tim Horan and I were on a roll. We talked every morning super early to discuss targets and planning. He'd come out for business trips every once in a while, and I have a great story to tell about him.

Tim was a short, well-built dude. Athletic build. I was tall and skinny with tattoos and spiky hair. One of my favorite hobbies was snowboarding, so I invited Tim out to give it a try. One Saturday morning super early we jumped in my truck and headed up to Mountain High Ski Resort in the San Gabriel Mountains. Now, I've taught a lot of people to snowboard and considered myself a pretty good instructor. I usually started them slowly, and kept them on their heels and toes, until they figured out how to use the rails of the board. We got Tim in some rental equipment and went up to mid-mountain to start. There were green (beginner) runs down from there. I didn't like to start people on bunny slopes. We exited the chair lift without incident, sat at the top of a green run, and strapped in. I told him, "Okay. Just stay on your heels all the way down this first section, real slow, and I'll follow you." He stood up, pointed his board straight downhill, and took off like a bat out of hell. I couldn't even keep up with him. He didn't do one S-turn or anything else to slow down. He flew all the way down to the bottom of the chairlift, and then wiped out in spectacular fashion. I have no idea how he avoided hitting or running over anyone on the way down. He got up, dusted off, and we went back up. He was cutting S-turns by the end of the day. One thing for sure, Tim Horan had balls.

By this point I was gaining tons of confidence. I was bringing in some good accounts. Tim (the owner) and I had a great relationship. He had come along on a few of my business trips and was a fun guy to hang with. He liked music, and we hit some concerts on our trips. One business trip in Vegas, I talked him into going to see Alice Cooper and Hank Williams III on back-to-back nights. One interesting thing I learned about him over the first year was that he was a huge American Civil War buff.

At one point in 2000, I hit pay dirt off cold calls, with an advertising agency called Ogilvy & Mather in West L.A. It was for their new corporate offices, and we were to put window perf on clear interior partitions, so they'd be opaque on one side and clear on the other. The job came out killer and got an article in an industry magazine for Imagic. My name wasn't mentioned. It was a $30,000 job.

I was bringing in opportunities to Imagic on a consistent basis but was only getting a small percentage of the work because of pricing. I was still learning about this, but it seemed pretty logical to me that you can't charge people prices way higher than market value. Most buyers from big companies are pretty sophisticated. This was another lesson that always stuck in my mind; I spent a lot of time trying to get myself acquainted with fair market value in the printing industry.

Another thing was turnaround and response times. I started to get complaints from people. Not about me, but about production and customer service from the shop. And as I learned more about the digital printing industry, I started to realize what kind of equipment was needed to be successful. And we didn't really have it.

As I was driving around, back then, I noticed printed signs everywhere. They punched me in the face as I drove down the street. The opportunities for sales were endless. One thing I noticed was wrapped buses. I started doing some internet searches and discovered that in order to perform this type of work, you had to be "TDI Certified." I immediately took it to my boss, Tom, the sales manager, and was told it was a dead end.

At the end of 2000, the Pittsburgh Steelers were under construction on a brand new stadium, Heinz Field. I contacted them and was able to weasel in on bidding on the banners for the stadium field walls. Tim (owner) and I scheduled a trip out to meet and measure. I had another opportunity for a job at the University of Cincinnati's football stadium, so we made a big trip out of it. Back in those days I wasn't paying for the flights or hotels, and didn't have anyone at home waiting for me, so I was totally good with a four-day business trip.

We went to Cincinnati first, and actually flew into Kentucky, which was right across the Ohio River. We had a great meeting at the stadium and then headed back to our hotel, which was right on the river (Ohio side). When we got back, Tim asked what I wanted to do. He wanted to go out at night on every trip. I thought about it, and said I wanted to go to Kentucky. So, we ended up going to dinner in Covington, Kentucky. We had a fantastic meal, and then hit up a bar across the street for a couple of beers. One thing I will always remember about Kentucky is the girls. They were super hot, and their Southern accents melted me.

On the flight from Kentucky to Pittsburgh the next morning I was chatting up a really cute flight attendant. She was telling me about this concert that night featuring cover bands. We figured out that the venue was about 45 minutes from our hotel, and I told her I might show up. We had a great meeting with the Steelers, and after we returned to the hotel and Tim asked what I wanted to do, I told him – later, dude. I'm taking the rental car and going to a concert. He was fine with it, and I ended up having a really fun night with that girl.

We still had another day built into the trip, but I had no idea why. I found out soon enough the next morning. Tim wanted to go to Gettysburg, to the Civil War battle site. I was a bit of a Civil War buff as well, so I was super stoked.

It was about a 200-mile drive from Pittsburgh to Gettysburg. We found the site and did a self-guided tour. We both knew where we were on the battlefield at all times – Little Round Top, the Peach Orchard, Devil's Den, Pickett's Charge. It was super rad.

On the way back to Pittsburgh we decided to take the scenic route through the top of West Virginia. Tim told me to drive, and about an hour in I found out why. He wanted to enjoy some Jack and Cokes out of a Coca-Cola can the whole way back. He was a super cool boss.

Late 2000, I was doing pretty well. I was losing more opportunities than I was winning, but I definitely had the most bids. Tom, my direct boss in sales, dropped a bomb on everyone in the beginning of 2001. He was leaving to take a partnership at a company called GP Color. I was pretty crushed. Even worse, they made David the new sales manager. Remember him? The guy who was upset I had gone after and landed the Angels account.

He was still holding a grudge after more than a year, and it didn't seem it would go away, so I started talking to other print companies in the area. I had a few people interested but was still too green in sales for the big companies. And they just weren't seeing the angle of going after the sports and sports stadiums market.

David started holding weekly sales meetings, which we'd never done, but seemed like a really good idea to me. The only thing was, in the meetings we never really talked about sales. Everyone was just gossiping and bullshitting.

One day about a month after Tom left, David called me into his office. I sat down, and this is exactly what he told me: "You're terminated for lack of sales. There is no room for discussion." That was it. I had been fired.

Ironically enough, after I left, Imagic did go get TDI approved and bought an 8-foot Vutek printer. And they ended up doing really well. They became the biggest producer of bus wraps in the entire country and then got bought out by Circle Graphics. My buddy Sean still works there to this day.

CHAPTER 6
SUPERCOLOR / INTERNATIONAL COLOR POSTERS

"OC Life,"

- D.I.

I didn't want to work in Los Angeles any longer. Especially since I lived in Long Beach now, in the house in which I'd eventually start Screaming Images. I missed living in Orange County, and I guess this was sort of my compromise. I had talked my buddy Jason into moving down there too, to be my roommate.

SuperColor was the only company I called after the firing by Imagic. I did some research, and they had 16-foot and 10-foot-wide printers. I walked in the door for an interview with requests for proposals (RFPs) from the New York Jets and Atlanta Falcons in my hand and was hired on the spot. Just two days after my last day at Imagic.

We negotiated a $40,000 base salary with 5% commission on all jobs. This was better than my last job, where I was paid zero commissions on all the jobs I had sold.

I was already established with a morning gym routine, and wanted to expand on it, so I found a super nice gym in Irvine, not far from the Super-Color shop (also in Irvine). I started getting up at 3:45 a.m. so I could hit the gym, get my workout in, then shower and be at the shop by 7 a.m. I got into a routine of loading a backpack with my work clothes the night before to save time in the morning. I'd have a cup of tea and be out the door. This allowed me to beat traffic heading in. It turns out the traffic between Long Beach and Irvine, mostly on the 405 freeway, was a total bitch. I was leaving SuperColor at 4 p.m., and it was taking literally an hour and a half to drive 22 miles to get home.

The owners didn't mind me getting there at 7 a.m., which was way before anyone else, but they pushed back a little when I began leaving at 3:30 p.m. to try to beat some traffic. I just said I'd be on my phone the entire commute and would hop back on my computer when I got home. I ended up talking the Angels baseball team into sticking with me, and this made my bosses feel more comfortable about it.

SuperColor had a huge building in Irvine. The upstairs area where the owners, executives, and salespeople worked was opulent. Granite counters, glass fixtures, marble columns – super high-end. Everyone upstairs had a private office, including myself. It was by far the nicest working space I'd ever had. They issued me a PC laptop for my office, which I wasn't really too stoked about – I was a Mac guy. They signed me up with an account for a sales program called ACT! They also gave me a company cell phone that doubled as a walkie-talkie. The owners liked using the walkie-talkie feature to determine where I was when not at the shop. I didn't really dig on it at the time, but as the years went by and I became an owner myself, I totally understood where they were coming from.

The downstairs/production area at SuperColor was impressive, too. They had six grand-format printers: three 10-footers and three 16-footers. They had a ton of floor space, and a big, huge square finishing table (which I would later emulate at my first small shop). They had an upstairs cat track that was a viewing area for people coming into the shop for press-checks or quality control. They had a shop engineer, and just about every piece of finishing equipment you could imagine. These dudes spent a ton of money setting up their shop.

The two owners were brothers, Peyman and Arman. They seemed like totally nice guys. Peyman was older and seemed more in charge. Arman spent most of his time downstairs with production. They seemed to be doing really well, and both wore nice clothes and drove really nice cars. I never asked their nationality, but assumed they were of Persian descent. Not that it matters.

They were always nice, helpful and open to suggestions.

One thing Peyman really liked was exhibiting at trade shows. I went to a couple right off the bat. We had sales meetings every Friday at 4 p.m., and Peyman asked us to bring our top five prospects. There were three of us sales reps working out of the shop, one in Texas named Marty, and another girl named Jody (can't remember where she worked remotely). I do remember she was super cute, and we did attend a few trade shows together.

In mid-2001, I picked up a new client via cold calling – Free Car Media. The CEO was named Drew, a super cool dude. Again, vehicle wraps were still fairly new, and FCM had a model where they would sell car wraps to advertisers, then find people to wrap their personal cars with the ads – and pay their car payment. Hence the name, Free Car Media. The cool thing about this account was they'd wrap 10 to 20 vehicles for every company they sold an ad to – so it was a lot of print work. It became my most consistent account.

As stated earlier, the Angels stuck with me, even though they had some hesitation initially. I capitalized on that and got the Anaheim Ducks from some pretty persistent cold calling. Also, KROQ and the Carolina Panthers were still with me.

The Carolina Panthers had a huge job they wanted me to bid on that didn't involve printing. It was more aesthetics, using fabric banners. The owners of SuperColor said they weren't interested.

* * *

There was a trade show for the International Association of Assembly Managers in Dallas (I believe), and I asked if I could exhibit there in early 2001; they approved. They let me help design the booth – and I wanted to come up with some sort of attraction to get people's attention. I decided to set up a little putting green in my booth to get people in so I could talk with them. Furthermore, I talked Peyman and Arman into buying a new set of killer golf clubs that I'd give away at the end of the show for everyone who submitted their business card. It worked, and my booth was packed the entire show, landing 500-plus potential new connections. A valuable thing those guys (Peyman & Arman) taught me about business was it takes money to make money.

Don't be afraid to spend the dough.

The guy who won (wink-wink) the set of golf clubs was the director of operations for a brand-new arena being built in Puerto Rico. Of course, he invited me down for a vendor's pre-bid meeting, and SuperColor agreed to pay my expenses to go there. It was a quick trip; one-nighter. I walked the arena with about (20) other potential vendors, and most of them were from the United States. The week after I returned, I received, as agreed upon, the signage package RFP. It involved a lot of things besides banners and wraps – mainly rigid signs. Wayfinding, directionals, bathroom signs, you name it. The entire package. Not sure why, but the owners of SuperColor declined to bid. Yeah, it was difficult, and yeah, it was different. Once I started Screaming Images, I never turned down a bid like this. I'd partner with someone strong at the applications I wasn't and won the jobs most of the time.

Regarding all the other connections I made at IAAM show, I got a ton of opportunities to bid. I didn't get any of the work. They all responded with the same reason: your prices are too high; not in line. It became a recurring theme. I brought in a ton of opportunities and lost them all on price.

Next thing, Peyman decided I needed some sales training. He signed me up for a sales class that was going to instruct how to not sell on price. I attended the once-a-week classes for about two months. Of ten people in class, nine sold insurance. It was a total waste of time. I completely understood selling quality and customer service, but to do that, your quality and customer service had to be way better than the other vendors. Ours wasn't. If you have an experienced buyer in a market like, say, sports, they have been buying prints for a long time, and know the per-square-foot price ranges of the market. When a vendor submits a bid double the price they usually pay, that vendor will not get the job.

* * *

Tim Horan was still with me. American Athletic and SuperColor co-opted a booth at the Major League Baseball Tradeshow in Dallas. It was all set up by Tim. We had a killer booth, and I was totally excited.

Of course, if Tim and I are in Dallas, we have to stop by and pay our respects to Billy Bob's, the world's largest honky-tonk. We rolled up to the front door like we owned the place – Tim in his pressed polo, khakis, and loafers, and me in a Hawaiian shirt, shorts, Converse All Stars, and spiky hair. The place was huge and absolutely packed. I had a couple of cowboys comment on my attire as we entered, but I let it go. I figured they would just get even madder if I jumped on the mechanical bull, which of course I did. Pretty sure I broke my thumb that night hanging onto that fucking thing. I wasn't letting go no matter what. Tim, though, rode it like a champ. The cowboys were all impressed. We had a blast at Billy Bob's! Chatted up cowgirls, two-stepped with older ladies, and drank many, many bottles of Lone Star beer.

The first day of the show I was like a kid in a candy store. There were famous retired baseball legends everywhere. Every day I'd skip out the booth for a bit, go down to the booth of the vendor that sells hot dogs to the stadiums, and have a custom dog. Then I'd hop on a cart shaped like a beer keg and head over the batting cages and take some rips. This wasn't any regular old batting cage either – it threw curveballs, sinkers, sliders, and could be programmed to exact speeds and exactly where the balls crossed the plate. It was amazing. We had a ton of traffic at our booth, and I was having the time of my life.

Something amazing happened on the show's first morning. I was sitting with Tim right before the doors opened, and Bill Russell came walking into our booth to say hello. I'm talking Bill Russell, legendary shortstop for the Los Angeles Dodgers. I'd been a Dodgers fan my whole life and knew all his career stats from baseball cards I collected as a kid. He sat in our booth and talked with us for almost two hours. The next morning, he came back and did it again. The third day also. I was kind of friends with Bill frickin' Russell!

The third morning, I was called by my old friend Jenn who used to work in the Angels marketing department and was now working for the Houston Astros. I had emailed her ahead of time letting her know I'd be in Dallas and seeing if she had any time to meet. She said come on down.

So, I looked at Tim and said: "You want to go meet with the Astros after the show?" He said, "Hell yeah! But you know it's 250 miles, right?" Shit!

The weather had been really nice in Dallas up to this point. But when I went outside in the afternoon, the skies began turning gray. Someone in a big jacket walked by me real fast and said: "The weather's about to turn." What the hell did that mean? I lived at the beach.

It meant ice storm, and Tim and I drove in it all the way to Houston and back. Slipping and sliding all over the highway in some little rental car. But at least we got to meet with Jenn, check out Enron Field (the name was changed the next year for obvious reasons), and add the Houston Astros to our list of potential clients.

By the time we returned to our hotel in Dallas, it was way after midnight, and our flights out were first thing in the morning. I called my bank to check on funds in my very slim bank account, only to discover I was overdrawn. I was in Dallas, and completely broke – couldn't even pay for parking at the airport. Thankfully, Tim was able to loan me a couple hundred bucks to get me through the next four days until I got paid.

* * *

Something I always noticed, and was super curious about, at the shop: I never saw the presses running. Every week in our sales meeting there was a girl talking about tons of work for GES and Freeman, which I learned were tradeshow houses. They were always talking about Las Vegas, too. Maybe the presses ran at night on a second shift or something. I had no idea.

I was doing really well with my Free Car Media account; we printed tons of vehicle wraps for them. I was using this work as leverage to get other vehicle wraps and had connected with a couple of marketing agencies. I wasn't super busy, but I was hustling hard every day. However, I hadn't heard from the Angels in a while.

One day I was on the production floor doing quality control on a couple of my jobs, and a guy came walking in the shop. I asked him how I could help, and he answered that he was looking to speak with someone about doing installations. I just so happened to have a Ford Explorer that was to be wrapped, and already had the files printed, so I asked him to send me a quote and some pictures of past vehicle wraps he'd done. He sent them that evening, and SuperColor hired him to wrap my Explorer. He did a great job and ended up being my main installer for wraps for many years. And, he ended up going on to create a huge media company that did all the building wraps in San Diego; a total success story. He got it by hustling – even if it meant going door to door.

As for me, I was still broke. I lived paycheck to paycheck, always having to make sure I had enough gas in my truck to get back and forth to Irvine every day, especially the last three or four days before payday. I was working hard, but very down on myself. I remember one of my buddies was getting married and we were all supposed to go to Mexico on a surf trip for his bachelor party. I had to back out last minute – I told them I couldn't get out of work. The truth was, I couldn't afford it. I was making myself tuna sandwiches to take to work every day because I couldn't afford to go out to lunch. At my lowest point, I had to take my little loose change cup I kept in my bedroom and stop by the change machine at the grocery store on the way to work. I got $28 bucks out of it for gas, and it barely got me to work and back until the next paycheck.

* * *

The Angels were having a good season in 2002, and it appeared they would make the playoffs. I was on my way home from Irvine one day after work, and my old (323) area code phone rang. It was Robert from the Angels.

He wanted to talk to me about playoff banners. I went and saw him the next day.

I was still talking to the Carolina Panthers about the fabric/aesthetics job. I had continued putting numbers together. Even though the owners of SuperColor weren't interested in this job at all, I just couldn't let it go.

There was a dude who sat in an upstairs office at SuperColor every day. He never joined any of our meetings, and never interacted with any of us. He was there all day every day. One day I asked Peyman who he was, and he said the guy had his own business called Graphics Unlimited. He had two big accounts. I won't mention the names, but one was a really popular clothing company, and another was a pretty huge software company. I saw his work on the floor all the time. Huh, I thought.

I was still having the same problems I had in Hollywood. The quality wasn't great, the customer service wasn't either. And the prices were super high. I was getting overruled on everything I tried to do and was having a hard time bringing in new customers.

I did end up bringing in the Angels playoffs job, though, and it was a huge job – the whole stadium. And we'd have to turn it around again, with another opponent's logos, if they advanced to the next round.

They played the New York Yankees first, in the Divisional Series. We did all the banners in the concourses, all the street banners on Katella and State College bordering the stadium, gate banners (which were new for post-season), billboards, the tops of the dugouts, as well as ancillary stuff up in the outfield terraces. It was a ton.

It was a super short turnaround. We didn't know the opponent until Sept. 28th. We had seven days to print and install everything (luckily, they were starting on the road, which gave us three additional days). But it would get even tighter if they won a series, and advanced.

SuperColor did a good job getting all the prints produced in time, and I brought in a guy named Robbie to handle the installation for the whole thing. We were all working 24 hours a day. I was managing the whole job and didn't get any support from the shop outside of the printing. I was entering orders, monitoring the press schedule to ensure things were being printed in the order they were installed, running back and forth from the stadium to the shop for pick-ups and deliveries, and managing installation as Robbie and his team weren't familiar with the stadium.

I was working my ass off but having the time of my life. I was right in the middle of the frickin' Major League Baseball playoffs! I had become an Angels fan too – it's hard to avoid when you're working at the stadium almost every day. I'd walk around at the stadium during the day and people would yell, "Hey, James!" Such a good feeling.

The Angels offered us a ticket package for purchase for the entire post-season, and I talked SuperColor into buying them. Two seats for every game, all the way through. In the case the team was eliminated, there would be a credit for the games not played.

The Yankees won the American League East and had a League-high 103 wins. The Angels had placed second in the American League West, squeaking by to take the wild-card playoff entry. Everyone was expecting the Yankees to steamroll the Angels, and that we wouldn't have a second round of print and install work.

The Yankees won the first game at home, 8-5, and it wasn't looking good, especially in a best-of-five series. But the Angels came back and won game two, 8-6, and all of a sudden were coming back home with the series tied.

I was excited out of my mind for all of this – but no one at the shop really seemed to care. So, I had the tickets all to myself. The first home game was Oct. 4th, a Friday – an afternoon game. I had two tickets, so I took a date. The seats were pretty good! The Angels still had an uphill battle but won the game 9-6 to take a 2-1 lead in the series. Toward the end of the game, I was getting messages on my walkie-talkie SuperColor phone from the owner, Arman, who seemed pretty interested now with the fact that the Angels looked to be one win away from advancing to the next round, which meant a ton more print work.

Game 4 was the next day, another day game, and I had options. One of my Angels contacts offered me two seats behind home plate in the field level dugout seats. So, I gave my two SuperColor seats to my KROQ contact, Mike. The energy in the stadium was incredible, and I was so excited I was shaking when the game started. My seats in the dugout suite were right next to the Angels on-deck circle. Darin Erstad had hit the ball really hard his first two at-bats but was 0 for 2. David Wells was pitching for the Yankees, and Erstad came into the on-deck circle in the fifth with the score tied 2-2 and two out. He had his head down taking practice swings and I was talking to him saying, "You got this, you're all over this guy, you already smoked the ball off him twice," and he just kept his head down nodding, hearing every word I said. David Eckstein hit a single and moved Benji Gil to third. Erstad came up and ripped a single on the first pitch, scoring Gil from third to take the lead: 3-2. It was hands down the most exhilarating sports experience I'd had to date.

The Angels won, 9-5, taking the series in four games. On to the American League Championship Series! And another round of full print and install for the stadium. The SuperColor guys were starting to pay attention now, as we had to turn the entire stadium's graphics again. We began preparing pre-press files that night, full sets, with two possible opponents – the Minnesota Twins or the Oakland A's.

The next day, Oct. 6th, the Twins beat the A's in game five. Since we were the wild card team, and the Twins had the better record, thankfully the series started in Minneapolis, and we had until Oct. 11th to get everything printed and installed.

I was still on my own with all the management and logistics. To be fair, the SuperColor guys did have their hands full with all the prints. What I didn't realize at the time was that this was hands-on experience that would be invaluable down the line with Screaming Images. Everything was completed in time again, and the Angels were super stoked on me. The atmosphere around the stadium while we were installing everything was electric. I'd never been involved in anything so killer, and I was super stoked myself.

The SuperColor guys still weren't asking about the tickets, so I kept them for myself again. Now we had a seven-game series, and the Twins won game one at home, 2-1. The Angels came back to win game two, 6-3, and headed back to Edison Field in Anaheim with the series tied, and three straight games at home. There was no stopping the Angels at this point. They were absolutely on fire and swept all three home games to make it to the 2002 World Series.

On Oct. 14, the San Francisco Giants beat the St. Louis Cardinals in game five of their series, to win the National League title and set up a World Series between two wild-card teams.

This time, the series would start in Anaheim, on Oct. 19, which meant we had five days to turn the whole stadium again. It was a little different at the stadium for this round – MLB takes over the entire stadium's operations for the World Series, which meant we weren't working around people we knew (Angels staff), and it took away a few shortcuts. But it was okay –SuperColor was busting out the prints, Robbie and I had our install systems down, and it would get done on time no matter what.

A couple days before the World Series started my Angels marketing contact gave me a heads-up that they had given my cell number to the local news, and that they would call. They did, and we set up an interview at the SuperColor shop with a local news crew (can't remember which one).

The SuperColor guys were all of a sudden interested in the games. The World Series was the hottest thing in town, and now that they'd been on the news everyone was hitting them up for tickets. I was able to hang onto tickets for the first two games but would be watching the last two (if it went that far) from home.

A fun story from around that time. I'd been taking my buddy Jason with me to the games during the ALCS with the Twins. We were having fun, drinking beers, and cheering on the Angels. After they won game 5 and clinched the World Series, the parking lot was going absolutely nuts. We got back to his truck and realized we had finished all our beers during pre- game tailgating and were stuck there with no beer. And no one was going anywhere, they were all celebrating, we were going to be there for a while. We saw a group of people close to us with an ice chest full of beers and walked over and asked if we could buy a couple. They said no. Jason said, "C'mon – this is the guy that printed all of the banners here for the playoffs!" (I was silently wishing he hadn't done that), and the group of people said, "Yeah right!" and still wouldn't part with two beers. We went back to Jason's truck and just waited the crowd out. The interview with me at the SuperColor shop, about printing the banners for the World Series, showed on local TV two nights later. The next day I was having lunch at an El Pollo Loco in Irvine, minding my own business and reading the sports page, and some dude walked up and tapped me on the shoulder. He said, "Dude, I saw you on the news last night. We didn't believe your friend's story about you printing all of the Angels banners for the playoffs. I'm sorry, man, I wish we would have given you guys those beers…" Haha.

The Angels ended up winning the 2002 World Series in dramatic fashion, in seven games. I was so stoked, even with the fact that I had to watch the last two games at home in Belmont Shores (where I had parties for both games). I had the time of my life. I had done the print and install for the World Series and had been hands-on involved. I needed to get more of this high.

Another pretty major thing happened during the course of the Angels postseason home games. I was taking either a date or Jason to the games, and I was drinking pretty heavily at them. That's what I had always done at baseball and football games, ever since I was old enough to drink at stadiums. It was late in one of the games against the Twins, and I was walking around in the outfield terrace area between innings when I ran into the vice president of marketing from the Angels. I was shit-faced. He walked up with a huge smile on his face that disappeared as soon as he noticed that I was completely drunk. He just shook his head and walked away, and I was humiliated. From that moment on I stopped drinking at sporting events. And anywhere else there was a possibility I'd run into clients. It actually wasn't that hard. I replaced beer with sunflower seeds at the Angels games. And I did apologize two days later, in person, once I was 100% again, to that VP. He said to forget about it, and that he would do the same, and he kept his word. His name was Robert, and he was one of the coolest dudes I ever worked with.

* * *

At this point I was working on some pretty high-profile jobs and bringing in a good amount of work – but I was still broke. I had a pretty good commission check coming for the World Series job, but they wouldn't tell me how much. I'd never even seen the final quote on the job. One thing I really wanted to buy, but couldn't afford, was a new pair of gym shoes. I had worn my other ones down to shreds. I went in and asked Peyman if I could get an advance on my commission, and told him what it was for, and he said yes and gave me an advance of $100. I remember very well running right down to the mall and buying a pair of red and white New Balance gym shoes.

One of the major traits I was developing was, once I got my hands on a job opportunity, I wouldn't let go. I was still working on Big League Dreams, trying to figure out the best way to do the crowd scenes on the outfield walls. I kept trying to explain to the SuperColor owners what a massive opportunity it was, but it seemed like it was something they'd never heard of and had no interest in. I kept in touch with BLD on a regular basis. I wasn't going to let it go. I was also still working on the big aesthetic job for the Carolina Panthers, that the owners had rejected a couple of times already because it didn't involve printing. I wasn't letting go of that one, either. I continued to bring in opportunities and continued to not get the jobs. The prospective clients were always straight up with me: your price is too high. We can get it for less. They loved the way I communicated with them, and wanted to give me the jobs, even to the point where they'd share the other quotes with me. But no go. SuperColor wouldn't budge on prices.

I was also getting a lot more comfortable cold calling. And, armed with the pictures from all the other work I'd done, doors were opening up easier. I just needed to get past the price hurdle. And this was the case when I started talking to the Anaheim Mighty Ducks about their graphics for the playoffs at the end of 2002.

SuperColor was all about exhibiting at local shows, and I was their guy for this. It didn't bother me – I loved to be around crowds and was never afraid to talk to people I didn't know. At one of these tradeshows, I met Scott from International Color Posters. ICP was located in Lake Forest, also south Orange County, and Scott was vice president of sales. I told him at the show about the World Series work I'd just done, the other Angels stuff, Free Car Media, KROQ, and the opportunities with the Mighty Ducks, Carolina Panthers, and Big League Dreams. I asked if they had 16-foot presses and he said they did. He said I should come check it out sometime. We left it at that.

The guy who ran his own little business out of SuperColor showed up every morning around 9 a.m. He always had print jobs on the floor. He was always dressed sharp and drove a really nice car. This was on my mind a lot.

One morning Peyman called me into his office and told me he was lowering my base salary. He said it was to motivate to sell more. I didn't really agree – I had the opportunities, but just wasn't getting them because of price. Whenever I tried to talk to the customers about "quality" and "service," their response was, competitors had the same presses and bought their materials from the same places. And I thought to myself, they were right. That same day I gave Scott a call and set up a tour at ICP.

The biggest thing I was looking for at International Color Posters were the 16-foot presses. And they did have them. They looked different, and a little older than those at SuperColor, but they were definitely 16 feet wide. I had Big League Dreams on my mind with these. I was still pretty new into the "digital print" world and didn't have a lot of knowledge about what was good and what was bad equipment-wise. I told Scott I was having problems winning jobs because of prices, and shared some of the info from competitors' quotes I'd received, to see if they could match or beat them. He said yes. I told him I had requests for quotes from the Ducks, and wanted to show them material samples, and he said yes. I told him I wanted to print some tests for Big League Dreams on the 16-foot presses and he said yes. I told him I wanted $45,000 a year base salary ($5,000 per year more than SC), and he said yes. We shook hands, and I agreed to make the move.

I arrived the next morning and gave two weeks' notice to Peyman. He said it was okay, and that I didn't have to give two weeks, I could just move on. He had my final check cut, and we parted ways.

One of the other stipulations I had made with Scott was that I bring my prepress guy with me from SC, as he had the Free Car Media jobs wired. He agreed, and Josh followed me over to ICP. They had a really nice building in Lake Forest; about the same size as SuperColor, just laid out differently. I turned in my bid for the 2003 NHL Finals to the Anaheim Mighty Ducks and was awarded the job. I ran some test panels on banner vinyl, with a special ultraviolet ray- protective coat I found on the interweb, and Big League Dreams approved them. We immediately did some replacement panels for their Cathedral City (Calif.) park and they were super stoked. Then KROQ gave me a big banner job for a music festival, and I was off to a good start at ICP.

Scott and I had a fun trip to a tradeshow in New Orleans during my time there – I talked him into exhibiting at the IAAM show. When we exited the plane and went over to claim our bags, mine never came out. An hour later, the airline informed me that my bag had somehow ended up at another destination, and it would be delivered the next day. I needed clothes for the show the next morning, so I went over to the GAP (totally not my style) and bought a pair of khakis and a light blue short-sleeve shirt. The next morning,

I wore them to the show, totally expecting to get my bags that afternoon. Nope. Had to wear the same clothes the next day. Called the airline the next afternoon – still no bag. I couldn't really afford to buy another set of clothes I'd never wear again, so I wore the same clothes for the third consecutive day. By now it was a joke among all the friends I'd made and the other vendors with booths around us. It was actually funny, and I wasn't all that bummed out. I ended up not getting my bag back until I returned home. But one thing I did pick up was a new customer that would lead me into the concessionaires at sports stadiums: Centerplate. Dirty clothes and all. Bango.

Lake Forest was even more of a haul than Irvine from Belmont Shores. I talked to Scott about working a couple days a week from home, and he approved. I was going to the gym in Long Beach that was at Pacific Coast Highway and the famous big traffic circle in town, and everything was working out well.

It only took me through the first KROQ job to figure out that ICP's 16-foot presses were different. They were NUR Blueboards, super slow, super low-resolution printing, and severely outdated. They worked okay for the BLD crowd scene banners, because they were viewed from a distance, but this wouldn't fly for the Ducks or KROQ banners. As for Free Car Media, ICP really struggled with getting the panels for wrapping vehicles right. I knew it wasn't a setup problem, because I brought my prepress guy with me, and everything went smoothly at SuperColor.

The owner at ICP was a French guy named Eric, and I'm pretty sure I never spoke with him once. I heard rumors that he was a hothead, but never saw anything personally to substantiate it. I kept hearing that he didn't like the *Free Car Media* account, and that account was kind of my bread-and-butter. The service at ICP also wasn't great, and I was getting an earful from customers I brought with me and promised everything would go smoothly. It got to the point where I was uncomfortable to go to work at the shop, so I was just working from home most days. I kept thinking about that guy who ran his own little business out of SuperColor.

For the NHL Finals for the Mighty Ducks, we ended up doing the huge windows outside The Pond (the name of their arena) and a big, huge banner that hung from the upper-level seats. I really wanted to pull out and do this one on my own, but the timing was bad, and I didn't want to affect the Ducks in any negative way, so I decided to have ICP print this one, and I'd handle install independently. I remember sitting in the arena's parking lot in my truck while the windows were being installed and talking to a friend on my cell and telling him I was going to start my own business, and him saying, "Yeah right." This guy was one of my best friends, and he clearly didn't think I could do it.

After the Ducks job finished, things still weren't going well at ICP. It wasn't Scott's fault – he kept me posted on everything – but I pretty much had decided it wouldn't work out. I was going to start my own business and vend out all my printing to someone else so I could be in control of the customer service, quality, and pricing.

Me with legendary Dodgers shortstop Bill Russell
at the MLB tradeshow in Dallas

CHAPTER 7
BELMONT SHORES /
S.I. BEGINNING

"My War"

- *Black Flag*

I kept working on the Carolina Panthers job while still with my last two employers. I brought it up to both owners, but neither were interested because it didn't involve printing. To them, it was just aesthetics. But it was money? A good profit margin job? I never understood that.

By the time I left (was let go, actually) ICP in Orange County, I pretty much had this job in the bag. I had all the pricing and logistics 99% complete. I had been working with the Panthers since the mid-90s. They liked and trusted me.

I knew I was leaving International Color Posters. It just wasn't a good fit. They didn't care about their customers, and their equipment was outdated and slow. The sports graphics circles I was walking around in were super fast-paced and the people who worked in them were sophisticated buyers. Which is to say, they knew a ton about print and finish quality, proper resolutions, how long it took to do jobs, and around how much they should pay per square foot. And, since they were being solicited by vendors from all over the country, they didn't have to put up with anything less than absolute highest-level customer service. I also knew ICP was my last stop before I struck out on my own. It was nerve-wracking, and I didn't have any kind of monetary cushion to fall back on. I knew if they let me go, as opposed to me quitting, I could collect unemployment for a bit while I got the ball rolling on my new business. I felt a little guilty about it, but not much.

I'd had a name for my new little business on my mind since the Super-Color days. I was going to call it "Structure Graphics." My self-reasoning was,

I was putting graphics onto structures, right? It seemed technical. I still wasn't yet thinking with my punk rock/business mindset. And I hadn't been down to Long Beach City Hall and signed everything up yet, thankfully. I wasn't going to do anything official until I was 100% cleared of my employer. That is just the way I've always rolled.

I was at the gym the morning ICP would let me go. I knew it was coming, because I was given a heads-up by the sales manager. I was on an elliptical machine, and the guy in front of me had on a T-shirt that said "screaming" something-or-other on the back. I think it might have been some kind of skateboarding company or something – we were in Orange County after all, right? As I carried on with my time on the cardio machine, my brain started rolling on this. Screaming this, Screaming that. SCREAMING IMAGES! I knew the first second it popped into my head, that was it. That my new little business would be called Screaming Images. It was perfect, I thought. It fit my personality. And I felt like it emboldened me.

I went on into ICP, was let go, and got my final check. No severance pay, just the last paycheck straight-up – even though I had brought a ton of high-profile work there. They hadn't capitalized on the opportunities I brought in, and that was not my fault.

I had four big customers I was worried about. I hoped to get at least two to stick with me, and my new little business. I had the Carolina Panthers job I'd been working on, which I really wanted to become the first Screaming Images job. So, I had them, Big League Dreams, Free Car Media, and KROQ radio. I decided to call them all on my way back to Long Beach from Lake Forest. I had no idea how it would go.

I called Scott from the Panthers first. I said right off the bat that I had left ICP and was starting my own business, and that it would be called Screaming Images. The first time I said S.I. out loud to someone it felt really weird. First thing he asked was if he would still be dealing directly with me, which was a Yes. Then he asked if the quote would change, and if I had finalized it yet, which was No. The last question he asked was if I was going to be able to guarantee the work with the new company. Yes. That was a tough one. All of a sudden, I would have to be a lot more responsible. He said he was staying with me. Next call was to Wayne at Big League Dreams. We had a big sports park job on the horizon, and I would be in really good shape if I could keep this one with S.I. He asked pretty much the same questions and then gave me the green light. He would stay with me, too. The calls with Free Car Media and KROQ went about the same, and by the time I pulled up to my little house in Belmont Shores, I had secured all four accounts. Time to get busy.

This Carolina Panthers job was aesthetics to cover up the plumbing and electrical conduits on the ceilings in the main concourse. It consisted of two sizes of fabric banners, just Panthers blue, and the banners had unique shapes. Kind of concave. I was told these had to match exactly for size and shape. There were 170 of them that were 45-feet wide by 24-inches high, and 55 of them were 25-feet wide and 24-inches high. I went out to Charlotte and the Panthers facility team put me up in a lift to see how they were attached, so I could determine what kind of finishing we needed. By finishing I mean how the banners are built, so they can be attached. Most common ways for this are either pockets for poles, or a string of reinforced holes, called grommets. I headed back home to finalize the quote 100%.

I completed the quote, emailed it to Scott, and he approved immediately. I asked if they could send one of each size to me in Long Beach so I could match the shape, size, and color. They did, and I had them within a week. The next step was to get a material and color approved, so I drove out to pick up some blue samples of a material called Sunbrella, which is an outdoor fabric used a lot for boats and marine-type stuff, from a company in City of Industry called TriVantage. I picked the color I thought was closest to Panther blue and bought enough to make a full-sized sample for Scott's sign-off. I also got a few small swatches of different blues just in case. I took the Sunbrella material and the sample banners from the stadium to my friend Leslie at AAA Flag &

Banner in West Los Angeles – she had already quoted me on the trimming and finishing for this job. She told me to come back tomorrow to do quality control on the finished sample.

I ran back to West L.A. the next morning to check it out. I compared the size and shape of the new sample Leslie had completed and also checked that the finishing had double- reinforced stitching and grommets. Everything looked great. We packed it up and shipped it out to Charlotte, N.C., to Ericsson Stadium. The samples arrived the following week, and were immediately approved, including the color I had selected.

It was time to send the invoice for the deposit. I have to admit I was a nervous wreck, as I had never done anything like this and was 100% responsible for this job, at an NFL football stadium. It was a big deal.

The total quote was $54,100. I asked for a 50% deposit, which came out to $27,050. I had to pay 100% up front for the Sunbrella material and pay upon shipping to AAA Flag & Banner for the finishing, and this all came out to $33,050. I was short $6,000 between what I collected on the deposit and what I needed to pay out. Please remember here, I was just a broke-ass punk rock guy from Long Beach, and I didn't have anywhere near that type of money. I only had one chance at getting this money. I called my best friend, Chris, who was a successful business owner, and hoped he'd lend me the money short-term. He did, and I was covered. Now I just needed the job to go well so I could pay him back. Shit.

The due date for the banners to arrive in Charlotte was July 28th, 2003. I received the deposit, bought the material, and took it all down to AAA the second week of June. We had two weeks to do all the cutting and sewing so I could get it on a truck at ground freight rates to get it to the stadium in time, so they could in turn get them up in time for their first home game which was Sept. 7th. I had given them 30-day terms on paying the balance; but that all depended on everything being right and going up correctly. I had done extensive quality control on the banners before they shipped out, but I was still super nervous.

Everything went out the door on time and the banners arrived the third week of July.

Everything went up, fit perfectly, and the colors and finishing were perfect. I sent out the final invoice for the balance and they paid it in two weeks. First thing I did was pay my friend Chris back the $6,000 he loaned me.

I also had a credit card debt of about $6,000 that was past due, which seemed insurmountable, and I had been harassed and threatened about it by a collection agency almost every day for the 60 days prior. I called this collections guy, got the total, and paid the whole credit card balance. This left a profit of about $14,000. It was the most money I'd ever had my entire life.

I guess I should backtrack a little here. When I first started telling my friends in mid-2002 that I planned to start my own business, no one believed I could do it. I could tell by the looks on their faces. I had a couple of them, who were already successful, tell me I couldn't start a business without capital. That's exactly what I ended up doing. Matter of fact, I had almost $10,000 in personal debt when I started Screaming Images. Sheer hustle, do-it-yourself attitude, and guts. That's how I did it. Punk rock style.

There's a lot more to all this when you think about it. If you don't have any personal money stashed or capital to subsidize things, you don't have funds for things like bookkeepers or workflow software. I had to do it all myself. I was crafting invoices in Adobe Illustrator (thanks to the skills from my prepress background) and I had folders on the desktop of my antique (junk, really) 1990s Apple computer, and I would put the invoices into a folder called "invoices out." When they were paid, I'd move them to a folder called "invoices paid." That was how I kept track of who owed me money. I bought a big plastic container bin and a box of manila folders and kept all my expenses and vendor invoices in labeled folders. Same for receipts. At the end of the year, I'd get everything out and spend a whole day adding everything up and figuring out my business expenses and taxes. I didn't hire an actual bookkeeper or get a QuickBooks account for the first three years I was in business (more on that later).

The first big expense after my successful Panthers job was to buy a newer-model used Mac. It was a Quicksilver model, about three years old, and I think I paid $1,200. I was riding high on the hog with this, as I was doing almost all the design stuff myself. I did hire someone to help me to get a quick website up that was really just a one-pager as a placeholder. It had logos from some of my customers, a few pictures, and a loop of a T.S.O.L. song playing on it. I got permission to use that song from singer Jack Grisham himself.

Another expense was printing the "slick sheets" I designed to send to prospects. So, there was the print cost and postage. Keep in mind this was still late 2003 into early 2004, and that's the way it was done then. I'd make lists of people at stadiums around the country, both baseball and football, and snail mail them these slick sheets with hopes of getting a response (haha). I was emailing invoices to people back then too, which also wasn't really the way it was done in those days (I didn't have a printer at home to print the invoices, and envelopes and stamps cost money).

I vividly remember one day sitting in the parking lot of Staples on Ximeno and PCH in Long Beach, about to spend $50 or so on more slick sheets, and freaking out about spending the money. I had received a letter in the mail that morning from unemployment, and my benefits would run out in two weeks, and they wouldn't be renewed. I still had some money in the bank, but rent at the little house I shared with a roommate in Belmont Shores was $750 a month, plus half of the utilities bills, and if I didn't get more money coming in soon it would run out. I had to start working harder.

I had a little desk in the corner of the front room of that house where I worked. I bought it at IKEA for $50 or $60. The house was only 600 square feet, so there wasn't much privacy. I worked all day, every day, and was determined to make all this Screaming Images stuff happen.

In late 2003, I brought in a big one when I was awarded all the printing and installation for Big League Dreams' new sports park in Redding, Calif. I went there in January 2004 to check out the park under construction and get some measurements and pictures. One of my installers and I drove up one afternoon, checked into our hotel near the sports park, and went to dinner. After dinner there was a bar next door, so we stopped in for a beer. Right upon walking in I spotted a super cute, tiny blonde girl that had her arms sleeved with tattoos. Now, back then tattoos weren't all that common. So, we were onto each other pretty quickly, as I was also sleeved. Her name was Michele, and she ended up being my girlfriend for about a year. It was nice to have someone local when I went up there for work, which was pretty often; she also came down to visit me in Long Beach (and also eventually in Las Vegas). She was a super nice girl, and we are still friends to this day. And she still lives in Redding.

Big League Dreams was a super cool client, as I was such a fan of baseball and still playing baseball and softball at that time. They built these huge sports parks that had restaurants, big fieldhouses for soccer, events, and multiple softball fields. Their angle was, they made these softball fields as replicas of major league baseball stadiums – past and present. They built in big facades in the outfields, to look like stadiums such as Wrigley Field, Fenway Park, and Yankee Stadium, and my job was to print and install crowd scenes in the bleachers and add nuances like bullpens and other features that were relevant to whatever famous stadium it was. Redding was their fourth park, but it was the first I did myself from soup to nuts. The other three parks were in Cathedral City (the original), Chino Hills, and Jurupa (Riverside), all in Southern California. I had done some updates and repair work at those other locations prior to starting at Redding.

Redding had three fields, the aforementioned Wrigley, Fenway, and Yankee Stadium. These were the three anchor fields that would end up being at every location. Cathedral City and Jurupa also had three; but Chino Hills had six fields. More on that later.

Being such a fan of baseball, and with my design background and knowledge of the history of these stadiums, I was allowed to have a small hand in Redding on the design of these fields. Some of the stuff in the earlier parks was a little outdated and I, along with Wayne from Big League Dreams, planned to fix that. This park in Redding had 30,000 square feet of printed graphics in the outfield facades alone. There were also graphics for the clubhouse, offices, and wayfinding signage for the parks – as well as some little nuances like broadcaster booths, etc. It really was super cool. For the outfield walls we did vinyl banners and one of the touches I brought in was adding a liquid ultraviolet coating to these banners in production. The banners sat at an angle on the bleachers, taking a direct hit from the sun, and BLD had a lot of problems at other parks with fading and cracking graphics. Problem fixed.

They'd been using a design company out in Palm Springs, and that's the company that had generated the crowd graphics since BLD's first stadium opened. The files were really low resolution and had a repeating pattern of the same people in the crowds, if anyone really looked closely. Not horrible, but something else on my list to fix for the next one. They used the architectural and engineering drawings for sizing, from which to build the graphics. I had gone there for a survey trip before we started pre-flight on the files, but didn't double-check all the bleachers' sizes myself. This is one of the big lessons I learned on this job. You might remember from an earlier chapter I alluded to the fact that everything didn't go perfect on this one. I had assumed that since the Palm Springs design company had also done the other three locations, that this plan worked. Lesson No. 1: never assume. Never trust supplied dimensions, never work off architect's drawings. You need to measure every single thing yourself.

The next issue we had was 100% on me, and probably showed a bit of a lack of experience on big projects like this. Remember, at this point I was vending out all my printing to National Posters Digital in Chattanooga. They had no idea what a Big League Dreams sports park looked like. It was on me to help them understand exactly how the panels needed to be produced. I knew in my head how it needed to be done, but I did not properly convey all of this information. The outfield facade crowd scenes were all produced in one big panel. Which meant 300-foot-wide banners. There is a double-check on this in the printing industry, called proofs for approval. These were delivered in PDF format via email and approved by the customer before printing. National Posters' customer in this case being me. I guess I just checked the overall sizes and didn't make sure they had been divided into 10-foot-wide panels for installation, as they should have been. All on me. I had fucked up.

Needless to say, there is no way to install 300-foot-wide wide banners onto these facades correctly. First off, those banners weighed a ton. I hired three guys I knew to go there and install; as soon as they opened up the banners and saw they hadn't been cut-paneled into sections, they pretty much walked off the job site. Again, this was all my fault. Did those installers handle it well? No. There always is a solution, and we eventually found one. Maybe since they knew me personally, they thought this was okay. And again, I took 100% responsibility for the screw-up. So, besides the lesson on giving more details to the printer, and checking the prepress proofs better, I learned another valuable lesson. Never ever hire your friends. (I wish I would have remembered this lesson 12 years later.)

Going to the customer, Wayne, was not any fun. But he stayed cool and helped me work out a solution. We were able to salvage most of the printed banners by cutting them into manageable panels ourselves. Wherever we had fallen short, National Posters worked with me to get panels reprinted – they were a great partner. I hired and brought up another installer and explained the situation. He understood, got to work, and worked his ass off. The end result was just about perfect – and that installer ended up working with me and getting a ton of business from S.I. for over a decade.

After all was said and done, I got paid, paid off the vendors, and was still able to make a pretty good profit. I had impressed Wayne from Big League

Dreams with my hustle, tenacity, and out-of-the-box thinking. I had been accountable and solved the problem, and he recognized that. I would never end up having bigger supporters than Wayne and Jeff from Big League Dreams. I also picked up a pretty damn good installer and learned some valuable lessons. I also cemented my relationship with my printer in Chattanooga. Big League Dreams in Redding opened to the public in April 2004. Time to move on to the next one.

The Anaheim Angels called next. I had done the World Series for them in 2002 when I worked for one of the Orange County companies. They were one of the customers I called when I started Screaming Images – and they stuck with me. A lot of people don't know this, but the iconic windows at the stadium's main entrance, with graphics of players on them? The tops of the dugouts, too. Those ideas came from me in 2001.

Before opening day, we did the windows again, the tops of the dugouts, all the interior and exterior banners in the concourses, and at the gate – plus a handful of the concession stands. The whole job went totally smoothly. I had been working in that stadium now for several years.

One of my favorite S.I. stories is the time the Angels called me last minute to put a Benji Molina sign up on the outfield wall for that night's game. It was about noon. The sign was promoting Benji as a write-in candidate for the MLB All-Star Game, and it was the last day of voting. I had to have it printed locally, and when I finally got to the stadium the Angels were already taking batting practice, and my installer was going to have his back to home plate putting the decal up on the right-center field wall. Don't worry, I said! "I brought my baseball glove – I will stand behind you facing the plate and catch everything that comes our way." It took him about 40 minutes to put it up and by the time he was done I was running all over the outfield shagging fly balls with Tim Salmon and Garrett Anderson. Someone from the stands yelled down at me, as I was running around on the field in jeans, a t-shirt, and Chuck Taylor Converse All Stars, "Who are you?!" Haha. Another brilliant

LinkedIn opportunity 10 years too early.

* * *

I had submitted bids for work at a couple of NFL stadiums in Spring 2004 – for the Carolina Panthers and Washington Redskins. I heard in June that I was awarded both jobs. August would be a busy month for little S.I. For the Panthers, we would be redoing their end zones and updating the artwork for the infamous "Cat's Eyes," and for the first time ever doing all their exterior light pole banners. There were 225 of them, with the logo for the new name of the venue, Bank of America Stadium. For the Redskins, we would be doing their entire stadium field wall banners – including building new pads and modifying 125 pads from 5 to 3 feet high. Plus, graphics in their end zones.

But it was only May, and we had a ton of work before then. I had picked up a small concert venue right by Angels Stadium called The Grove via cold calling. It was a super cool venue; I had been to a bunch of shows there. They had three big exterior banners outside the main entrance to the theater that they changed out for all their shows. The banners were 12-by-19-foot and we were handling both the print and install. We did banners for acts like Alice Cooper, Switchfoot and G. Love & Special Sauce... also for their corporate events and sponsors like Wells Fargo.

Another customer keeping us busy was Free Car Media. Their deal was they paid people's car payments in exchange for letting them advertise on their personal cars. Occasionally they'd get a big campaign and would rent a bunch of the same kind of vehicles, wrap them, run the ad campaign, then remove the wraps and return the vehicles. Risky business! Good thing that from day one I used only 3M pressure-sensitive vinyl. It was hands-down the best wrap product, not even close. Their material was so far superior that I used it even though 3M's customer service was dog shit.

Between May and July of 2004, we did a ton of work for FCM. We wrapped: 14 vans for Adelphia; eight VWs for Interim; six PT Cruisers for Verizon; 12 vans for El Pollo Loco; six Mini Coopers for Esprit; and a few more I can't remember or find details about. Drew from Free Car was a super cool dude, and he always paid us promptly.

By this point we were also wrapping all of KROQ's vehicles for their promotions department. I was having a lot of fun in those days; I have to admit. KROQ was by far my favorite radio station, and I was not only working for them but also hanging out in their studios at least a couple times a week. Steve from KROQ ended up being a super close friend and we still hang out to this day.

Another thing we did for KROQ was all their annual music festivals. When June rolled around, we were down at Irvine Meadows Amphitheater (RIP, miss that place) for the 2004 KROQ Weenie Roast. That year some of the featured artists were Beastie Boys, Bad Religion, The Strokes, Cypress Hill, and Velvet Revolver. I would have attended this show even if KROQ wasn't my client. My sales style was starting to really show through. I was going after things I liked. Music and sports being the main two.

For these KROQ shows, we did event branding and stage banners, basically. They used to build big truss structures at the entrances to the venue, and we would cover them with mesh banners. It was nothing like the branding for festivals nowadays, but it was definitely different for that time and KROQ was blazing the trail for future festival producers for sure. The guy building the truss for all those KROQ shows was named Charley, and his company was called Stage Tech. He also became a big customer over the years, and we are still friends to this day.

By the time I arrived on festival days, all my work was done. I was still in my 30s then, and I was usually with a huge group of my friends, so it was party time. My KROQ friends never cared, because they were partying themselves. And they always took care of me with passes and killer seats. Another lesson learned early on: take care of your folks and they will take care of you.

Something that happened at that Weenie Roast I'll never forget. Me and my buddies were walking out of Irvine Meadows after the show ended, and you had to walk through a huge truss structure to get to the walkway that led to the exit. There were people climbing all over the truss tearing the banners down to take them home. They were literally swinging from banners that were halfway torn off the truss! My friends were all yelling to me asking if they should stop them. I said, "Fuck no! Get me a camera!" But this was back before cell phone cameras and social media. That would have made for a hell of a LinkedIn post.

* * *

Two things that were super important to me wherever I lived were record stores and bookstores – and I was lucky to have good ones living in Long Beach. I'd never had much money, and was almost always in debt, but I always tried to budget for one book a month and one or two CDs. I clearly remember one Friday afternoon sitting in the parking lot of Fingerprints, a record store on 2nd Street in Belmont Shores. I had just returned to my truck after purchasing three CDs, which was something I couldn't remember ever doing. I had money in the bank, no debt at all, and jobs in the next two months that would net me about $40,000 in profit. My hard work was paying off. I went home with my new CDs, but the first thing I ended up doing when I arrived was calling Mom and telling her all this. She was proud of me, and it was a great feeling.

* * *

The third week of July came around and it was time to get started on the two NFL stadiums. I had my installers in Maryland at FedEx Field (Redskins) starting July 22nd. The scope for the first phase was wrapping all the pads on the sidelines with their burgundy team color. Robbie had a six-man team, and they started out gangbusters. The banner vinyl that National Posters had produced in Chattanooga was a perfect color match. So, what this process consisted of was printing individual banners for each pad, with six inches extra on all four sides, so it could be wrapped around the pad and attached with staples on the back.

Keep in mind, these pads were on TV every home game and had to be wrapped super tight and look flat and perfect. The old vinyl banners had to be removed first. I'd estimate approximately 300 pads needed to be done this way. When I arrived in Maryland on July 25th, they were already almost half-way done, and Robbie had sent two of his guys ahead to (the newly renamed) Bank of America Stadium in Charlotte to start prepping pads there.

I stayed a couple of nights in D.C. and split the time between supervising the pads install and walking the stadium with Redskins executives. What was going on at the stadium was that they had a company called Staging Concepts that was adding additional seats to the bowl, and we were working behind them. Once we finished wrapping the sideline pads, we were going to head to the Panthers to do their end zones, and then circle back to Redskins to finish up the pads and graphics once Staging Concepts had completed their work on the additional seating.

It didn't matter how long I was away from home back in 2004 because I didn't have any pups yet. So, I was planning to be gone for 10 days. I flew into Baltimore for the work at the Redskins' stadium and then drove a rental car from there to Charlotte to manage the work for the Panthers. I loved rivers and Civil War battle sites, so I was super stoked to do the drive back and forth, which was about 450 miles each way, through the South. Cool stuff for a city slicker like me. I was feeling pretty proud of the success I was having, so… I rented myself a 2004 Cadillac DTS. I was so used to always being broke, that being able to do this financially was exhilarating. I will never to able to describe how happy I was feeling back then.

I left Landover for Charlotte on Tuesday morning, July 27th. This date was totally planned, as Tuesday was the day new albums were released, and one of my favorite bands put out their new record that day – the Old 97's – their new album was called *Drag it Up*. I listened to it on repeat the whole drive, both to Charlotte and back. Great album. And a very beautiful part of our country.

I arrived in Charlotte in the afternoon and the boys already had one of the end zones prepped. Same process as the pads at FedEx Field – except these ones had printed graphics, so lining up artwork was crucial. What we did here was design the end zone to its overall size in one graphic – then we had to break it all out into individual panels in prepress and add bleed to put around the back and staple on. And none of the panels were the same size, so we had to be really careful. There were 68 panels in the east end zone and 71 in the west end zone. The boys had a system they perfected doing this same style of wrapping pads with graphics for the Anaheim Angels, so it was going pretty quickly. What they did was set up a worktable that would hold three pads at a time. They'd wrap the one on the end, then line up the graphic on the panel in the middle, then move everything over to the right and add a new one on the front.

For the graphic, we were just redoing the same art we had designed in 1999. Back then, when I was still with Imagic, we had built the designs in Photoshop, and the eyes we used were super low-resolution. We redid everything in Vector which made the files way smaller, and easier to manage size-wise. Plus, the image was crystal clear. In the four years the "Cat's Eyes" had been up, the graphic had become iconic in Charlotte – and several other teams were copying us. We had budgeted for four days at Bank of America Stadium in Charlotte but finished in three. I got Scott to walk with me to approve everything, and then we were off, back to D.C.

We arrived back in Landover on the afternoon of July 30th to learn that the Staging Concepts crew was nowhere near ready for us, so we had two days of sitting around before we could start shortening the height of the new pads in the sections Staging Concepts were extending. The only way to add seats at field level was to make them go further down onto the field – which is the reason why we had to shorten the height of these pads to three feet, from five. We needed 125 pads to do this. We had to remove old vinyl off the pads, use power saws to cut through the plywood and foam to change the height, and then re-wrap them with the new vinyl we'd produced in Chattanooga. We also had to move down the z-clips, which were used to attach the pads to the walls, on most of these pads.

Once we could start working again, we were three days behind schedule. I had already left to return to Long Beach. Unfortunately, we were not lucky with the weather, and it rained two of those three days. We had to be out of there so they could get ready for their first preseason home game. The boys gutted it out and worked in the rain – we had no choice. But halfway through the first day, and I will never forget this, Mike and Chris from the Redskins came out onto the field and gave all of the boys Redskins rain ponchos and sweatshirts, as well as a Thermos of coffee. The Redskins executives were super good dudes. The Redskins would end up being my customer the entire 20 years I owned Screaming Images, and a key job they gave me in 2011 was instrumental in helping to open my first shop and buying my first pieces of printing equipment.

Something to mention here is a reminder that in 2004 there were no smartphones yet, and laptops weren't really a thing in my little world. Every day that I was on the road for this trip, I had to go to an internet café to catch up on my emails and take care of all my other customers.

The Redskins and Panthers both paid me by the beginning of September, and I paid Robbie and the boys. They did a great job. Both teams couldn't have been happier with the work. I sure could have made a big splash with all this stuff if social media existed then. It was a pretty big accomplishment for a guy who worked at home in his underpants.

* * *

The Angels called again in September and asked me to prepare for some postseason graphics. They had once again won the American League West Division. I worked with their designer on the files for all the usual items – big windows at the entrance, tops of the dugouts, big banners at all the gates, and a couple of big banners on the side of the stadium, and all the light pole banners on Katella and State College boulevards. One thing different about postseason is, you have to be prepared with art files for different teams depending on how the other divisions and the wild card shake out, and you have to be able to turn a lot of prints very quickly. They ended up playing the Boston Red Sox, Oct. 5 to 8, and got swept three games to zero. Super bummer. By the way, that was the last season they were ever called "Anaheim" Angels. The next year they would controversially change the team name to "Los Angeles Angels."

2004 was a great 12 months for Screaming Images. In early November I fulfilled one of my lifelong dreams: I bought a boat. It was a ten-year-old 21-foot Hallett and to me it was the best boat in the whole world. But by the beginning of 2005 I began realizing I was missing one really big thing: the companionship of a dog. So, I started making plans that would ultimately have me leave southern California and move my little business to Las Vegas.

My life was changing pretty quickly. I loved living the beach life, and all my friends especially, but I was partying way too much on the weekends. Weekdays I never partied, always went to bed early, and always went to the gym in the early morning before work. I started realizing that if I wanted to keep this snowball of success going, I had to become more responsible. My lifelong friend Wolfie (John) had followed his in-laws out to Henderson, Nevada a couple years earlier, and I was good friends with them, too. The houses were new, really nice, and affordable. I was going to do it in 2005.

* * *

On Dec. 11, KROQ had their annual year-end music festival: the KROQ Almost Acoustic Christmas. This year it featured artists like Gwen Stefani, Interpol, and Jimmy Eat World along with a bunch of others. KROQ always took good care of me, it was always fun, and I always got a good-sized job out of it. It would be my last job of 2004, as on the 16th I was heading to London, England, to visit my grandma for two weeks.

My grandma was my favorite. When I stayed at her house, I felt at home. I had to join the gym down the road every time I went there because, otherwise I would have come home 20 pounds heavier. She fed me non-stop. Plus, all she had at her house was a tiny little bathtub I barely fit in, so the gym showers were nice. It was a pretty posh gym, and the older guys always looked at me funny because of the tattoos, but the staff always remembered me every year. "Back to visiting grandma?" Yes, I was.

2005 started out hot work-wise. We wrapped two vans for ESPN in Washington, D.C., in late January, then started working on the newest Big League Dreams sports park. It was in League City, Texas, just south of Houston, with a May opening.

I was super stoked because this park would feature six replica fields – double the size of Redding. That means double the square feet of printing and double the profit. Plus, now that I had one under my belt, they allowed me to make upgrades to the designs of the stadiums myself. Besides the three standard fields – Wrigley, Yankee, and Fenway – they added Ebbets Field (old home of the Brooklyn Dodgers, no longer existing), Crosley Field (former home of the Cincinnati Reds, closed in 1970), and Sportsman's Park (home of the St Louis Cardinals and Browns from the early 1900s to 1966). Both Ebbets and Crosley had also been featured at the Chino Hills, Calif. park, but Sportsman's was brand new, and I had a ton of fun helping design it.

The architectural drawings were once again supplied to us, but I was not going down that road again. Robbie and I went to League City in early February to measure all six stadiums ourselves. It took us three full days, but it was a super fun trip because we stayed down in Galveston which is a totally cool little town right on the gulf. I designed everything, National Posters in Chattanooga printed it, Robbie installed it all, and they paid us immediately. This job went perfectly – I learned my lessons well. Wayne and the BLD crew couldn't have been happier.

While we were finishing at Big League Dreams in League City, I was also working on all the stuff for the Anaheim Angels season opener. We were splitting the Angels job with another vendor, but it was plenty of work. And

I was just stoked they were keeping a little guy like me involved.

* * *

In May 2005, I began the process of getting a home loan approved and hired a real estate agent in Henderson. First time I'd done anything even close to this. My credit wasn't great, but it was decent. I had a pretty good chunk of money put away – but back in those days there were loans requiring no down payment. But being self-employed made it a little difficult to prove my income, plus I had only been in business for 2-plus years. I had a friend in the industry, and he helped me through the process. Back then there were a lot of "interest only" loans, with the premise being you pay your mortgage that way for a year, and then come back and refinance it into a 30-year fixed once you have some equity and your credit rating is stronger. He did present me with other options, but I had a couple of friends in California who had done their home loans this way successfully, so I went for it. More on how that turned out later.

On my first trip to Las Vegas to meet my real estate agent I decided to stop and see my old friend Frankie. He was my buddy Wolfie's father-in-law, and I had been friends with him for 5-plus years. I even used to stay at his house in Henderson when I went to Vegas for work. After we chatted for a while, he told me his neighbor two doors up was considering selling his house, but hadn't officially put it on the market yet, and asked if I'd like to go check it out? Sure! It was a great neighborhood. So, we went up and walked through it, and it was a really nice house – and only 7 years old. It had a pool, RV parking for my boat, and I thought to myself this might be a good spot for me and Scout (I had already named the puppy I was going to get, even though she wasn't even born yet). I said goodbye to Frankie and then headed out to meet the real estate agent to look at more houses.

She took me all over town showing me places that I didn't really like. She was trying to push me into other areas of town that I didn't want to live in. I wanted to be in Henderson, specifically Green Valley, because that was where Wolfie and Frankie lived, and I wanted to be close to friends.

I headed back home to Long Beach that night, with another house-hunting trip set in two weeks. I went back out and had given the real estate agent very specific instructions on what I was looking for: Green Valley, pool, and some sort of grass (not always a given in the desert). I met her and we went and looked at about 15 houses I had absolutely no interest in. I called Frankie and asked if he could find out if I could look at that house on his street again, and he set it up. I said goodbye to the agent and headed back over there. I walked through, and then asked the owner how much he was asking. $375,000. I accepted, and we decided to do it all without an agent. I didn't really know what I was doing, but it seemed like he (the owner) did. I headed back home to Belmont Shores, tripping out that not only was I about to become a homeowner, but I was also moving out of state away from all my friends and family.

Once back home I got together with my buddy who had helped me get pre-approved on the loan. We got all the paperwork together and he sent it to the seller – but suddenly, the price had gone up to $385,000. And I didn't have an agent to protect me. I could have backed out but didn't. It was a great spot, I thought to myself, and what was $10K in the long run?

Back at home now, it was early August, and my new Green Valley home was in escrow. My roommate at the Long Beach house moved out to live with his girlfriend, so I had to cover the full rent on the house for the last two months. I was staying busy with a lot of smaller stuff – a lot of Free Car Media wraps, KROQ was rewrapping their whole fleet, and I was doing the sponsor billboards for all five Big League Dreams parks, including the design. Everything was still going really well.

Escrow would close Sept. 1st on my new pad, but I wasn't planning on doing the full move until two weeks later. The reason was, I had to go to New Orleans the first week of September. The Saints contacted me and wanted me to bid on the field wall graphics that were part of their 2005 renovations.

Hurricane Katrina had just happened about a week prior, so I was trippin' out a little bit. When the flight was coming into New Orleans I could see all the damage of Katrina. I hopped in a taxi to head to the stadium and the driver warned me it might be a pretty gnarly drive. Oh shit. I arrived at the Superdome to discover they had turned it into a shelter for hurricane victims. As the Saints operations guy walked me down to the field to measure, I saw hundreds of victims laying on cots in the concourses. It was awful.

My return flight didn't leave until early the next morning so I decided to see if I could get down to the French Quarter for dinner and a couple of beers. I found a tiny restaurant on a side street in the Quarter and had a killer authentic Cajun meal. There was a little bar right across the street, so I decided to go over there afterwards and have one more beer before returning to the hotel. I went in, sat down at the bar, and ordered a beer. There was a cute little girl over in the corner by herself and she was looking at me funny. About halfway through my beer she came over and introduced herself – her name was Ruby. She was local, and I told her I was from Long Beach, Calif., and was just here on business for one day. Then she asked if I wanted to go for a ride. Sure, I said, having no idea what she meant. I followed her outside, she unlocked a huge bicycle and told me to get on the bars. Okay! For the next three hours she rode me around on the handlebars, and she was just a skinny little girl. We stopped at a bunch of local places and had more drinks – she was giving me the locals tour.

Around 1 a.m. I told her I really needed to get back to my hotel, that I had an 8 a.m. flight the next morning – and she said she'd come with me. Okay again! My hotel was in a really cool, super old building, and somehow, we fit her bicycle into the elevator to go up to my room. Security just chuckled. She spent the night and when I woke up in the morning, she was gone with just a note that said, "Thank You." I had no idea how she got her bike back down that elevator by herself. Only problem now was, I was late getting to the airport. I ran my ass off down the concourse, but my plane was gone by the time I arrived at the gate. I spent the rest of the day on standbys and doing flight connections, and didn't get home until after 10 p.m. that night. God bless New Orleans. I didn't get the Saints job, by the way.

On Sept. 15th, 2005, I locked up the Belmont Shores pad for the last time, left the keys in the mailbox for the landlord, fired up the moving truck and headed for Sin City.

Redskins End Zone 2004

Carolina Panthers - First S.I. Job 2002

Big League Dreams Redding - Wrigley Field

Carolina Panthers
"Cat's Eyes" 2004

Angels Stadium
Windows 2004

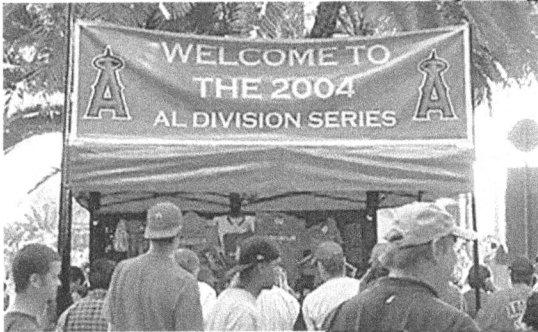

MLB Playoffs 2004

NHL Finals in
Anaheim 2003

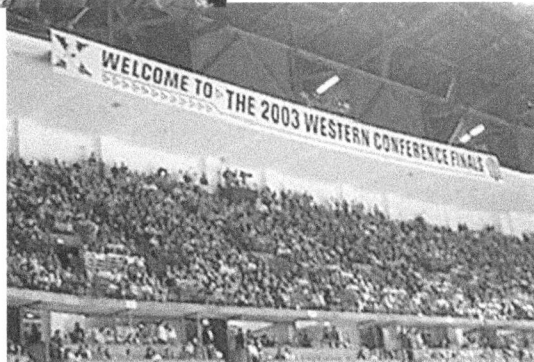

CHAPTER 8

WELCOME TO NEVADA

"Another State of Mind"
- *Social Distortion*

I arrived at my new home in Henderson, Nevada on Sept. 15th, 2005, around 5 p.m. with my long-bed truck stacked with boxes and a 20-foot U-Haul truck filled with every single thing I owned. I drove the U-Haul, and my little brother Chris followed in my truck. I now had to get him down to the Greyhound station in downtown Las Vegas so he could get back home, and we were running late on him catching his bus. He didn't like to fly.

By the time I got back from dropping him off, it was around 6:45 p.m. and I had two trucks full of boxes and about an hour of daylight. I started the arduous task of emptying the contents of the trucks into the garage, so I didn't have to leave them on the street overnight. A few neighbors came by to introduce themselves, as Frankie, my friend two doors down, had told them I was arriving. After they'd all left and I was getting back to moving boxes, an older red-haired lady snuck up from nowhere, just as it was starting to get dark. She told me she was on the homeowners' association board, and that I should watch out for my neighbors, and specifically named a couple of them. Huh? She seemed like trouble, and I confirmed all this in the morning with my new friends/neighbors. It wouldn't be my last run-in with her. Welcome to the neighborhood.

Once the boxes were all in the garage, I set myself to the one task that was mandatory for that night – setting up my office, so I could get to work first thing in the morning. It was a Thursday, and I had to work the next day. I got my little IKEA table from Belmont Shores set up, got my new/used Mac out and set up, connected to the internet, and I was ready to roll in the morning.

It was already late, so I had no time to set up my bed upstairs. I had closed on the house on Sept. 1st and had some brand-new furniture delivered by RC Willey, so thankfully I had somewhere to sleep. I also had the internet and cable set up on the 1st and tested it with a laptop on a trip that week. I couldn't miss any days of work. Right before I laid down on my couch to crash for the night, I went outside and stood in the street for a while in my new neighborhood. It was so quiet! No screeching tires, sirens, or gunshots. I wasn't in Long Beach anymore. Right before I went back inside the realization hit me hard that I had just moved out of the state I'd lived in my whole life, and away from all my friends. I was tripping out. I'd better make something out of this.

I had a list ready for my tasks the next day, and after running through my emails in the morning, I got after the biggest and most important one: finding my Scout. I'd been talking to a breeder in Pahrump, a small town 80 miles northwest. That morning, I secured the first female of the litter, due to be born at the end of October. The next most-important task was joining a gym. I had been driving back and forth by a big gym called Las Vegas Athletic Club right off the 215 freeway on my trips out to Henderson. Checked that one off the list. I found a record store called Zia's on Eastern Avenue, and a Borders bookstore right off of Stephanie and Warm Springs. I was now officially a Nevadan.

* * *

First order of Screaming Images business was the 2005 Major League Baseball playoffs for the Angels. They drew the Yankees in the Division Series, and we'd do the graphics for the whole ballpark. I spent a lot of time driving back and forth from Henderson to Anaheim that first month, including trips there and back the same day, plus working there all day.

Another twist was, since I had just bought my first home, and it was in Las Vegas, my family from England was super excited and wanted to visit. My cousin Melissa called and said she wanted to come out. I said, Cool! How long will you stay? Six months? Okay!

The Angels defeated the Yankees 3 games to 2 and moved on to face the White Sox in the American League Championship series, which was played Oct. 11 to 16. My cousin arrived in time to join me at both of those home games. Oh yeah – I also had season tickets now. Being British, she knew nothing about the game or rules of baseball, and I had a good time teaching her while we were watching games. All the print and install work for both series went super smoothly, but unfortunately the Angels lost to the White Sox, who went on to defeat the Houston Astros in the World Series.

* * *

Scout was born Oct. 26th, 2005. The breeder sent me pictures, and I was already in love. There were three females in the litter, and I already knew which one she was. She opened her eyes two weeks later, and I was then allowed to go meet her and hold her for the first time. This beautiful girl would completely change my life. I went and visited her once a week, and then on Dec. 7th brought her to the home she'd live in her entire life. My cousin Melissa held her in her lap in my truck on the drive, and Scout had her first of very many truck rides – 80 miles. She was six weeks old.

Another amazing thing happened that December. Two days after Scout came home, my grandma arrived from London for a month's visit. It's a very long flight, so she doesn't come out too often. There was a little battle between Mom and I about whether grandma would go to L.A. to Mom's house or come to Vegas to stay with me. I got a call one night from grandma and she was crying saying she didn't want to go to L.A., that she wanted to come to Vegas. So, I called Mom and let her know she would have to get out of the house and come to Vegas to see my grandma. It was the first time I ever had to overrule Mom.

Mom came out for the first two weeks, which meant I would have grandma to myself for the last two weeks at my house. So, now I had my grandma, Mom, my cousin, and baby Scout in my house. Scout was running around and chasing balls all over the house, biting our toes, leaving toys strewn everywhere, and my heart was full.

Man, I loved my grandma. Hands down my favorite person in the world ever. I would get up in the morning and go to the gym, and on the way home I'd stop and get every newspaper I could find. Grandma was always sitting in the chair she had chosen as her spot in my den, waiting for them. I'd then head into my home office to start my workday, and after an hour or so I'd look out in the backyard, and she would be out there sitting by the pool with Scout right next to her, both of their faces up to the sun. Every night I would make her dinner, and then right before she went to bed, I would give her an ice cream, and then walk her up the stairs to her bedroom and say goodnight. In my mind it was paying her back for all the love she'd shown me on all those trips out to her house in London. With Scout, my grandma, and my new home – those were probably the best two weeks of my life.

I'll never forget the day she left to go back home. We moved all her bags downstairs and loaded them into my truck. She, my cousin, and I all exchanged hugs, and my cousin said goodbye. The last thing my grandma did before she left my house was walk over to Scout's playpen and give her a hug and kiss and tell her what a good girl she was. When she turned around to walk out, she had tears running down her face. My two best girls had built a huge bond.

Grandma called me every Sunday morning after that; it was our new little ritual. The first thing she asked every call was, "How's that Scout?"

* * *

So, now it's mid-January, and I'd had a great time with my family the last month, but it was time to get back to work. Not going to lie here: I was feeling a little overwhelmed with all my new financial responsibilities. The new house mortgage was more than three times my rent at the little house in Long Beach. If I wanted to keep this bitchin' new life, I had to get back to hustling.

Right out of the gate in 2006, I was buried with work from Free Car Media, Mojo Sports, and Big League Dreams. By this time, I was pretty much

100% in charge of all graphics for all BLD parks. They trusted me completely. There was a guy at BLD named Roger, who was in charge of sales for them; selling partnerships, sponsors, and events. They were on a mission to plaster their outfield walls with sponsor advertisements (like Major League Baseball teams), and I was their guy for not only print but also design. It was pretty simple art to build, and I was charging $100 a pop to build ads that were taking me about 20 minutes to make. Plus, the print. I was doing four to five of these "billboards" a week. It was keeping me busy and paying my bills.

I had sent Scott from the Panthers pictures of all the pads we built for the Redskins in 2004, and at the end of January, he called me with a quote for 112 pads for their practice facility, which was pretty much connected to Bank of America Stadium. The only catch was, I couldn't build them on-site. I would have to do them in Vegas and ship them out. Never to be deterred, I came up with a plan and recruited a couple of friends, one of which was my next-door neighbor, to build the pads outside of their work hours and on weekends.

So, when I say "pads," I mean the safety pads that are on the sidelines and endzones walls. They're basically made of three-quarters-inch marine-grade plywood painted on all six sides, 3-inch-thick high-density foam hot-glued to the plywood, then wrapped with 20-ounce stock colored vinyl. You then cut in a "weep hole" at the bottom for condensation to escape so the wood and foam don't get damaged. It was great work, great margins; but took up a lot of space. My friends were building the pads in my next-door neighbor's garage, wrapping 10 at a time onto a pallet, and then we'd wheel the pallets into my garage to store until the job was completed. The whole process took a little more than two months. Then an 18-wheeler transport truck picked them up right in front of my house, and off to Charlotte they went.

At the same time, I did 175 black windscreens for the practice facility, and 210 light pole banners for the outside of Bank of America Stadium. And they invited me to a game that season to stand on the sidelines. I loved the

Carolina Panthers.

* * *

One sunny Saturday in March I had nothing to do, so I went up to the corner store and grabbed a *Las Vegas Weekly* to see what Scout and I could get ourselves into. I found an ad showing the Sin City Rollergirls had an open practice that afternoon at Freedom Park. Perfect! I threw some ice-cold beverages into a cooler, grabbed a lawn chair, and Scout and I were off. I got there at the beginning of their practice and set up camp. First thing I noticed was that they were dressed up like cavewomen, and the name of the team was the NeanderDolls. Rad! They had an old banner about 1-by-2 feet hanging on a fence. It had a plumbing logo or something on the backside, but they had hand spray-painted the team's name on the front. Hmmm…

I sat and watched for about an hour, and Scout and I were having a total blast. The girls were skating really fast and were super aggressive. Towards the end of the practice something happened on the track, and next thing I knew they were all fighting! With each other! Even though they were on the same team! It finally broke up and they all hugged it out – what a trip! I had to get involved with this. I hit them up after practice and said I'd donate a huge banner with their name and logo on it. They loved it, I loved them, and my little graphics business had its first sponsorship. I am still friends with Ivanna and Trish to this day.

In April I picked up two new customers. One was local: AREA 108, a radio station which was like KROQ in Vegas. I picked them up on a cold call. And also, Havasu Speedway out in Lake Havasu City, Ariz., who were referred to me. I was on a roll.

I landed a huge one in May. I had already been to Pittsburgh to meet with the Steelers about the new graphics package for Heinz Field, and right as I arrived in Arizona for my annual Memorial Day boating trip to Lake Havasu, they called and said I got the job. My biggest job to date. Made for a pretty good holiday weekend.

To celebrate this Steelers win, I decided to take a vacation to Bora Bora in mid-June. I'd been hanging out with this younger girl off and on for the past six months, so she was in the right place at the right time. It wasn't serious, but she was cute (and fun), so off we went for four nights in Tahiti.

I returned to a seriously stacked schedule. Big League Dreams had another brand-new sports park opening in October, and I had to get on the graphics package. I was super stoked about Manteca, Calif. because it would be the first of their parks to feature a replica of Angel Stadium, and they all knew about the work I'd done for years at the real one. I ended up designing the whole stadium myself. It was super fun and came out killer. BLD also knew about all the pads I'd been building for the Redskins and Panthers, so I also got to do the backstop pads for all six stadiums. Robbie was on board for the install again, and everything went perfect when it was all installed in September.

While I was working on the designs for BLD Manteca, I also had to get the ball rolling on the Steelers job. Our scope was the field walls of the stadium, the hall of fame area in the east concourse, banners on the rotunda, decals in the hall leading to the locker room, and light pole banners on the streets surrounding the stadium. In addition to the Steelers work, we were also awarded the field walls and some big exterior banners for the Pittsburgh Panthers college football team. They had seen the preliminary designs we did for the Steelers field walls and asked us to do something similar for them. What was super unique about this job, and what won us the work, was the application system we came up with to hang the banners on the sideline walls. The idea was a collaboration between Robbie and I, engineered and installed by him and his crew. We set up a system where the Steelers field wall banners stayed up all season long, and the Pitt Panthers banners were installed over them the Friday before the games on Saturdays and removed immediately after the game. I won't bore you with the details, but our system ended up being copied by several other stadiums after they saw how we did ours.

Everything went off perfectly and on time – and the Steelers were especially pleased with that little trick we pulled off with their Rolling Rock sponsor logos in the end zones mentioned earlier. And once again, one of my business theories was confirmed: take care of your folks and they will take care of you. The Steelers and Panthers invited me out on a weekend where Pitt played on Saturday and the Steelers played Sunday, and I got to watch both games standing on the sidelines. The highlight of that weekend was on Saturday, when an incomplete pass bounced its way over to me, and when I picked it up and threw it back to the referee, Mom saw it on TV. Priceless.

* * *

My little business had fallen into a pretty comfortable pattern at this point. I had my day-to-day work that was paying my bills, along with several large jobs throughout the year that I was making really good margins on. I'll mention this again several times throughout this book – this still did not let me feel comfortable. Being comfortable would make me complacent, and I needed to keep hustling. I was living a blessed life, but I knew it could all go away really quickly if I slacked off. Whenever my friends came out from SoCal to visit, they always tripped out that on weekdays I spent all day in my home office working, every day. Throughout all the years I ran my business out of my home, I always started no later than 7 a.m. and worked a minimum of 9 hours a day.

In the last quarter of 2006, I had steady work. No more big jobs, but everyday stuff from the usual clients. I was still making lots of cold calls, and my sales style was really taking shape. I was going after things I liked, and that I knew a lot about. In October, I picked up another radio station, Jack FM, and was awarded more vehicle wraps for the local Vegas station AREA 108. Then in November, after five years of working on it, starting before the S.I. era, I landed an account that would become one of my all-time favorites. I got my first stage backdrop for my favorite band, Social Distortion.

In December, I went to London to visit grandma. Scout was a year old, and I had her staying with a girlfriend of mine who also had a Labrador, named Joey. I joined the gym, ate a ton of grandma's cooking, and hung out with my English pals. But one thing was different on this trip – I really missed Scout. So much, a couple of nights I even cried. I couldn't wait to get home and see her. She had become a huge part of my life.

The night I returned, my friend picked me up from the airport and I was reunited with my Scout. When we got back to my house a couple of neighbors saw me pull up and came over to say hello and see how the trip went. My friend and neighbor Frankie and his wife Lovie were also English. I was happy to see all of them, but I was exhausted and couldn't wait to go to bed. Once they had all gone, Scout and I went upstairs to crash out. As soon as I climbed into my cozy bed for the first time in two weeks, my phone rang with a number I didn't recognize. I was going to let it go to voicemail, but the sales guy in me was forced to answer. It was a guy named Patrick from the NBA and he'd been given my number by his boss, who was the senior vice president of events and attractions for the league. I had gotten this SVP's email address out of my handy *Sports Business Journal* almanac I purchased every year for $999 because it had every sports contact in the country, along with their email addresses. A year earlier, when they announced the NBA All-Star Game would be in Las Vegas in February 2007, I searched for the highest-position NBA guy for events that I could find in the SBJ almanac, and sent a cold email. Apparently, it had worked. By now it was pushing 11 p.m. Patrick said he'd like to talk to discuss the possibility of me doing some print work for the All-Star Game, and asked if I could meet him at 7 a.m. at Mandalay Bay to discuss my capabilities. SHIT. I wasn't prepared but agreed to meet.

I got up at 2:30 a.m. and put together a presentation to share with him using pictures from past stadium and event print-and-install jobs. Thank God for those designer skills I picked up from my Jordan & Horn days – I never would have found someone to help on that timeline. I arrived at Mandalay Bay, found the café we agreed to meet at, and sat down at a table at 6:59 a.m.

He rolled in right at 7 a.m. looking like a million bucks, like he'd just had a full night's sleep. We shook hands and he sat down and asked me how I was doing. I said to him, straight up, "I'm fucking exhausted." Profanity and all. I then explained how I'd just returned from two weeks in England and was dozing off when he called the night before, and had risen at 2:30 a.m. to prepare. He just laughed and I could already tell we would get along. He gave me some small jobs for the game so he could test me – and we ended up having a decades-long relationship. I am still friends with him. Another funny story to add here is that he eventually ended up knowing my grandma! Over the next several years he called her house in England twice when I was visiting her, looking for me. Both times I was out, and when I got back she'd say "That nice man from the NBA called again." Haha. She had no idea what the NBA was.

* * *

When 2007 began, weighing heavy on my mind was my pipe dream of opening my own print shop. Every single industry friend I spoke with said they thought it was a bad idea. Clearly, they didn't think I could pull it off. But I was determined. I loved being the underdog, and I loved when people doubted me.

Early January, I got a big job from the Angels for their 2007 Fan Fest. It was held every year in their parking lot at The Big A and drew thousands of fans. It was a tight turn with us also having the NBA coming in hot. The Fan Fest was Feb. 11th, and the All-Star Game was Feb. 18th. Printing everything was easy but install for Fan Fest was also in my scope. I didn't find out until the last minute that both my Southern California installers were booked and couldn't shift their schedules. I had to hustle for a solution at the 11th hour. I was supposed to install everything on the 10th but couldn't pull it off; my Angels contacts were freaking out. I promised I'd get it done before the gates opened. I left my house at 10 p.m. the night before the festival with one of my Vegas buddies and had recruited three of my Orange County/Beach friends to meet me there at 2 a.m. The majority of the work was hanging mesh banners on fences, and vinyl banners on activations – thankfully not much wrapping work or I would've been in trouble. My friends all came through and worked their asses off, and we got everything done before the gates opened. I passed out Angels tickets to my buddies, plus some cash, and limped back home to Henderson and Scout that afternoon.

Mid-January, we started working on the NBA All-Star Game stuff. Work I had gotten from the coldest of cold calls – and an email. Patrick was testing me, so our scope was pretty small. We had a couple hundred linear feet of All-Star Game-branded mesh banners that went up at the Mandalay Bay convention center. We also had some mesh banners for an Adidas sponsorship activation in the parking lot, a bunch of banners for a T-Mobile activation, and some "VEE" banners we did for one of their production partners. National Posters Digital in Chattanooga was pumping everything out in record time, and I made all deadlines – though I did have to eat the freight since it was a Las Vegas event. I couldn't really charge them shipping since I was a Las Vegas company.

I hustled my ass off for about six days driving back and forth for drop offs and watching over installs to ensure everything went perfectly well. I'd see Patrick every once in a while, driving by in a golf cart – he saw my presence there, which was good. It's what I wanted him to see. My entire scope was pulled off flawlessly and ended up including a handful of last-minute rush jobs that my partners in Chattanooga helped bust out. Huge moment for my little company – I had successfully pulled off a job for the NBA's marquee event.

At the end of February, my little sponsorship of the Vegas roller derby girls started paying off. I got jobs from the teams in Dallas and Philadelphia. It wasn't a ton of work, but it was a lot of fun. I also got opportunities to bid on jobs from the Dodgers and Colorado Rockies – all from cold calls and emails out of my little *Sports Business Journal* almanac. I was getting my money's worth out of that subscription and making really good headway in the sports market.

By March, I figured if I wanted to keep all my accounting straight I needed help, so I hired my first outsourced bookkeeper. Her name was Marisa, and she was awesome. She instructed me to buy a laptop so she could download the QuickBooks software to it. QuickBooks Online already had been out for a few years, but she said it wasn't the best option for my little company, and that we should just use the software. She gave me some training on how to create invoices and helped me set up templates, so they included my S.I. logo. Invoicing would be my responsibility, but she would do everything else. I was feeling very high-tech! It was a PC laptop, and I was a Mac guy, but I figured it out. How the rest worked was – I would put all my paperwork and receipts in labeled folders, and she would pick those up, along with the laptop, once a month, and keep it for a week while she did all the data entry, then bring it all back to me.

* * *

In late March I was preparing to do the big entry windows and dugouts for the Angels for the 2007 season. I had spent a significant amount of time on the road (Scout was covered; I had a roommate at my house by then), and lugging around a laptop everywhere (to keep up with my emails) was becoming cumbersome. A couple of my friends had BlackBerry phones for emails and calendars, so I took another step up in technology and got one. I remember pretty clearly, during the installation of the windows, my installer Wes tripping out that I was doing emails from my phone. Things had come a long way since the days when the account executives at Jordan & Horn used beepers.

In late March I also got a small job from the Dodgers. Not the one I was bidding on, but still: progress. I did get the Rockies job I bid on, for their dugout tops. They did their dugouts with banners attached to the top with Velcro, which was the total opposite of how we did the Angels dugouts. Whatever the customer wants, right?

In April we got another job from the Pittsburgh Steelers for 100 light pole banners, and 10 stadiums from our customer Mojo Sports. Mojo installed pitching cages at Major League Baseball stadiums, and they were a huge fan favorite. We designed and printed all the banners for their cages. The owner Joe had started his company around the same time I started S.I., and I had worked with him since Belmont Shores. It was pretty cool to work together as both our companies grew.

In mid-May I got a late-day call from my old buddy Patrick at the NBA. The Finals were in San Antonio this year, and he asked if I could put banners on buildings. "Of course I can!" Can you be in San Antonio at the basketball arena tomorrow morning? "Of course I can," I responded automatically. Shit! I booked a red-eye flight last-minute and headed out that night. Thank God I had the roommate at that time and Scout was covered, or I couldn't have gone. A lot of people don't realize it from the outside looking in, but these are the kinds of things you have to do to win new customers and get them to trust you. Sports graphics was a very demanding industry.

I arrived in San Antonio around 8 a.m. the next morning, rented a car, and drove off to AT&T Center. Patrick wouldn't be there, but he had me meet the vice president of operations for the Spurs. They wanted to put two huge banners on the front of the building. The problem was, they were kind of tear-shaped, and they had never put anything up there, so they didn't have an artwork template or sizes. He asked if I could figure that out. "Of course I can." He asked what I needed to do, and I asked if they could get me on the side of the building. He took me to the engineering department and introduced me to the lead rigger. The rigger asked if I had ever rappelled a building, and I said yes, lying. I was kind of scared of heights, to be honest. He harnessed me up, gave me some safety instructions, and over the side of the building we went. I had an old trick from doing templates for vehicle wraps that I would apply to this, just on a way bigger scale. I only needed three dimensions, assuming both sides were mirrored sizes, which I was told they were.

The funny story here is, while I was up there hanging from a rope, my phone buzzed with a text message from Patrick. "Swanson, that better not be you on the side of that building! I saw your MySpace!" Too late, dude. I already had my dims. I guess the Spurs' V.P. ratted me out.

The next step in my template trick was getting a picture of the tear-shaped sides of the building from a level height. The Spurs had a boom lift in the parking lot and sent me up in that. When I got home, I scaled the pictures up to the dimensions I'd grabbed on the side of the building in Illustrator, drew up my templates, and handed them to the NBA.

Because of how far the building was off the parking lot, we needed to use a cherry picker instead of a boom lift to install the banners. I once again enlisted Robbie for the install. It was basically a crane with a little basket hanging from the cable with Robbie, one of his guys, and a 300-pound banner all in it. The tear-shaped banners fit perfectly, and the install went off without a hitch. It was the craziest job I'd pulled off to date, and also the most risk I'd ever taken.

Needless to say, Patrick and all the NBA folks were super stoked. They ended up giving me a bunch more work for the Finals and said to expect to hear from them more often. I was beside myself – I was really pulling all this off. I couldn't wait to get home and tell Scout.

* * *

Summer of 2007, I lost the Free Car Media account. One reason was the vehicle wraps market was getting totally saturated, and I think the CEO, Drew, a serial entrepreneur, was moving on to greener fields. One bad thing happened to me, though, from the vendor I'd been using. I had switched over to them for this account because the volume was a little overwhelming, and everything was super quick turns. Plus, shipping was less from Burbank, Calif. where they were located. I'd been running the billing through them and then they were kicking me back the money from my margins. I had a huge job with over 20 vehicles, and one of the owners just decided not to pay.

His exact words to me were, "What are you going to do? You're just a small business. We're way bigger than you. Sue me." And he was right. I was just a one-man operation, and in no position for a lawsuit against a big company, even though I would have won. Lesson learned. This was just the first of many times this would happen.

The Angels made the playoffs again in September and drew the Red Sox in the Division Series starting Oct. 3rd in Boston. The Angels had a strong season, won their division, and everyone's hopes were high. They added several building banners and a bunch of new branding up in the outfield concourse for the postseason – a lot more work than usual for playoffs. Unfortunately, they ended up getting swept by the Red Sox and only played one game at home.

I hadn't gotten any jobs from the Panthers or Redskins that year. Not even anything to bid on. I got a design request from the Steelers for huge banners to go on the bridges of the three rivers that met right in front of their stadium, but the banners never came to fruition.

* * *

The whole country was in a pretty major financial crisis as the end of 2007 came around, and I was starting to see it workload-wise. It was slowing down a lot. I did get a couple of super fun jobs in December, though. One was a stage backdrop for Tiger Army, a band I loved, and the other was a full-size bus wrap for Microsoft, who I was really hoping to wiggle my way in with, but these small jobs weren't big money-makers. As always, however, Big League Dreams kept coming through. I had billboards for their parks almost daily, and they had two new sports parks opening in 2008. They both had eight replica fields; these would be my biggest jobs to date money-wise.

We started production on Big League Dreams in Gilbert, Ariz. in early January 2008. It had eight replica fields, seven of the usual suspects, with the new one being Chase Field, where the Diamondbacks played. That one had to be designed from ground-up. I'd never been to a game at that stadium – but was familiar with its unique features, such as a swimming pool just beyond the fence in right-center field, and huge industrial-looking girders on the upper sides to support the retractable roof. I designed some features for those two items along with the bullpens, dugouts, etc., and got the design approved right away. At this point, for BLD, I also did their whole directional and wayfinding sign packages – and with parks being built this size, they were quantities of 200-plus. I helped National Posters in Chattanooga with the idea of testing direct prints on Dibond (faux metal material) with their new Inca flatbed printer, and that's how we ended up doing them. I also developed color schemes for the directional signs that were proprietary to each city/park. Since I was designing all of them myself, by this point, all I had to do was pick up the last park's package, change the colors, and add and delete some signs per the architect's specs. It was a lot of work, but pretty easy. And very profitable.

There was one thing about Gilbert, though, that was drastically different from all the other BLD parks. They had built the bleachers for each stadium out of precast concrete. So instead of just heavy duty stapling the crowd scene banners to the bleachers, we had to use drills and concrete screws. It tripled the labor.

We of course finished everything on schedule, Robbie once again on the install, and everything was beautiful when completed. I was especially proud of the Chase Field replica I had personally designed.

* * *

The NBA All-Star Game was in New Orleans in February 2008, and I'd already been pre-warned by Patrick they had a long-standing vendor there, so my scope would be different. The local vendor would do all the direct work from the NBA, but I had a chance to help with the work from their production partners, including, once again, VEE. Any of the NBA's events were massive, and they were like a well-oiled machine. It was a trip working for them. They had so many partners. I'd been learning the sales ropes for the last five years and had picked up a pretty good trick: any email (from anyone) that was forwarded to me, I read down the entire thread to see who else was copied to it. Once the job we were working on was complete, I would ask the main customer for permission to contact the ancillary partners on the thread and let them know I was who did all the print and install, and to mention that I would also love to work directly for them. This was going very well and would become my biggest tool in building new sales over the next 15 years. Using this method over those last two events for the NBA, I was able to get a good amount of work for All-Star/New Orleans.

∗ ∗ ∗

Big League Dreams in Mansfield, Texas was on deck, and we'd been working on artwork files since early February. Once again, eight fields, and this had a new one: Ameriquest Field, home of the Texas Rangers. I'd actually had an opportunity to visit that stadium for an invite-only party for a softball tournament I played there (Dallas) six months earlier. For the party we had full access to everything – dugouts, locker rooms, all of it. I knew BLD had a park coming to Texas, so I took a lot of pics and made design plans for this stadium.

Thankfully they'd returned to building the bleachers from plywood, and everything went super smooth. Robbie once again on the install.

I had been super fortunate so far in 2008. In the middle of a disastrous financial crisis in our country, which was being called The Great Recession, I had three major projects that gave me a little financial comfort against everything going on.

∗ ∗ ∗

Besides the business worries, though, the housing market of the entire country was crashing. Vegas was one of the cities hit hardest. I had paid $385,000 for my house and was now being told it was barely worth $200K. People were walking away from houses everywhere around me; others were being foreclosed on, and it was a horrible mess. For me, I loved my home and my neighborhood and could still afford the mortgage. So, I decided to just ride it out. Plus, it was the only home Scout had ever known, and by now she was the most important thing to me in the whole world.

One more bad thing had happened, though. I lost the Angels account. Ownership brought in a new marketing team, and my main contacts all left. By this time "sponsorships" were becoming a thing in sports, and big companies were swooping work from little guys like me. More on that later in this chapter.

Another thing happened then: Facebook. I'd been on MySpace since early 2006, but Facebook was bigger, and *everyone* was getting on it. I already used MySpace to post work stuff, but once I figured out Facebook, I started doing it more often. By the end of the year, I would also have a business page besides my personal one and was posting pictures and descriptions of my work on both.

* * *

I was hitting the cold calls harder than ever. My daily routine was to contact 25 new people a day. I'd pick a target, say, the SEC (a conference in collegiate sports), hospitals, hotels, and then make lists. I went after spaces I was already doing work in for the most part, but I was also including things I'd see driving around town. I'd send myself notes via emails. I'd been getting a lot of work from Havasu Speedway, which was one of those small, local stock car racetracks. So, I did a Google search for similar ones in the United States and got a list of about 50, and contacted every single one, including sending pictures of the work from the track in Havasu. Generally speaking, I'd get one hit back on a hundred cold calls sent out. I had some luck with the racetracks and got a hit back from Mohave Valley Raceway in Arizona asking for quotes for their track billboards. I quickly turned them into a customer. Same thing with a list I created with local Vegas hospitals. I contacted every one and got a hit back from Sunrise Hospital; pulled them onboard as well.

In early May, Patrick from the NBA called once again. He said I'd been doing a great job, but he had done some searches and discovered Screaming Images was not incorporated, was a sole proprietorship. He had more work for me, but said I needed to get incorporated immediately. He also said he needed me to up my general liability insurance and get workers comp added. So, I hired a lawyer and incorporated S.I. as an LLC. I called my insurance broker and upped my business insurance policy to the NBA's specified levels, and then Patrick gave me another job: the 2008 NBA Finals.

It ended up being the Lakers vs. the Boston Celtics, and I was a lifelong Lakers fan, so I was super stoked. Turned out I was only doing the Boston side though, as the NBA already had a long-standing vendor in Los Angeles. They didn't know who would be in the finals until the playoffs finished, so everything would be a tight turnaround. The Celtics didn't clinch until May 30th, which happened to be right in the middle of my annual Memorial Day weekend boating trip to Lake Havasu. So, I sat in the garage working on my laptop at my buddy's house in Havasu, with my boat sitting out in the driveway, while everyone else was out on the lake. But that was okay. My little company was working for the NBA.

Two cool things happened in June. I picked up another racetrack, Bakersfield Speedway, and I got a call back from the Dallas Cowboys. I'd been sending them cold emails and pictures of my past sports work for about three years. If I didn't hear back from one department, I'd just contact another. I knew they were building a new stadium, and I wanted in on it; 2008 was the last year they'd play at old Cowboys Stadium. The person that called me was Stephanie, an executive assistant. She was getting bids on mesh banners for the exterior of the stadium for their last season there.

I got the bid specs the next week, and it was for eighteen 40-by-20-foot mesh banners, plus installation. Apparently, they had had trouble with keeping the banners up in high wind, which was why they were looking for a new vendor. So besides putting together the numbers for the bid, I had a 10-by-10-foot sample made by National Posters, which I funded. I shipped it to Stephanie so she could see the quality of my finishing – it showed a new method we were working on where seatbelt webbing was welded into the hems so the grommets wouldn't tear out. She loved the sample and the prices, and we were awarded the job. I enlisted Robbie once again on the install. The job went up in late July, in time for their first preseason game. I made enough profit off that job to pay my mortgage for a full year. In the middle of a great recession, my little business was hanging in there.

In August, I heard from the Pittsburgh Panthers about a rebrand for their field wall graphics at Heinz Field. Their old athletic director, Steve Pederson, had returned home after a brief stint at Nebraska, and they were looking to switch back to their old branding scheme from during his first tenure. It was a great job – design, print, and install – and I was super stoked. Something was still weighing on my mind, though. I hadn't heard from the Carolina Panthers yet this offseason… On NFL opening day 2008, Scout and I pulled up onto the couch at home to watch some football. The Panthers game was on at 1 p.m., playing at home. I loved watching games at the stadiums where we'd worked – and always called Mom to let her know they were on TV. As soon as the opening kickoff was in the air, my heart was crushed. They had new field wall graphics, including the sidelines. We'd only been doing the end zones since we started working for them in 2001. The sidelines were just concrete walls, and I had been pitching them to cover them the last three seasons. They had even changed the "Cat's Eyes" in the end zones – and in my opinion, they didn't look as good as what I had done.

I switched to another game, heartbroken. The next morning, I emailed my main contact asking what had happened? She told me a local vendor offered a "partnership" where they did work free in exchange for sponsorship opportunities at the stadium. She said she was super sorry, she had forgotten to let me know in advance, and I believed her. She promised they would keep me involved in other areas. This was a big harbinger of things to come in my biggest market – sports stadiums.

***

In September I picked up my first NBA team, the Oklahoma City Thunder. It wasn't a huge job, but a foot in the door. The team had moved from Seattle (where they played as the Supersonics), and I had been chasing them since the move was announced. Persistence pays off! I had sent probably a hundred emails on this and talked to probably 20 different people.

October and November were both super-scary slow. Thank God I had Big League Dreams and their design and print business for their billboards, or I would have had nothing.

In December, the Panthers came through with their promise to keep me involved and gave me 120 light pole banners for their divisional playoff game against the Arizona Cardinals. They lost that game, so no further playoff work that year for the Panthers.

I was super lucky in 2008. I had some big jobs from existing customers. I had lost the Angels but picked up a few new customers. Still, I had a really bad feeling about 2009.

* * *

January started off strong, though. Patrick called, and the NBA All-Star Game was in Phoenix in February. I would be completely responsible for his ancillary event – the NBA Jam Session. It was super exciting.

I ended up spending a full week in Phoenix installing, Robbie once again on board. There were huge towers, multiple stages, sponsor booths and activations, games and activities, and concession stands. It was like a little city. Everything went as smoothly as it possibly could have, and Patrick was stoked. He kicked me down a couple of tickets to the actual game, and I called my girlfriend from Vegas to come join me. We left town that night right after the game, because I wanted to get home. I really missed Scout.

During the installation of that event, one of the partners at Jam Session was TNT Sports. The TV station. They had some banners for their command center that didn't fit, and they saw me installing all my stuff, so they hit me up and asked if I could help them in a rush. I did, and they ended up being a regular client through the sale of my company.

Also in January, I did another stage backdrop for Social Distortion. Again, always super cool to work for your favorite band. Even got a direct call from band founder and leader, Mike Ness.

February began hot, too. A cold call to the San Diego Padres landed the opportunity to bid on some new pads for their outfield walls. Turned in my bid, got awarded, and ended up building and installing 150 pads at Petco Park.

Next big one in February was a huge win. I had read in Sports Business Journal magazine the past summer about the $250 million renovation the Kansas City Royals planned for Kauffman Field and started cold calling them right away. It took me four months, but I finally got a response, and the opportunity to bid. They ended up awarding me print and install for ten 19-by-11-foot mesh exterior banners. I was making that subscription money to the Sports Business Journal magazine and almanac pay off.

The ball kept rolling in March and April with eight new Mojo Sports stadiums ahead of baseball season. My buddy Joe was kicking ass and taking names, and I was so stoked for him. We also got another billboard order from Bakersfield Speedway. The K.C. Royals called mid-April with a rush request for some big windows in the outfield, so I booked a quick flight and headed there. I measured everything and was back home the same day. By this time, I had adapted to pretty brutal travel schedules, so I didn't have to spend that much time away from the office. Any time I spent traveling usually had to be made up, hour to hour, just to keep on track with the workload. I ended up getting the windows job and using a local installer. Everything went great, and I thought I had a permanent new account locked up.

May and June stayed steady, and I got my first job from TNT Sports – a huge logo'd rain tarp for their broadcast booth at Pocono Speedway. I also did new end zones for the Redskins and Pitt Panthers. I was getting really lucky with the work. Everyone else I knew in the print business was dead slow from the recession. No one was spending any money; but it seemed like the sports work was keeping me afloat. It was heavy on my mind, though. I knew if it dried up for me, too, I could lose everything.

At this point I'd been self-employed for about six years. I had a whole lot more stuff than when I started. I went from being in debt when I started S.I. to having about $60K savings in the bank now – but I was still never comfortable one day. Even though I worked from home, and didn't have to answer to anyone, I worked at least 10 hours a day. I liked my lifestyle and wanted to keep it. I knew that would mean to keep taking risks, and I was okay with that. But I was lucky, there was one big risk I hadn't taken yet: opening my own shop. That would be on hold until I was sure I'd navigated my way through this recession.

* * *

The gym I went to five mornings a week, Las Vegas Athletic Club, had a huge banner on the exterior I walked underneath every morning. I had made some cold call efforts but got nowhere. One of those mornings in early August, I arrived and noticed the wind had torn the banner from its frame, and it was hanging down low enough that I could touch it. I took pictures and showed them to the guy up front who checked membership cards and told him I owned a printing company and that torn, hanging banner was definitely a safety hazard for the gym. I left a business card and told him they could call, and I'd fix it right away. I ended up getting a call from the director of marketing, an awesome person named Kim, before I even finished working out. She asked for a quote on printing only, as they had a contract with an installer called Vision Signs. I delivered a quote within an hour of getting home and she approved it right away and sent me art. I had the banner printed and rushed from Chattanooga, and I hand-delivered it the next day. I had to eat the overnight shipping but wasn't worried – my focus was for a long-term client, not a one-time profit. One step back to get two steps forward, and it worked. I would have LVAC as a client until the very end. I also picked up Vision Signs. This success triggered even more determination for more local work.

I finished August 2009 with more billboards for Bakersfield Speedway, and my first-ever job generated from my social media efforts! I was called by Topps, the dominant producer of baseball and trading cards, seeking a quote on a box truck. They were referred by someone who'd seen pictures of vehicles we wrapped on my Facebook Business page. And I got the job. New tool for sales! I was super stoked.

In September I picked up a referral to the WNBA from Patrick and printed 30 big banners for the league. Besides that, the month was dead slow. Same for October and November. I had Big League Dreams stuff, but not much else. Those two months I didn't even make enough money to cover my bills.

In December I heard from Kim at Las Vegas Athletic Club again, and she sent me a job for big exterior banners at all six of their locations. Once that job was done and installed, I went to England to visit grandma.

* * *

Let's back up a bit to convey the goings-on of my personal life. I had been in Nevada for a little over four years, and self-employed for a little over seven. I'd dodged a few bullets and took a few hits business-wise, but I was doing really well on a personal and financial level. I had gone from living paycheck to paycheck and watching my print company employers not caring properly for my customers, to 100% customer satisfaction and not having to worry about paying my bills. I knew it could all dump at any moment, which kept me motivated to work hard. I got up early every day, went to the gym, and started work by 7 a.m. I was healthier than I could ever remember being, and a lot of it was due to curtailing much of the partying. I still had some drinks on weekends, but never on weekdays. Work was too important to me. I had also completely cut out all the drugs. Plus, I had Scout to care for now, and that motivated me more than anything.

I had made a lot of friends around town and had a pretty good social life. The launch ramp I used at Lake Mead was 10 miles from home, and Scout, myself, and our friends went out on our boat just about every Saturday from April to October. By then we had upgraded our truck and boat. Thanks to *match.com*, I had a pretty good dating life, too. I met some really nice, fun girls. A permanent relationship wasn't really in the cards for me at that time, and I was up front with them all about it. Besides, they didn't really care for my sleep and work schedule during the week very much. I would go to bed at 8:30 p.m. and get up at 4 a.m. They all said the same thing: I worked too much. And I was okay with that.

Life was *really* good, but I knew I had to keep hustling to keep it. I had little motivational messages all over my home office, things like, "Do you like your life?" Yes, I did, and it kept me working hard. Plus, Scout. I loved her more than the world and she was counting on me.

* * *

The year 2010 started slow, which I expected. I spent most of January making lists and hitting cold calls hard. I'd made some "sales sheets" that prompted me to make at least 25 cold calls a day. I'd put the name of the potential customer on it, how I contacted them (call, email, socials), then added columns for results, and next steps. I kept completed ones in a storage container so I could revisit and look at the dates and notes any time.

I always started calling sports teams in January, too. Teams I already worked for, teams I had spoken with but hadn't gotten jobs from, and teams I hadn't yet contacted. There were a lot of opportunities between the professional leagues and the college level, meaning NCAA. Something started happening that caused me a bad feeling from conversations I'd had last year: they were all asking for partnerships. To be specific, they wanted me to print and install stuff for free in exchange for advertising my business via their stadiums and all their assets. That wouldn't work for me with how I'd set up my business. And to be honest, it wouldn't have worked for me in any way.

I understood where they were coming from, and that one of the biggest reasons they did it was the Great Recession. They didn't really have any money to spend. But the reality of it was, they ended up going with local vendors and at least some semblance of a partnership. When I had first gotten into the sports graphics market it was a specialty, but now everyone was figuring out they could probably do it, too. I was once again – like the Union vs. Macintoshes situation back in L.A. when I was with Jordan & Horn/Techtron/Wace – at a crossroads.

I had to diversify. To that point my sole focus had been professional sports teams and stadiums. There was so much other work out there. I would just have to be smart and work harder. I had to separate myself from competitors; make myself stand out. It was time to show my punk rock roots.

I still had one super fortunate thing going – Big League Dreams. I was working my ass off for them, and they showed some pretty major loyalty in return. Aside from the new parks they built from the ground-up, I still got the day-to-day work designing and printing billboards for all eight parks. And this year I would get a special one: a new BLD park in Vegas, featuring a stadium they had never replicated, Dodger Stadium, my hometown field. One different thing about this one, though. Nevada passed a new law, and I would need a contractor's license for the installation.

In early January, I called the Nevada State Contractors Board and was directed to attend an orientation/onboarding meeting to learn what was needed for the license. Financial information was easy, but there was a big test I would have to take, and I was given the curriculum to study beforehand.

I got a big handbook to prepare, and decided I needed two full weeks to study. I booked an appointment for the end of January. I arrived at the state building at the scheduled 8 a.m. – and I was pretty nervous. I hadn't taken a big test since high school. They were projecting the test to take three hours, and after you finish you press a submit button, and after about a minute it flashes with either a "pass" or "fail" screen. I took the test, finished right on time and hit the button. I was shitting my pants. I could lose this Big League Dreams job by not passing, and with it my biggest customer. After about 30 seconds the screen flashed: "PASS!" Carry on! This license would open up many doors.

* * *

January and February were pretty slow months overall. I got more work from Bakersfield Speedway, another huge job for LVAC for all six locations, and picked up a Marriott Hotel near the convention center from my cold calls. Nothing big, because most folks still didn't have any money to spend. When they did have money, their budgets were tiny. Across the board my customers all loved me due to the customer service, communication, and accountability. They wanted to get work done, and in many instances would share their budgets to see what all they could fit in. Many, because of corporate rules (besides the recession), would have to get three quotes for every job. A lot of times they'd share quotes with me to see if I could match, because they wanted me to get the work. I always matched, even when it meant smaller profit margins, or in special cases just breaking even. I wasn't trying to make as much profit as possible off of every single job. I wanted lifetime customers – and really, just get through to the other side of these hard financial times with them still on my team. I considered every one of my customers friends and partners.

Good ol' Joe from Mojo Sports was *really* ramping up and sent me a bunch of work in March. I also picked up a new account via relentless cold calls, Crown Imports, which distributed Corona beer.

Cathy from Crown Imports, who would eventually become one of my biggest allies and staunchest supporters, invited me to Harrah's to measure their new space for some wall murals and signs. Easy work, print and install, right up our alley. We met in the space one morning in mid-March. Her, myself, and a representative from Harrah's. I recognized this dude, but it took me a second to figure it out. "Lance?" I asked. Yep, it was him, one of my childhood friends from Eagle Rock. Small world! Job went perfect, I had a lot of motivation on this one, and Lance and I picked our childhood friendship back up and ended up riding our Harleys all over southern Nevada.

I also landed a couple of new hospitals in March: UMC and Mountain

View. My neighbor John had been doing some freelance sales and brought in UMC. I then proclaimed us as "hospital graphics experts" and called every hospital I could find. I called it "snowballing it." Like a big snowball going downhill that keeps getting bigger and bigger. It was becoming one of my biggest sales strategies. I did it with everything.

I had another first in March: I was asked to speak before a class of business students at the College of Southern Nevada. My bookkeeper Marisa's daughter was a member of the class. I was told to be prepared to speak for 15 minutes, and this could include a slideshow if I wanted. There would be three other business owners doing the same, and I was speaking last. I arrived early because I was interested in hearing the other business owners. The first two went through their speeches at the agreed-upon time limit. The third speaker was a woman and the first words out of her mouth were, "non-profit." She then repeated those words every other sentence for the next 40 minutes. She must have said "non-profit" a hundred times, with no slide show. She went way over the allotted time, and the class was falling asleep.

When she finally finished, I knew I had to do something to fire the class up. When I stepped up to the front, I put a picture from the NBA All-Star Game on the screen, and the first words I said were: "Hi, I'm James, owner of Screaming Images, and we are a FOR PROFIT BUSINESS." The entire class erupted in laughter – I had them in my pocket. I went through my 15 minutes, they asked a ton of questions, and wanted me to keep going, but the class was ending. It was super fun, and the first of many times I would end up speaking in front of students and crowds.

In April, I somehow wiggled into a project with Deutsch, the advertising agency. I always had those old sales reps from Jordan & Horn in mind, and everything they taught me. We wrapped six Volkswagen Tuaregs for them. I also picked up what would become my biggest partnership ever that month – Punk Rock Bowling.

Punk Rock Bowling started over the last few years as an annual Vegas bowling trip organized by Mark and Shawn Stern from the band Youth Brigade and the Better Youth Organization record label. It slowly evolved from just a Vegas bowling trip to a few bands playing, to this year, a full-blown three-day music festival. The bands they inked included T.S.O.L., Adolescents, 7 Seconds, and Ill Repute. Some of my old faves. I had to get involved.

I sent them a cold email from their website's "Contact Us" tab, and said I was an old- school punk rocker from L.A., who happened to own a local print company, and was a "festival graphics expert." Mark Stern responded personally and put me on the guest list for a local show they (Youth Brigade) had that month at a restaurant in Vegas. We struck a deal and partnership that night that would last for 11 years, until I sold S.I.

This second sponsorship with this little business of mine would pay great dividends, and I'll lay a lot of that out later. I would leverage it into hundreds of thousands of dollars in revenue in stage backdrops for bands – with some of my all-time favorites. And I'd also become friends with a lot of people from punk rock bands who were my heroes while a kid. All that for doing a few free banners for Punk Rock Bowling in 2010. One step back, 10 steps forward.

* * *

Also, in April we started on Big League Dreams Las Vegas, brand new contractor's license in hand. Big League Dreams had hired a "construction manager" for this project, who reported to Wayne. I had to deal with him directly; his name was Gary. I was one of only two contractors, at every BLD park built from scratch, that was written into the contract with the general contractor. The only other one besides me was the contractor who installed the field lights. The GC chose all the other vendors. I controlled all creative and archived art files and knew more about the graphics for their parks than anyone from BLD even. This all from Wayne's trust that I had built up over the last eight years and five brand new sports parks.

Nonetheless, Gary gave me a really hard time, and I didn't know why.

By this time some of the bigger printers around the country had caught wind that I'd been printing hundreds of thousands of square feet of banners and signs for BLD via my social media efforts (mostly still just Facebook Business at this point). I guess a lot of them were hitting up Gary and he was trying to displace me because they were really big companies, and I was just a little one-man show.

This is the origin of one of my biggest social media and business rules: Don't worry about competitors, just worry about yourself and doing your job. In the late Facebook days and early LinkedIn days people always used to ask, "Aren't you worried about other people seeing what you're working on and trying to take it away from you?" No, I wasn't. As long as I worked hard, was honest and accountable, giving customers fair market value on square-foot prices and the absolute best customer service and communication, I absolutely was not worried about losing a customer to a competitor. Take care of your folks and they will take care of you.

The new BLD Vegas had the three regulars: Wrigley Field, Yankee Stadium, and Fenway Park. In addition, they had Crosley Field (always one of my faves), Angel Stadium (which I had personally designed for the Manteca Park), and now Dodger Stadium, which as I mentioned earlier would be the first time they replicated it for one of their parks. I knew this stadium better than any other, as I had grown up six miles from Dodger Stadium, been to hundreds of games, and they were my favorite team since I was a kid. My BLD folks were thrilled with all my designs – especially the iconic Dodger Stadium scoreboard. I had designed it to replicate the exact moment Kirk Gibson hit the famous home run against the Oakland A's in the 1988 World Series. Super fun!

Everything went off seamlessly, on budget, and on time. I was so excited that I came out of my brief retirement and started a Screaming Images softball team to play there. I actually recruited my team off of Craigslist – and ended up having a couple guys on my team named Bill and Dennis who, besides being killer ballplayers and absolute sluggers, would also become great friends. We went undefeated and won the A League our second season. And Vegas BLD was one and done for Gary the construction manager.

* * *

Beginning of May, I heard from my friends at TNT Sports, and we did a couple more rain tarps for their broadcast booths. I was slowly working my way through other departments there by asking for introductions to other people. I hit pay dirt when I was eventually connected with Trevor at their scenic department.

I caught an even bigger one in May, when Chris, Senior Vice President of Operations for the Washington Redskins, finally gave me a crack at the "tower banners" by letting me do one test print and install. I'd been working with Chris since 2002 when he was still the operations manager there at FedEx Field. We'd always had a good relationship – he was tough, but fair. I wasn't surprised that he kept moving up in operations until he finally held the top spot. The tower banners were huge: 50-by-50-foot mesh exterior banners that were installed into big metal frames along the top perimeter of the stadium. There were eighteen of them. Every time I traveled to Landover, Maryland to work at the stadium, at least half of them were in disrepair, torn and flapping. I knew enough by then about big exterior installations to see that the frames didn't have a very good (or easy) installation system. I'd been bugging Chris for three solid years to give me a crack, and he finally did. It was huge. The creative on our very first tower banner was Virginia Lottery.

In June I got my first payoff from my partnership with Punk Rock Bowling – Reggae Fest in Vegas. It came via Brian from Bogus Productions who had handled event production for the PRB festival at Sunset Station. I also got a small job from Enterprise Rent-a-Car which was the result of relentless cold calls and emails. But the biggest one I secured in June was from Sunrise Hospital for 45 light pole banners – including the hardware for hanging the banners. I had to rent a bucket truck to install in the hospital's southwest parking lot. It was the first time I ever did light pole banner hardware, and the experience would pay off huge the next year.

July was pretty slow, but I picked up Mountain View hospital and got my second job from Corona. The country was still in a recession, but I was starting to fall into a plan that I called "the long game." I wasn't just looking for jobs to make as much money as possible. I was looking for long-term customers and relationships I could keep forever.

Since most professional sports teams now sought partnerships, and I still really wanted to be involved in sports, I started going after sports agencies. All of course listed in my trusty *Sports Business Journal* almanac, which I still bought every year. I was getting better with my sales pitches, which were always super casual, and by now was getting about one response for every 25 cold calls/emails. In August I picked up an agency called The Marketing Arm for a small job. They were what I guess you'd call one of the earliest progenitors of experiential marketing in the sports space. It was a good win, and I planned on playing the long game with them. I also picked up another racetrack, the Las Vegas Motor Speedway Bull Ring track, for whom we did some track billboards.

Also, in August I heard back from Chris with the Redskins. The test tower banner we installed did well and already outlasted those the incumbent vendor had done. He ordered four more! It was then that I also put the bug in his ear about starting to slowly replace his old, outdated tower banner frames.

September was pretty slow, but I got a couple of nice wall murals from Cathy at Corona and landed a good-sized job printing vinyl banners for the WNBA Finals (via my old buddy Patrick). October was slow as well, but I picked up a few new customers: the Black Angels (stage backdrops), Live Nation (amphitheater backdrop in North Carolina), and Bruno Mars (stage backdrop). I had been hitting the music industry cold calls hard. I was developing another big sales style: going after things I liked. It makes hard work fun, and it's easier to talk about things you know a lot about.

In November, I heard from the Redskins again, and they ordered another tower banner. Chris also said they had interest in building new frames for the towers next season and wanted to get going on a test frame after the season ended. He hooked me up with another guy from the operations team named Sean to get the ball rolling.

December was slow, which was pretty normal. I had the usual BLD stuff, a couple of small Corona jobs, and some LVAC jobs. But one great thing happened – I got my first job from Kawasaki. It came from contacts I met in my days playing softball in the old Advertising League in West L.A. Scout and I just kicked back at home the last two weeks of the year.

Overall, 2009 and 2010 were not great years financially. Mainly it was the recession. There were a few pretty big printing companies I knew of that didn't make it through. I was starting to realize that I had a pretty unorthodox business style – and it was working. The most important thing to me was the relationships. I told all my customers: if they were honest with me, I would be flexible. I took a lot of jobs over the last two years at smaller profit margins to help customers fit the scopes of work they wanted into their budgets, with hopes it would all come back around. It was a big risk but paid off in spades. I had been in business now for nine years and felt I had a big year right around the corner. Not bad for a punk rock guy without a college degree.

* * *

I was ready to hit 2011 hard. I'd diversified quite a bit the past two years, and I felt like the economy was finally turning a corner. First job I got in January was for three 25-by-20-foot stage backdrops for Social Distortion's upcoming House of Blues tour which kicked off in Vegas. They were touring on their new album, *Hard Times and Nursery Rhymes*, and the record cover was one of the backdrops we'd make. At this time, I was having my fabric backdrops printed by a company in L.A., because National Posters didn't have dye-sublimation capabilities. The band's plan was to start the show with the

"Skelly Car" backdrop which had the famous S.D. skeleton riding in a classic hot rod. Then, when they got to the part of the show where they played songs from the new album, they'd "kabuki drop" the first backdrop and the new album cover backdrop would appear. Then, when they got toward the end of the show, they'd do another drop and fly the classic Social Distortion "Skelly" logo while finishing with the old-school songs.

They were playing two nights in Vegas, and I was going to both. On the way home the first night I got a frantic call from their manager. Someone had stolen the skelly car backdrop after the kabuki drop! Could I get another one printed by tomorrow? I woke up my L.A. dye-sub printer in the middle of the night and she reluctantly agreed to do it, but I would have to drive to L.A. to pick it up, which I agreed to. I went home and crashed out but was woken up in the morning by S.D.'s manager. They found the backdrop. They caught one of the backstage guys on camera carrying it out the side-stage door all bundled up in a ball. That was a big-ass fabric banner! I was shocked he got it out the door without anyone seeing him! Anyhow, the dude was caught and agreed to return it before that night's show. Crisis averted.

I do want to mention here what an incredible feeling it is to be in a venue in your new hometown, watching your favorite band with a bunch of your buddies who also love them, and watching three banners that you produced via the business you started yourself from scratch get kabuki-dropped during the show. What a motivator. I was high as a kite.

* * *

End of January I decided to take a few days off to do some snowboarding up in Mammoth Lakes with my buddy Jason. On the first day we rode in the morning, then took an afternoon break at the main lodge. As we walked down the side of the building, I noticed a door that said Administration. We went to the deck of the lodge and got a table, and I told my buddy I'd be right back. I confidently walked in through that administration door and asked the first person I saw where the marketing office was, and they said two doors down on the left. I guess they weren't too concerned about me with all of my snowboarding gear on. I went down and knocked on the open door and met the girl in charge of Mammoth Mountain's marketing. Her name was Casey. I gave her my quick little spiel about being able to print anything, and she responded that she was actually looking for some big banners that her local vendor couldn't handle. I gave her my card and when I got back to the office two days later there was an email from her waiting for me with specs for an estimate. I sent off the quote within 30 minutes, and within an hour I had a good-sized order from Mammoth Mountain Ski Resort. New customer! I'd end up being Mammoth's main print vendor for several years until Casey left.

In early February my lists and cold calling system paid off again when I got an opportunity from the Ohio Valley Conference to bid on the graphics package for their annual basketball tournament. I had made a list of all the smaller conferences in the country, got the contacts info from my trusty old SBJ almanac, and sent cold-call emails to every single one. Out of the twenty or so, I got one hit. My returns were getting better. I sent out the bid, won the work, and was the vendor for the OVC for many years after. Right after that, I got another hit on a cold email: the Shamrock Music Festival in Maryland. I sent a message to the "Contact Us" button on their website, got a response, and got the job. I ended up working with Shawn the rest of my S.I. career, and he would go on to introduce me to at least a hundred new clients over the next decade. I also got one more cold-call hit that month, CBS Outdoor. It was a small job, but that was all I ever needed, a foot in the door.

* * *

March brought a pretty major surprise. I received a message on Facebook – my niece Brittany's mom had agreed to let her come visit me. Brittany was the daughter of my little brother David, who had passed away in 2002. Mom and I had known her when she was a baby, but for some reason when she was three, she and her mother disappeared. It crushed Mom. We'd been looking for her for years, and I had found Brittany's mom on MySpace a few years earlier. We started chatting and she was at first reluctant to let Britt come visit because her memories of me were as a "mean punk rocker/big brother" to her boyfriend (my little brother). Mom told her: "No, James has changed a lot, he has his own business, owns a nice home, and is very responsible." Go Mom! Britt was finally coming to see me in the summer, and Mom would come out to Vegas. There was a twist though. She didn't know anything about her dad (my little brother), and her mom asked me not to say anything. I wasn't sure I could do that. Especially after I talked to her on the phone, and she asked me, "Why doesn't my dad want to see me?" That was going to be a tough conversation.

They were in San Antonio now, and she had never flown on an airplane by herself. She was 16. The only flights we could work out that were within their schedules had a connection. I gave Britt a pep talk and bought her airline ticket. Well, her flight from San Antonio ended up leaving two hours behind schedule, and she ended up missing her connecting flight in Los Angeles. I'd been talking with American Airlines the whole day and they assured me they would get her to me. Once she arrived in L.A., I spoke with them again, and they said sorry, but they couldn't get her to Vegas that night. She would have to spend the night in the airport and take a flight in the morning. No way! I started panicking trying to think of a solution, and I was about to throw Scout in the truck and drive out to pick her up. Then I had an idea – maybe ask Sam? I had an awesome longtime friend in Hermosa Beach named Samantha, who lived not far from LAX. I called her and she agreed to go get Britt, take her to her place for the night, and then take her back to the airport in the morning. Life saver! It wasn't an ideal situation, and poor Britt was scared, but I just knew she'd love Sam, which she did. She arrived the next morning, we packed our bags, hooked up the boat to the truck, and headed to Lake Havasu. Britt has visited me every year since, and sometimes twice. She is the closest relationship I have, and I love her with all my heart. More on her later. And, *shame on American Airlines for stranding a 16-year-old girl.*

***

I kept rolling in March with cold hits. I picked up work for local music festival "Extreme Thing," The Academy of Country Music Awards show, and the City of Henderson. For Henderson, I started doing the big 15-by-15-foot mesh banners in front of their box offices at their amphitheater. Print and install. We'd keep that account until they tore that amphitheater down to build a minor league hockey stadium.

The year 2011 was kicking ass. I'd like to mention all the companies sending us continuous work but will try to condense it for brevity's sake.

In April I got a Corona job out in Laughlin wrapping a tiki hut on the beach, which I afterward parlayed into picking up the Harrah's Laughlin account and four of their huge shuttle buses. I also got the biggest banner we'd ever done – a massive 142-by-41-foot Corona banner we printed and dropped off the side of the parking garage at the Flamingo so it could be seen at the Imperial Palace (later known as The Linq) pool. This banner was a little too big for National Posters, so I started using Circle Graphics for these oversized ones. I got that new printing contact because my old boss from ICP in Orange County was now working there. They were based in Denver.

***

When I went to bed at night, I usually turned the ringer off on my phone. For some reason on the night of April 11th, I didn't. My phone rang about 3 a.m. which was really rare, so I knew it was something bad. When I picked up the phone and looked, it was a call from England. My grandma, I thought. I answered, and it was my uncle Paul. No, he said. Your Mom. All my wind went out of me. I couldn't even speak.

Mom had left two weeks earlier to visit grandma in London. One day, while standing outside my grandma's retirement flat, she had a pulmonary embolism and died on the spot. It was totally unexpected. My grandma, obviously, was a wreck. My uncles Paul and Tony, her younger brothers, handled everything there. I felt helpless. Thank God for them. The first thing we needed to do was get her body home.

My brother Chris and I decided we would wait to have her memorial gathering. We wanted to wait, so when we had it for her, everyone could be happy and tell awesome stories about her. A celebration of her life. That's the way she would have wanted it, I know.

Mom had been my biggest supporter ever since I started Screaming Images. She believed in me when no one else did. We talked on the phone every single week and she told me how proud she was on every call. And that she loved me. My heart was completely broken, but I knew she would want me to keep working, so that's what I did. It was the only thing I knew how to do. She never got to see Brittany, but at least she knew I had her on my radar now and that she would be cared for.

* * *

I kept the streak hot into May and June by picking up more new customers, such as 100.3 The Sound radio station (three vehicle wraps), Miller Lite beer (wrapping two kayaks), Warped Tour music festival (four stage banners), and then a *huge* one, R&R Partners. These guys handled all the printing and graphics for the Las Vegas Visitors and Convention Authority, and I had been chasing them for at least two years. The guy's name was Pat, and it turned out he was a Premier League (English soccer) fan like me, so we hit it off right away. It was just a small job wrapping a wall, but that was okay. Remember, a foot in the door.

I want to mention that during these last six months, I also picked up a kick-ass local installer named Chris, who would become a big part of my little business for the next nine years.

* * *

At this point with S.I., I was busy as hell. I started getting up earlier so I could get to the gym earlier so I could start work earlier. I was working 6:30 a.m. to 5 p.m. as a set schedule – but I was on-call and working from my phone wherever I was every waking hour. I was seeing results from all the hard work, and it was motivating me big time.

I was buzzing through my new issue of *Sports Business Journal* one morning when I saw an article that the PAC-10 athletic conference was expanding, to 12 teams, and rebranding as the PAC-12. The article included the new logo. All I could think of was, damn! There will be a lot of printing that goes along with this rebrand, and I need to get a piece.

See, even though I was a one-man operation working from home, I had this mentality that came from not only the fact that I had worked for some pretty big companies, but also from my punk rock background. I had a little mantra, "*Why not us?*" Someone had to do this work; why not me? So, for the PAC-12 I did a Google search for PAC-12 marketing and found Heather who was the vice president. I looked her up in my handy-dandy SBJ almanac and got her email address. I crafted a personalized email (never ever, under any circumstances, send generic or copy-and-paste emails; more on this later) that had a ton of info on my background, my experience in the sports market, and at least 20 pictures of past work in this space. She responded pretty quickly and said she actually had an event in Vegas the next week and needed a board with the new logo for the presentation. I said it would be on the house. I ate the cost of printing and shipping the board from Chattanooga and drove down and handed it to her in person. She was super cool and appreciative, and said I would hear from her again. And I would. She would become one of my biggest advocates, and we would have a working relationship that still lasts to this day.

Then I got the biggest job S.I. job to date: rebuilding all the tower banner frames at FedEx Field for the Washington Redskins. I had partnered with a general contractor named Hudrock from Baltimore at the end of the previous season and built a test frame, and I guess they loved it! We got awarded 15 new frames and tower banners. It would be huge.

* * *

We'd had some success building pads at baseball and football stadiums, so I spent a good amount of time making cold calls for this product. Hard work and diligence paid off once again in July when I was called by the University of Utah up in Salt Lake City to redo all the pads for their fieldhouse. I booked a flight right away and was off on a day trip to SLC to meet and greet, measure, and get the ball rolling.

I was still subjecting myself to some pretty brutal travel schedules. Partially because I was so damn busy, and partly because I had Scout at home to worry about. Which I always did. I missed her when I was gone. I took a lot of red-eye flights, getting that night's sleep on a plane. For example, when I worked in Landover at FedEx Field for the Redskins: I'd take a red eye, usually departing Vegas around midnight, into Baltimore. I'd land around 7:30 a.m., get a rental car, and arrive at the stadium around 9 or 9:30 a.m. I'd work there all day and then catch a 5 p.m. flight back to Vegas, and I'd get back home around 10 p.m. that night. Then, of course, in my office the next morning by 6:30 a.m.

Another development around this time was, I'd somehow tapped into the rap market for stage backdrops. That July, we had a 20-by-10-foot stage backdrop from Warner Brothers Records for a rapper named Theophilus London.

By the beginning of August, we were already heavy into the new tower frames for the Redskins. We had eight new frames and banners scheduled to go up that month. We were also still getting banner jobs from Mammoth Mountain even though it was summer. This month it was stage banners for their "Summer Series" concerts. Another big banner job also came through for Mountain View Hospital for 400 linear feet of mesh banners on construction fences for their remodel. We wrapped up a super-busy summer by picking up the stage banners for another new music client, Silopanna Fest in Maryland, via our new friends at Shamrock Fest.

We started September by finishing the last five tower banner frames and prints. The Redskins were super stoked, and we got a big payday. We also started working on Big League Dreams' newest sports park in Perris, Calif. Six replica fields on this one. There was a catch much like the Vegas park – the general contractor wanted me to get a California contractor's license. No problem.

This time I thought I'd get smart and hire a consulting company to help get the license. They were actually based in Vegas. I went there, heard the spiel, and paid the fee. The way it worked, they said, was that California had three tests and they had the questions and answers to all three. When I went to take the test, it would be one of the three. All I had to do was study the questions and answers. Done. I somehow found a way to cram in studying before the test date.

My test was at 10 a.m. on a Friday in mid-September. I left my house in Henderson that morning at 3:30 a.m., figuring if I arrived early, I'd hop into a Starbucks and do last-minute studying. The test was in San Diego. I arrived at the facility on time, signed in, and was taken into a room with a computer terminal for the test. It was the same deal as Vegas – hit "done" when finished, and the results come in a minute or so. I was left alone in the room and logged in to start the test. As soon as the first page of questions popped up, I knew I was in trouble. I didn't recognize any of the questions.

The three tests I studied before the trip were kind of weird anyway. The questions didn't really have anything to do with printing or installation – or even business questions, for that matter. They were more like questions related to construction. I had asked the consultants about it, and they said it was right, it was just the way California did it. I flipped through a few pages to see what else was there, and it had nothing to do with what I studied. I had two and a half hours' time limit, so I just figured I'd do the best I could. I used every second of that two and a half hours before I hit the Done button and was shitting my pants. One minute later the result came through: Pass. Rad. Common sense and logic got me through the test. I was now a California contractor. I sped back home to Scout.

In October my hard work for the Redskins paid off, and I got awarded the field wall banners for the Army-Navy football game at FedEx Field. I also picked up a new sports client in Vegas via cold calls that was super fun, the Lingerie Football League. The league was short-lived, but I can tell you those girls were badasses and could seriously play football. And they literally wore lingerie under their helmets and shoulder pads. They played hard and had the battle wounds to show for it.

In early November I hit potential paydirt. I was called by R&R Partners with an RFP for light pole banners and hardware *and* maintenance for 210 light pole banners on the Las Vegas Strip, the airport corridor, and Convention Center way. Besides the hardware for the poles, the RFP was for 1,152 light pole banners, as they would be switching out for events 16 times the first year. All 210 poles. I had done several small jobs for Pat already, and knew I had a shot if my price was right. And I had a plan I thought would help win the bid: I started looking at bucket trucks to purchase. I knew the four companies I was bidding against, and knew they didn't have one, and most likely didn't have the guts to buy one. It would give me a big advantage on install pricing since the competitors would likely have to include bucket rentals in bids.

In December I picked up another hospital: Southern Hills. We wrapped some big windows on the side of their building facing the 215 freeway. My install partner Chris was on the job and killed it. We had the usual work still coming in from the regulars – Corona, LVAC, Mammoth, BLD – but Scout and I were able to take a well-deserved break between Christmas and New Year's Day. We went snowboarding in Brian Head, Utah. Scout loved the snow.

I was ready for 2012. My little company had kicked ass in 2011, and I had some hot ones on the stove already. I had one thing on my mind: buy a printer and open my own shop.

* * *

I heard back from Pat from R&R on the light pole bid from November, and he wanted a test print and install, including hardware, at the convention center – 10 sets. I provided two options for the hardware and pushed for the higher-end product. It was spring-loaded, which would extend the life of the banners, and they also came with a 10-year warranty. That's what we went with on the test. I "rented" a bucket truck from an electrician guy I met at Sunrise Hospital on one of our installs. I had Chattanooga print me a couple of Screaming Images magnets to put on the truck during the install. Everything went great, as usual, and we were on time, as usual.

In February I got a small job for Baylor University's baseball team. I had been hitting the cold calls on collegiate sports pretty hard, and it was starting to pay off. I also picked up a 20-by-20-foot fabric stage backdrop for another rapper, Mac Miller.

My old buddy Patrick contacted me in early January and asked me to quote on a huge job for the NBA All-Star Game in Orlando the following month. Besides the usual scope for his off-site "Jam Session," he had a huge job printing mesh banners for a closed-in area surrounding Amway Center. It was 4,000 linear feet. I got the job, and he said he needed me there the *entire* week. In return, besides the fact that he gave me all that work, he hooked me up with VIP passes for all the ancillary events. It would be a fun week, but I didn't look forward to being away from Scout that long. She'd be okay, though. She would be with her friend Joey and my friend (Joey's mom), Kim.

One of the things in our scope for All-Star Orlando was a huge tent cover for their broadcast booth. I had a ton of experience with these by now from TNT and NASCAR. There was a very specific way you had to reinforce the edges that I had developed with Chattanooga. Toward the end of set-up, weather reports were showing some nasty stuff coming in. It was reported that our area might experience "microbursts." *What?* They were supposed to be pretty gnarly.

The riggers from the arena suggested we take the cover off the tent, but there really wasn't time. They then suggested we cut some slits in it for the wind to pass through, and I said, "NOOO!" No way. That would compromise the integrity of the banner, and it would rip right off. They said okay. At the end of the day, I left to go up to my room and then was called an hour later with news that the cover had flown off the tent. They cut slits after I left. The event started the next evening. Shit! I called Chattanooga and spoke with the night plant manager, Josh. By some miracle of God, National Posters got me another roof and we did a counter-to-counter delivery for the next morning. It was set up on time. I had great partners. And I also had Patrick on my side even harder.

Historically for me and little S.I., March was slow. Not this year. We didn't really have any huge jobs, but I sent out 49 invoices, breaking my record by far. I guess this might be a good spot for an update on my bookkeeping. Marisa, my original bookkeeper, was awesome. But she was a wife, and a mom, and had a young family with a lot going on. She left her private business to take a job with the county to give her time and schedule more stability. She left me in the good hands of a very nice lady named Peggy, who'd worked for Marisa before the move to the county. Peggy picked up everything seamlessly, and everything went great for about a year. Then Peggy decided to retire. Peggy left me in the hands of a very nice lady named Marilyn. We were still doing everything the exact same way. She would retrieve all my paperwork and the "accounting laptop" once a month, keep it for a week for data entry, and return it. I still handled all invoicing. An additional thing Marilyn started doing was printing out accounts receivable reports, which were becoming pretty substantial, so I could better stay on top of it all.

That month, I started getting regular work from Kawasaki. Plus, besides all the usual stuff from Corona, Big League Dreams, LVAC, etc., we also got good-sized jobs from Oklahoma City Thunder of the NBA, Extreme Thing music festival, and a 40-by-20-foot fabric stage backdrop for rapper Wiz Khalifa. Then we got a job that couldn't have had better timing – forty light pole banners plus hardware for Mountain View Hospital. Print and install. As soon as we finished that job, I sent pictures of the install over to Pat from

R&R to remind him that we were the local light pole banners experts.

In April we landed ten jobs from Corona beer, including a Pacifico bus wrap in Florida. We'd been working all over the country for the last decade, and I'd developed a pretty extensive network of installation partners. Something I was working toward was getting my little company 3M Certified. We also got another job for the six exterior banners for LVAC, which was becoming a great account. Then I pulled another new client out of my hat with my networking/cold call skills: the Oklahoma City Barons, a minor league hockey team. Their stadium was across the street from the NBA arena. I had been working on all these accounts with Brooke from Walker Companies. She was definitely one of my favorites.

In May I was called by John from the Pitt Panthers (NCAA). I had sent him pictures of the tower banners we did for the Redskins, so he sent two massive mesh exterior banners to go on the side of Heinz Field. I also landed a sizable wall mural at Qualcomm Stadium for the San Diego Chargers, coming from my old softball buddy Brian who was doing some sales for S.I. on the side. A year of cold calls to a big company that supported beverages in casinos and events, Back Bar, finally paid off, and we finished the month with two more festivals, Brambleton, and of course Punk Rock Bowling.

* * *

By this time Scout was six and a half years old. She was my A-1 and my partner in everything. A couple of friends had Labradors that had lived to be ten and a half, and I was terrified of that day coming. I was so busy with local work that I spent a lot of time on job sites, measuring, and having meet-and-greets, and I hated leaving her home. I was feeling she needed a buddy for when I was away, so one day at the end of May we went down and looked at the Henderson Animal Shelter. I really was just looking, and Scout was outside in the truck in the parking lot waiting. As I walked down the row of cages there were a bunch of beautiful pups wagging tails and jumping up to greet me. When I got down to the end, there was a dirty little black pup laying in the back of the very last cage, shaking and looking up at me. I got down on one knee and held out my hand, and she crawled (literally) to the front of the cage. I put my hand inside and started petting her on the head, and she started crying. Just lying there, crying, looking up at me with these beautiful dark eyes. I went back up front and said I had interest in the black pup in the last cage, and the response from the girl at the desk was, "Really? We thought she was unadoptable." Not anymore, I said. We arranged to have her brought into a room to meet us, and I went outside to bring Scout in with me for the meet. When they opened the door, this little black pup crawled in on her belly and immediately went to Scout and laid down next to her. After the attendant left the room and closed the door, I called her over to me and she crawled over and laid her head up on my lap and started crying again. I said, "That's it, you're coming home with us." I went up front and informed the lady there that we would adopt her. It took a few days as they had to get her spayed and do a house and yard check on our home. On June 1, we brought her home to Rancho Ridge. She was six months old, and we named her Ranger.

* * *

In June, I finally got the call. We were awarded the light pole banners job by Pat at R&R Partners. Between printing 1,150-plus banners and providing the hardware, installation, and maintenance, it was a $300,000-plus job. We would be switching out banners on the Strip for 20 events per year, so I had to rent a storage unit for all the banners. And I bought that bucket truck I had been eyeing. It was a 2001 Freightliner with a 40-foot working height. It was my biggest business purchase to date, and it was hilarious when they dropped it off in front of my house. My neighbors were all, "What the hell?" Haha. This job would be a game changer for not-so-little-anymore S.I.

The Chargers were stoked with the wall mural we did, so they sent us a *ton* more work in July. We had 10 concession stands, a handful of exterior columns, and a massive wall wrap for Bud Light, their beer partner. Much of this work was from the stadium's concession company, Centerplate, and that was duly noted for my future sales efforts. We also got five more tower banners from the Redskins, who were thrilled with the new tower frames we'd built the previous season. Also got a stage backdrop job from another rapper, Big K.R.I.T. I guess that Suge Knight connection I made in Hollywood in '99 was still paying off.

* * *

I started August looking at printing equipment and for a building. That pipe dream was super close to becoming reality. I'd learned over the previous 10 years that you had to make yourself really uncomfortable to move forward, and I was about to do that big-time. My best friend Chris owned a commercial building over by Sam Boyd Stadium and he had a tenant not paying their rent. It was about 3,000 square feet. I went and looked. It was kind of close to my house, but pretty far away from the Strip.

August was another good month workwise. We were called again by Baylor University, this time for football, and we printed and installed a massive 78-by-21-foot banner on the backside of the football stadium's scoreboard. I started cold-calling hard on concession companies for stadiums, which led me to a small job with the Oklahoma Sooners (NCAA), which led me to an introduction to their creative director, Scott, which led to a job with 29 wall wraps for the Sooners. I shit you not, it was that easy when you put in the effort.

In early September we landed a big job doing two huge exterior banners for the OKC Barons hockey team. I had sent them pictures of banners we did for Pitt and the Redskins, and Brooke and I got the job. I sent my trusty contractor from Washington, D.C., Craig Hudrock, to handle this install. I also got another rapper backdrop, Kushed God.

* * *

On Sept. 13th, I took the call I'd hoped to never get. My beautiful grandma had passed away in her sleep. She was 91 years old, and for the last few years lived in an assisted senior community that she didn't love. She was able to maintain her little house on Mead Way in Hayes, Bromley until her late 80s. She was always on the go – down to the market, down to the high street, down to see friends. I'd never had a closer relationship with any human. She meant the whole world to me, and I was crushed. My uncles had a very small service for her pretty quickly, and I couldn't break away to go to London because it was happening really fast and I was buried with work. On our Sunday calls, after she asked about Scout, she always asked this question next: "Do you have plenty of work?" I know that she, like Mom, would just want me to keep working. She was my other biggest supporter besides Mom. She taught me so much about how to be a good person. I don't think she ever even noticed my tattoos, bleached spiky hair, or the way I dressed. She just loved me for me. She was an amazing woman. I was determined to make her proud with my new shop.

* * *

In October I came to an agreement with my friend Chris to take over the lease for his commercial warehouse at 6504 Boulder Ranch Road, Unit B. My rent would be $3,900 a month. More than double my mortgage. The tenants he had there before had trashed the place, so he installed new carpets and painted the walls in the office area. I told him not to worry about the warehouse area, because I had special plans. I was going to take a combination of inspirations from the advertising agencies in L.A., Zappos, playgrounds, skateboard parks from where I grew up, and punk rock, and turn that warehouse into the raddest print shop Las Vegas had ever seen.

October and November were super steady with all the regular work which by this time was pretty consistent. In the beginning of December I took over the space on Boulder Ranch and started mapping out plans for the décor and setting up the equipment in the warehouse. I connected with a company called Montroy and bought a 64-inch HP latex printer, a SEAL laminator, a welder, grommet machine, and a bunch of other tools and racks I'd need to get started. I bought four brand new highest-end iMac Pros, desks for the front offices, chairs, carpets – basically spent my life savings. I was doing this.

Cheers to the risk takers.

* * *

It was 2012, and my life was really good at this point. I was still working at home, and my overhead was still low. I had my mortgage, a truck payment, and a boat payment, and my only other responsibilities were Scout and Ranger.

Scout was a godsend. She was 6½ at this point and was in her prime. She was a beautiful, sweet, smart, loyal, and loving companion. I loved her more than I loved life itself. She was the best boat dog in the history of the world. She would literally show first-timers on the boat where they should sit, and sit them down when they stood up while we were underway – such a pro. People would trip out on her. She was running and diving off the front of our boat and putting on a show all day. I was so proud to be her Poppy.

Ranger was doing well, also. She was finally coming out of her shell. She always went on the boat, but wasn't a natural like Scout, as she wasn't a Labrador (she was a retriever mix). But she was having fun. And she *loved* Scout.

I loved my house, my neighborhood, my neighbors. I had friends from SoCal visiting for weekends all the time, had a big party at my house for almost every UFC fight, and even had my uncle Paul, auntie Jan, and cousin Alice come out from England for two weeks. Scout and I took friends to the lake almost every Saturday on our boat in the summer. Life was really good.

I had business ideas and marketing plans running through my head at all times. I was having great success with my sales and was able to get into almost anywhere I wanted. S.I. was gaining a great reputation for customer service and quality, and I was riding that wave for all it was worth. I was building my first shop, set to open at the beginning of 2013, and the future was bright.

I did notice, however, that I was a total recluse during the week and on Sundays. All I did during the week was go to the gym, work, and read for a bit at night. On Sundays, I turned my phone off and slept all day because I was so frickin' tired, and wanted to start the week fresh, before just wearing myself down again. It was a lot. And it was starting to affect some of my personal relationships.

I just figured it was the price to pay as a business owner, and I carried on. I'd been self-employed at this point for over 10 years. But I was ready to tackle the next phase of S.I. Where it would take me, personal life included, remained a mystery. But I was super excited to get on with it.

Carolina Panthers Pads at Practice facilty — built in my garage

NBA Finals Banners San Antonio 2007

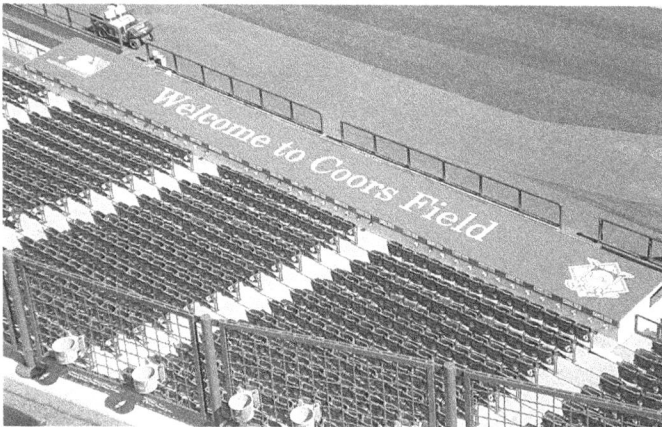
Colorado Rockies Dugout — banners attached with Velcro

Exterior Mesh Banners at Old Cowboys Stadium

Bucket Truck delivered to my house in Henderson

Washington Redskins - Tower Banners

CHAPTER 9
FIRST SHOP / 6504 BOULDER RANCH AVE.

"Give Me Fire"

- *GBH*

I knew it would be a drastic change to open a shop. I was going from working at home and vending everything out for the last 9 years to being responsible for producing about half of it myself. This was besides the fact that I was now going to have to commute and be in an office every day. The shop was only about a 15-minute drive from my house, but still... I had at least three people say I shouldn't open a shop, that I should just keep it simple like I had it. One was my old boss from Imagic in Hollywood, Tom; one was my friend Michele, from 3M; and one was my old boss, John. They used terms like "becoming a manufacturer," "learning curve," and "can of worms." I heard them, but I was determined, and for several reasons. No. 1, I was finally starting to get a lot of traction with local accounts, and didn't want to keep eating freight costs of shipping stuff from Chattanooga and Denver to Vegas. No. 2, profit margins. I was doing pretty well how I'd been doing it, but there was more profit doing it myself. No. 3, I didn't feel I could sell the company (my plan) without a shop or equipment, no matter how good my clients list was (and by this point it was already pretty good).

I'll tell you who was loving it: Scout and Ranger. Get to go on a truck ride every morning first thing? Yes, please. New place with people there other than Poppy? Yes, please. New smells and sounds? Yes, please. Not having to watch Poppy sit in his office all day at home? Yes, please. They were all-in.

They were of course restricted to the office area only – we had to keep the production warehouse free of dog hair. But they were okay with it. Such good girls. When I went into the shop, I always left the door open, and they just laid right there in the opening between the office and the warehouse watching us. Ranger was only 1 year old then, but she just followed her sister's lead. Scout was already 7, and a very good girl.

* * *

One big regret I had was that my grandma never got to see the shop. She'd been my co-biggest-supporter for years. Her and Mom knew better than anyone all the things I'd been through. They believed in me when no one else did. Those first few weeks in the shop, when I was alone there in the morning, I could sense her presence. She *did* know.

* * *

Once everything was set up, the grand opening party done, and it was time to start my new routine/life, I decided a 7 a.m. arrival to the shop would be appropriate. It meant I'd have to get up a half-hour earlier to accommodate the gym and all that, but all good. After the first week I realized it wouldn't work, and quickly adjusted to a 6 a.m. arrival. Besides writing the work orders and project managing, I was now also doing prepress, ripping the files, and running the presses. And doing the finishing. And we were busy. Oh shit.

This was all the last week of January, as the grand opening party was on the 19th (and a hell of a party it was), so let's back up a bit here.

I got the keys to the shop the first week of November. The front office still needed fixing by Chris, but he didn't really need to do anything in the warehouse/production area, because I had big plans for it. I was going to turn it into the most creative print shop in Vegas by building a punk rock, urban playground, spray-painted and plastered-up Man's Land. I would take a little bit of inspiration from the punk rock clubs, L.A. graffiti, the advertising agencies of Los Angeles in the '80s, '90s décor, the style of Zappos' corporate offices, and the neighborhoods and playgrounds I grew up in. It was going to be super fun.

My next-door neighbor was a handyman kind of guy who could build just about anything, and I'd been filling him in on my creative plans. One

Saturday evening in mid-November, we headed over to the empty warehouse with a couple of lawn chairs, a radio, and a 12-pack, and I laid it all out to him. I wanted corrugated metal sheets to separate all the areas in the shop – press room, prepress, finishing, storage, bar, etc. – and it all would be spray-painted with punk rock bands, graffiti, slogans, motivational messages, and other cool stuff. My installer Chris was an old punk rock tagger and was super stoked to help with the rattle can spray-paint work. We talked about stands for the corrugated sheets and decided to do some tests. We couldn't get any of the stands to hold the sheets up stable, and we determined we would have to frame the areas out and attach the sheets to the frames. Might as well powder-coat it all blue too, to match the Screaming Images logo colors.

What gave me the confidence to open this shop at this point: I'd been in business for nine-plus years; had built a pretty awesome clients list (including the new/local accounts); knew how to do prepress and run presses myself from back in my Jordan Horn/Techtron days in downtown L.A.; and by now had a ton of experience with the materials and with installations thanks to all my work with Big League Dreams, the NBA, the Redskins, the Panthers, and the Steelers. I'd also had really good years in 2011 and 2012 and banked enough cash to fund it all myself without any help – including the printer, laminator, and all ancillary equipment. This included spanking new top-of-the-line Macintosh desktop computers for prepress, my office up front, and the office that would be Matt's. Plus, all the expenses for the shop's décor. Much like when I uprooted from Southern California and moved to Nevada, I was taking a massive risk, spending my life's savings. I absolutely had to succeed. There was no other alternative. Scout, Ranger, and I would be homeless otherwise.

I had measured out and taped off the floor where all the dividers would go and gave my neighbor free reign to buy whatever materials we needed from the metal supply store. He spent mornings at the shop building frames before he went to his regular paying job. It took about 10 days or so to get the frames built, and then to hang the corrugated sheets. Then I was able to unleash Chris and the rattle can.

The biggest wall was what separated the press room from the rest of the warehouse, and that was designated the "punk rock wall" where Chris spray-painted the names of bands like Social Distortion, T.S.O.L., Ill Repute, Descendents, Wasted Youth, and of course, Black Flag. For the bar area – yes, we had a bar, and yes, I copied Imagic from my Hollywood days – we called it the "Corona Bar." Chris sprayed-painted accordingly, and we finished it off with Corona beach scene banners.

We covered every inch of the shop walls with banners of current clients and jobs – Kawasaki, Redskins, Carolina Panthers, Mayweather, Baylor Bears, NBA All-Star, Pitt Panthers – just to name a few. The cost came out of my pocket, though, as the little 64-inch printer I bought wasn't big enough to print them. I had my own shop's banners done in Denver and shipped, rather ironically.

Another of my ideas that worked really well was having six 4-by-8-foot chain-link fence panels built, with bases. We designed and fit a cool creative/banner on each one and used them as portable walls. We could fence off sections of the shop, create temporary walls, hide things we didn't want visitors to see – and I could also use them as trade show booth walls when I exhibited.

We built frames and set corrugated sheets in the front office to build out two offices – mine and Matt's. Chris rattle-can tagged those two walls with "Screaming" on one side and "Images" on the other, Hollywood graffiti-style. They looked killer.

Regarding Matt: I was introduced through an Orange County friend, and he came aboard a month or so before I opened the shop to do sales and business development. He was a super cool guy, and handy as well, and helped with the shop's build-out. He also learned to run the printer, and between the two of us we figured out the laminator, welder, grommet machine, and how to make hems on the banners using banner tape. It definitely was a learning process, and I couldn't have done it without him.

The only thing left, before the new shop was 100% rolling, was to throw a grand-opening party. I got the Vegascendents (Descendents cover band) to play, and Larsen's Steakhouse (business neighbor) to cater, while Corona donated a ton of beer. I arranged for an equipment demonstration for all my business associates, potential new customers, and friends, and pointed mini spotlights at all the graffiti. I made a playlist of old '80s new wave songs, and I designed invitations and sent them to everyone I could think of, including the local newspapers, the chamber of commerce, and even the mayors of Las Vegas and Henderson. The guy from Las Vegas Business Press came, the woman who ran the chamber showed up, and both mayors sent representatives.

The party was a great time and went way into the wee hours. We had a packed house, and the Vegascendents totally jammed. And, oh yeah, I might have jumped up there and sang a song or two with the band.

Now it was time to get to work. Thankfully January wasn't crazy-busy, and we could finally set up and get the shindigs out of the way. The main equipment pieces I purchased were a 64-inch HP 26-500 printer, and a Seal 62 Base 61-inch laminator with heat assist. For ripping the files to press I got ONYX rip software, for which we had to use a PC computer (boo!). The last two weeks of January were a good learning period for this equipment, while we pumped out live jobs for LVAC, Corona, and Mojo Sports.

Something surprising was how much material rolls cost. I knew the numbers, as in how much per square foot and stuff – knowledge I needed to calculate what to charge customers. However, I'd never put it together with buying full rolls. I had purchased my equipment from Montroy, and decided my best bet was to start a relationship with them by also using them for materials. Jamie the general manager was awesome, and she gave us a lot of support in those early days. On the first material order I just ordered a roll of everything: 3M PSV and laminates (two or three different kinds), window perf, vinyl and mesh banner, and some ½-inch 4-by-8-foot sheets of Gator Board. Jamie delivered them personally and gave me the invoice and I shit my pants. So, figure a 54-inch by 150-foot roll of material is 675 square feet – and that all adds up very quickly. But all good, it provided motivation to make the most of every roll. It's super easy to waste a lot of that 675 square feet if you do it incorrectly. Also making a huge difference was knowledge of what materials to use in which situations: indoor or outdoor, short or long-term, smooth or rough wall, etc. Some of those 3M materials only cost 25% of what the highest-end car wrap stuff cost, and a lot of people didn't know that. Creating programs to cause less waste and using the correct materials boosts your profit margins and also allows you to be more competitive with pricing to win work.

The plan for production, now that we had the equipment, was pretty simple. We would print everything we possibly could in-house, then source the rest out to Chattanooga or Denver. All wall wraps would be printed at the shop, and also all banners under 64 inches in the shortest dimension. For all rigid boards – Ultra Board, Coroplast, acrylics, Dibond – we would print pressure-sensitive vinyl in-house and then wrap the boards. Off we went.

February came in hot, and I got my first taste of being a manufacturer. We were working on the NBA All-Star Game, which was in Houston; that alone kept us busy. Then that little free poster board I did for Heather from the PAC-12 in 2011 paid off, when she began sending artwork for their first-ever men's basketball tourney at MGM Grand. We also had a big job in Oakland wrapping walls for Anheuser-Busch at the A's stadium. All this was in-house production. My 7 a.m. starts had gone at first to 6 a.m., which changed to 5 a.m. Matt couldn't keep helping me with production, as he needed to get going on business development. We needed to get help.

There was a design school in Vegas that kept hitting me up to send interns to our shop. I guess part of the checklist before students graduated was performing 100 hours of internship doing graphic design. The first kid they sent was Adam, and I loved him right away. I threw him right into the fire, and he was immediately designing and doing prepress for jobs from

Anheuser-Busch and the Angels baseball team (which we had won back, partially). He did a killer job and seemed like he was having fun. At the end of his 100 hours, I hired him full-time on an hourly rate, which was a really big deal for me, causing much stress! My first hourly employee. He worked with us through the summer, and then left to move to California to be closer to his family. He had done a great job and would be missed.

Another guy was graduating from the school, and he really wanted his internship at S.I. He was relentless sending emails and calling the shop. He'd found us on our Facebook Business page, and loved all the stuff we were doing, since he was both a big music and big sports guy. Finally, one day he just showed up at the shop and said, "Are you going to hire me or what?" And I had to say yes. We had our second intern.

Lee fit in right away. Besides doing prepress and design, he also wanted to learn how to run the press and the rip, which impressed me. He was also helping a bit in finishing. One thing that always sticks in my mind about Lee: he'd arrive at 7 a.m., and as he was walking in the door through the warehouse, he always looked at what was on the tables, inspected job tickets, saw what was on the plate production-wise for the morning. He would then walk to his work area, turn everything on, and get right to work. No fucking off, no loitering around, no outside drinking coffee and smoking cigarettes – right to work. This might sound pretty normal to some, but believe me, in my experience up to then (and especially after) it was outside the norm. As soon as his intern hours were up, I hired him permanently.

Another thing needed in those early shop days was creating a job ticket template, creating a system for tracking jobs, and figuring out how to move the tickets through the shop. I used an old job ticket from National in Chattanooga and revised it, and bought a bunch of clear job ticket jackets, borrowing from how they did it. We put little plastic job ticket baskets in prepress, at the printer, in finishing, in shipping over by the back door, and in the front office for completed jobs so I could invoice them. I'd create the job ticket, put it in a jacket, and drop it in prepress. The job jacket would then follow the job through the shop, then back to me when done so I could invoice. We tracked everything (including job numbers) through Excel spreadsheets. Pretty simple.

March brought bombardment. We had 57 jobs, and about three-quarters were in-house prints. We had stuff for the NBA All-Star Game in Houston, Angels Baseball, a huge 70-by-14-foot Corona banner at Wahoo's, 20,000 square feet of exterior/rough surface wall wraps for "Corona Beach" at the Monte Carlo (hotel & casino, now called Park MGM), Extreme Thing music festival, two 60-by-30-foot exterior mesh banners for Pitt Panthers, stage backdrops for the Black Angels and Middle Class Rut, 16 stadium jobs for Mojo Sports, and biggest of all – PAC-12. Something to remember here, there was additional time/work in the outsourced jobs now that we had a shop and a new workflow system. It wasn't as quick and easy as the days working at home.

The PAC-12 job was huge. I mentioned earlier how hard Heather fought to get us into MGM. Dennis (mentioned earlier as well) told her in a meeting, right in front of me, that she had to use his vendor. She said no way and put her foot down. No James, no graphics for the tourney. Dennis eventually relented, and away we went. The biggest piece, and first to go up, was called a "diamond wall," and these will come up a bunch more in this book. They were basically big-ass exterior building wraps, 50 by 35 feet or so; there were eight outside MGM on Tropicana and Las Vegas boulevards. Heather sent me the artwork, we placed it on the template provided to us and went into proofing and production.

These diamond walls were about 2,100 square feet. That means three-plus rolls of vinyl and three-plus rolls of laminate. That little 64-inch HP printer wasn't really made for this type of production, but that's how we did it. It took us three full days to print that thing. We were laminating as we were going. We had some help from a guy named Keith who I knew from my neighborhood, and another guy I hired to work in the shop who was the husband of a girl who'd been my roommate for a bit while she finished college. We could have installed it, too, but I felt I'd pushed Dennis hard enough with just getting in. We would end up installing everything but the diamond wall. I took the panels down and personally delivered them to the company installing it, which as it turns out was also the company we had displaced on the printing – MGM's current vendor. They were scheduled to put it up the next day. About 20 minutes into the install, they called Dennis and said it was printed wrong. Bullshit. We'd done extensive quality control, and it matched the template provided to a quarter inch. Dennis called Heather, then she called me, and I told her we matched the template. I offered to send my guy there with a cloth tape to confirm dimensions – and magically the other vendor said, "*OOPS*, we sent the wrong template." Yeah. Nice try.

So, we printed a few extra panels so it fit right, they put them up, and we were golden. Turns out there were two different-sized diamond walls. This was a dirty trick by the installers, which other vendors would try to pull on me many times in the future as I displaced them – supplying wrong dimensions. What I did in response was rent a lift, measure every single diamond wall, create to-scale templates for each, turn them over to MGM for no charge, and guaranteed their accuracy. The templates were MGM's to keep, with no obligation to go with us. But guess what happened? I ended up taking over the diamond walls almost immediately afterwards, and controlled them for almost 10 years, until after the sale of S.I.

Here's the reason I did it: take care of your folks. Get them to use you because they want to, not because they have to. MGM trusted me after that.

For the PAC-12, we did stuff all over the casino. It was a huge job. We did stuff in the lobbies, the casino, the restaurants, at the retail stores, the valet, on the gaming equipment and on the court. Print and install. I was a constant presence on site delivering stuff, helping Chris and the installers, measuring add-ons. Dennis was around and saw me every single day. Around the third or fourth day he approached and was being nice, and asked, "Are you local?" Yes, I am. "Do you have a shop?" Yes, I do. Then, he said, "Come talk to me after the tournament is done." Yessir.

My first impression of Dennis was super formal, suit-wearing, stuffy, executive type. But when we shook hands before he walked away that day, I noticed he had a full arm sleeve of tattoos under his fancy suit sports coat. We were gonna get along just fine. And he'd end up being my biggest advocate in Las Vegas. It was also a reminder to never judge a book by its cover.

The PAC-12 job went off without a hitch. Matt and I mastered the new equipment pretty quickly, and Lee also helped a ton to get everything produced. Chris and his team did a great job on the installation and strike (post-event tear-down), and Heather was super stoked.

* * *

The hot streak continued into April, with 49 jobs. Keep in mind here, besides all the production work, we also had to generate job tickets, keep the workflow systems updated, coordinate installations, invoice all the jobs, and collect the money. It was a lot. I was now getting up at 3 a.m., working for an hour at home then going to the gym and getting to the shop at 6 a.m., leaving the shop at 4 p.m. and going home and working at least another hour.

The two biggest jobs volume-wise were from Corona. Terrible's Casino on Paradise was rebranding to Silver Sevens, and Corona would sponsor the sportsbook, so we wrapped just about an entire wing of the casino with Corona's "Find Your Beach" imagery.

I asked Cathy for an intro to the GM of the property figuring there would be a lot more rebranding work, and she introduced me to David, who then introduced me to Estelle from Affinity Gaming. We ended up doing the entire interior, exterior, and all of their shuttles. Bango.

Also in April we did stage backdrops for Chevy Woods (another rapper) and Alkaline Trio. More work came in from Baylor University Athletics, and OKC Thunder basketball. We got a 53-foot trailer wrap in Washington, D.C., from Comcast; we did (for the first time) light pole banners for the City of Henderson; and then my favorite, Red Rock Harley-Davidson.

I bought my first Harley in 2011, fulfilling another lifelong dream. Vegas had three Harley dealerships, and I'd been hitting them very hard with cold calls. Finally, I got a positive response from the Red Rock dealership, who asked me to visit to show me something. I knew what it would be.

They had six huge exterior wraps above the main entrance that were in super bad disrepair. Cracking, faded; just looked horrible. That's what he wanted to show me. I knew from experience that those murals would be a bitch to peel, and it would need painting after removal. He also wanted the same artwork, but didn't have the art files.

So, that bucket truck I had bought a couple years back was coming in super handy. I sent Chris out for the peel and repaint, and he did a killer job as always. The art was another story. I came up with an outside-the-box idea, unsure it would even work. I had Chris send me up in the bucket truck to directly in front of each mural. With a digital camera, I took high-resolution photos of all six and went back to the shop to download the files. Once the files downloaded, Lee and I checked them for resolution, and determined they'd work. The only problem was the fading and all of the cracks. Lee and I took three each and started retouching them in Photoshop. Super tedious work! I told Fred from Red Rock how we were doing it, and he was skeptical…

It took Lee and I about a week to fix those files up, in between all the other work we had, but I was happy with the end result. We crafted some PDF proofs for approval and printed off some 100% sample swatches, and I ran them to Fred. He couldn't believe we had pulled it off. He signed off, we printed and installed them, and Fred was super stoked.

To back up just a bit here, when Chris was doing the peels, I got a good-sized chunk of the old vinyl to evaluate. Based on the color of the back of the film, and the thickness, I could tell whoever did it first hadn't used the right material. Based on my back experience of being in business for 11 years at this point, and in the printing industry for 26 years, I knew exactly what kind of base film and laminate to use to make this job successful. Red Rock

Harley wouldn't have this problem again. I also turned over the artwork files we had doctored as a show of confidence. They didn't have to use me again. What did I get out of that? The other two Harley-Davidson dealerships.

* * *

We stayed busy into May with jobs from all the usual folks. We did our sponsorship with Punk Rock Bowling for the third year and printed all their banners. We also did a festival in Maryland called "Death Fest." I was also emailed by Dennis at MGM. He would give me our first opportunity to work directly for them – a construction wall wrap. I was bidding against their current vendor. I did have experience with construction walls and was banking on my knowledge of materials to win the bid. Construction walls were temporary, and came down, graphics and all, when the job was done, and I knew the most cost-effective material for it. I ended up being right and won the job easily. It was a wrap for UFC 162 featuring a belt fight between the middleweight champ Anderson Silva and Chris Weidman. I was double-super stoked on this one because not only was I getting my first job for MGM direct, but I was also a huge, massive fan of UFC. We smashed it out of the park, Chris installing, then had our first UFC fight party at the shop. I usually had parties at my house for UFC, but then I figured out the cost of pay-per-view was the same at the shop – and it'd be much more fun. Plus, I could invite clients and get them in to see the shop. And get more work. Punk rock marketing.

Dennis was so happy with the UFC wall wrap that he introduced me to one of his counterparts over at Mandalay Bay, and in that same week we got a job from him printing four huge mesh banners for a tower by the pool.

Also in May, I saw an article in the local newspaper *Las Vegas Review Journal* which reported a group was working to renovate the historic Huntridge Theater. This struck a chord with me, as in the 80s it was a pretty legendary punk rock venue. My friends and I *always* talked about heading to Vegas to hit a show there, but it never came around. I wanted to be involved with this renovation for sure.

At this point in my career, I was having some pretty good success and was getting a lot of support locally with work and regular accounts. I'm a big believer in karma and wanted to start paying it forward. I did some research and found the folks in charge and told them I owned a local printing company and wanted to get involved. They said they were looking for a few big banners for the exterior of the theater, and I said, "Done." They asked what I wanted, and I said nothing. They asked how much, and I said, simply, "Donated."

On the day the banners were installed I rode my Harley down there to get some pictures. I met one of the main organizers and asked if I could go inside and check it out. He walked me in, and I went directly over to the room where the main stage was. I got goosebumps. I could totally feel the vibe. It reminded me of the old Olympic Auditorium in downtown L.A., main home of my punk rock youth. Punk rock had gotten me to where I was in life personally and professionally, and I was determined to pay it back.

We had 125 jobs between June and July. We did work for Carolina Panthers, San Diego Chargers, Washington Redskins, Warped Tour, City of Henderson, Mandalay Bay, MGM Grand, the Ohio Valley Conference, and rapper Slim Thug, to name a few.

As crazy-busy as we were consistently, the bookkeeping was getting super heavy.

Sometime in March, Marisa called, wanting to come back. Marilyn had done a great job, but I really loved Marisa and agreed to bring her back. Informing Marilyn of this decision was super hard and brought me to tears.

Collections were also getting backed up, and I hadn't really had time to stay on top of it.

We were a snowball racing downhill, becoming bigger and bigger. It was insane.

* * *

Back in May I had done some pretty heavy cold-calling in the collegiate sports market. I was sending everyone pictures of work we did for Baylor University and University of Pittsburgh athletics with hopes of getting some traction. In June, I received an email response from the University of Colorado in Boulder inviting me to visit for a mandatory meeting for the RFP they were arranging for a new signage vendor. I signed up.

Busy as I was, I decided to travel there the morning of the meeting. The meeting wasn't until noon, and the first flight out got me to Denver by 9:15 a.m., with a one-hour drive to Boulder. I figured I was good. I secured my rental car and arrived with 45 minutes before the meeting's start time. Coors Event Center had some construction underway, so it took me some time to find a parking spot. By the time I got in the building, I had 15 minutes until the meeting began. Well, I got lost and couldn't find the meeting. After walking around a bit, I found a nice girl named Marge over in the basketball office and asked for help pointing me in the right direction. By the time I found the room I was five minutes late. I wasn't sure what to expect, but I walked into a packed room. There were at least 20 other vendors there, most of them in suits and ties. I sported jeans, a T-shirt, and Converse sneakers. I also had arms sleeved with tattoos and jet-black dyed hair. All eyes were on me, walking in late. Whoops.

The meeting went well, and I could tell a lot of the vendors had no clue what they were talking about. We were all told we'd be receiving the RFP package the next week, and that the university's intention was to move fast on awarding. Once I got it the next week, I could tell it was totally out-dated in terms of the materials they were asking for and how it was laid out. I immediately emailed the main contact, Tim, and asked if he wanted some help updating. He said just fill it out as it was, and I'd get the opportunity to explain everything later in the process. Cool.

About a week later I got an email saying that I made the first cut, and it was down to six finalists. They sent a form with some additional questions, which I filled out and sent back immediately. Three or four days after that, I got another email saying I had made the final two and asking if I could visit the next week for one last meeting. Yessir, I could.

The next week I showed up, and was told the other finalist was also there, and that there would be separate interviews, and then an interview together. The CU athletic staff had formed a committee for these two meetings. The other finalist was from a company based out of Arizona that I guess had a local sales office. It was a younger woman, *super* good looking. I didn't remember her from the pre-bid meeting. We did the separate interviews first, and then we were put together in a room with the committee, her and I sitting in chairs facing them. Kind of like a game show. They started asking questions, mainly about materials, of which by this point I was an absolute expert. Advantage, me. That poor girl didn't have a chance; I buried her.

I heard back the next week that I was awarded a four-year, $500,000 contract with University of Colorado Athletics. This started a decade-long relationship, with two contract extensions. I grew to know just about everyone on campus and felt completely at home every time I went there. They became my staunchest supporters. Not bad for a tattooed guy from Vegas.

* * *

More cold call-work came through in August when we picked up jobs from Summerlin, Desert Springs, Centennial, and Spring Valley hospitals. We now had seven local hospitals as clients, and it was a lot of work. Most people don't realize, but hospitals are big business. They have full marketing departments, brand guidelines, big budgets, etc. Notice all the billboards on the highways.

More work also came from the baseball stadium in Oakland, the county fair in Maryland, a big job from Lingerie Football League, and then a really big one: our first exterior windows wrap at MGM. It was for the Mayweather vs. Canelo fight.

We ended up doing a ton of work for this Floyd Mayweather fight, starting a relationship that would last almost 10 years. The coolest part was Mayweather's team asked us to build an exhibit in the MGM Grand main lobby to display his fight outfits from his entire history of fights. To do this, we had to go to his house in Las Vegas to get them. I had some major history riding with me in my truck back to our little shop after we left his house. And we had another major fight party at the shop for this one – again a huge success. I picked up new clients every time we hosted fight parties.

As you may imagine, my personal life was starting to become a struggle. During the week I did absolutely nothing except go to work and gym. It was lucky if I had an hour a night to read before I went to bed at 8 p.m. I was still getting out on the lake every once in a while, on a Saturday, and that was all for Scout.

＊

In September the work started pouring in from the Colorado Buffaloes. We did jobs for golf, soccer, basketball, volleyball, and the film room. We got another huge exterior window wrap from Southern Hills hospital, and a nice 40-by-20-foot fabric stage backdrop for rapper Mac Miller.

October arrived, and we picked up another new beverage client, Dos Equis beer. City of Henderson led me into Clark County, and we did a big stage backdrop for Dutch Dinero. I also picked up another new client I'd been working on for a long time – Central Christian Church. Their parking lot backed right up to the street behind our shop, and I drove by their main building every day. I kept noticing they had a really torn up banner mounted on a wall right in front of their church entrance, so I walked in their door one day and offered to donate a replacement. They asked what I wanted in return, and I said nothing. We put the banner up, and two weeks later they called, gave me a huge, paying job – and we started a relationship that would last through the sale of my company.

November and December stayed steady, with a ton more work from MGM, Colorado Buffaloes, Central Christian Church, and Corona. We won an RFP to do a huge job at Anheuser-Busch's brewery in Fairfield, Calif., and wrapped five shuttles for Long Beach State University. Oklahoma Sooners called back for a bunch of wall wraps for their wrestling team, and we were notified by 3M that we were approved as a 3M certified installer. Our first print job from 3M came along with that news.

We also landed our highest-profile job to date the last month of 2013. We were awarded one of the huge building wraps on the exterior of MGM Grand. It was for KA, the Cirque du Soleil show. These wraps were 322 x 45 feet. Once I entered the bidding for this, it was kind of weird how it progressed. There were three other companies bidding, but we and all the other companies used the same printer and installer (I did not have the equipment yet to print these on my own, nor the swing stages required for installation). So, what it came down to, basically, was who marked it up the least. And that was me. I would go on to control all MGM building wraps from this one through the sale of S.I. and eventually put up over one million square feet of building wraps in Las Vegas.

All told, 2013 was a crazy year. I pulled it off. I opened my own shop. We did $1.3 million in business that year.

* * *

As 2014 began I had one big thing on my mind: I needed another printer. Staff-wise we were okay. We were working hard but handling it. There were four of us at this point. We were ready for another big year.

We carried right on in January. We had about 20 big customers consistently giving us work, and we came through for them every time. They weren't even putting these jobs out to bid anymore – that's how much they trusted us. I always answered my phone, I responded to emails promptly, the jobs were always finished (and either installed or delivered) on time, were always highest quality, and all at fair market pricing. I consistently posted pictures of our work on our Facebook Business page, and on my personal page. We were making a name for ourselves not just locally, but nationally. And we were running the shit out of our equipment.

Another thing I was having a lot of fun with was the punk rock reputation we were getting at the shop. I'd been in a lot of printing facilities, and nothing compared with what we were doing. Thanks to social media and word-of-mouth, we would get a lot of requests from people to visit the shop. A lot of vendors that wanted to sell us material and equipment, a lot of customers who wanted to see our capabilities, and a lot of people just curious to see it – including the editor from the *Las Vegas Business Press*. They all were greeted with tons of love at the front door by Scout and Ranger, which they loved. And as soon as they walked in, they were met by loud punk rock music blasting from the Sonos sound system speakers located all over the shop. We were definitely making an impression.

I was also making the most of my newfound reputation as the underdog. All my competitors were underestimating me because of my appearance and manner, and I was taking full advantage. This was something I learned from my L.A./Hollywood punk rock days. Never judge a book by its cover.

We had a great first quarter in 2014. I don't want to keep repeating the same old folks giving us work, but we did get another of those huge building wraps from MGM, this time for Hakkasan nightclub. Some of the new customers we picked up that quarter were: Rugby Sevens (who would remain a customer through their Vegas run's end), Speedee Mart (23 locations in Vegas), rapper Juicy J, Boulder Boats (where my boat had maintenance performed), Palm Beach Tan (three locations), Dodger Stadium (via Anheuser-Busch), and UMC Hospital (direct). We also did our first two diamond walls directly for MGM.

In April I was hot to get another printer. I was scoping out brand new ones, about the same size as the HP 26-500 we had, but wasn't opposed to buying a used one if I found a good deal. So, I was talking to Montroy, and also looking at a website called Global Garage.

We did end up buying a brand new Graphtec FC-8600 plotter in April, which was made for cutting vinyl and film into shapes. I had skipped over this while buying the initial equipment for the shop because of cost. As always, I stressed some over the spend, but here's what happened: we used it every day, and I couldn't believe we had lasted this long without it. This revelation would influence my buying decisions on every piece of equipment I'd purchase for the next 7-plus years.

* * *

At the start of summer 2014, I was really starting to feel the love from the community and wanted to start paying some of our success forward. I contacted Henderson and Green Valley Little Leagues to say that any teams wanting small team banners with the kids' names on them, S.I. would design, print and donate. I also called the Henderson Animal Shelter, which is where we got Ranger, and told them to never pay for a banner again – just call me. And we also started a program with them (that would last every year through the sale of the company) where we would donate 100-plus blankets in December, and plush toys in the spring, enough for every little buddy in there. I continue doing that personally to this day.

* * *

First week of April, I took a call from Corona asking if I could do a survey at a place called Chica Bonita, for some Find Your Beach wall wraps. I said sure, I'll go tomorrow. I figured it was another restaurant, so I went around lunchtime, and was hungry. I had a bad feeling when I arrived at the parking lot; it sure didn't look like a restaurant. Sure as shit it wasn't – it was a strip club. And not a high-end one. As soon as I walked in, I was cornered by several big Hispanic ladies, but was quickly saved by my contact, who was the manager.

Like a good vendor, I went about my business and got everything measured. And got the job. We ended up doing the entire interior and exterior – a good-sized job. This would have made for a great LinkedIn post! But since LinkedIn wasn't doing that yet, I had to settle for Facebook Business.

I want to step back here and describe what I was doing with the surveys. When they asked me to go survey something I always did it, and for no charge. Something that always stuck in my mind was when back in 2003, Scott from the Carolina Panthers did not agree to a survey charge and told me very simply, "That's the cost of doing business." I always remembered that, and how loyal he'd been. Another thing I did was, after completing a survey, create a to-scale template in Illustrator. Again, at no charge. I did them myself, they didn't take very long, and the customers loved them. The advantage to me was that, for one, I would get the artwork built onto my template at the exact size and scale I requested. Cuts prepress and RIP time way down. But the biggest thing I got was that customers loved me for this. I made everything super easy for them, and I was 100% getting their next 10 jobs.

* * *

Second quarter of 2014 we averaged 85 jobs per month; most in-house. We were getting bombarded by MGM, a bunch more work over at Dodger Stadium, Central Christian was slamming us, Affinity sent us out to Primm on the Nevada-California state line for some huge garage banners, and we were doing everything for (Floyd) Mayweather Promotions. This is besides all the other usual folks.

New accounts we picked up included Tecate beer, Live Nation (national), Verizon Wireless Amphitheater in Irvine, and the NHL – for which we did the NHL Awards Show, and ended up working with up until the sale of S.I. Nick from the NHL is one of the coolest guys I ever worked for. We did stage backdrops for rapper Ty Dolla $ign, BL'AST! (one of my fave punk rock bands), Wiz Khalifa (40-by-20-foot), Fu Manchu (another of my faves), and a bunch of posters and banners for Jack Grisham from T.S.O.L. for his new movie *Code Blue*. I did those for Jack as a donation. Remember, when I asked him back in 2003 if I could use T.S.O.L.'s song on my website, he said, "Of course you can!" Paying it back right there.

We also did Punk Rock Bowling music festival in May; our fourth year as a sponsor. New things we did for existing customers were big mesh banners in the valet area at MGM Grand (each around 50-by-7-foot), 110 new light pole banners for R&R Partners (new summer colors), a ton of mesh and vinyl banners for OKC Thunder (who had made the NBA playoffs), and a refresh on all 23 stores for Speedee Mart. We also picked up the Susan Komen Foundation for breast cancer awareness as a new partner for donating prints.

Mixed in with all these pretty big names was always a bunch of small jobs from mom- and-pop shops that occasionally walked into our lobby. I always treated everyone the same, big job or small. Everyone that had a job with us, that job was super important to them, and I answered my phone at 10 p.m. for both MGM and Joe's Pizza Shop. They were all important to me equally.

In June I pulled the trigger on a used 64-inch Epson GS6000 printer I found on Global Garage. It was shipped from California, and an Epson tech came and installed it. My vision was just to use it as a back-up for when the HP was booked (the ink was cheaper for the HP). We put it to work right away.

In 2013 a new music festival came to Downtown Las Vegas called Life is Beautiful. It was a pretty big deal, but despite my best cold-calling efforts, no progress. My hard work paid off in July when I finally got a call back from Ashley who did their marketing. We produced some half-inch Ultra boards for her as a test run.

In July we also did two more of the big building wraps for MGM Grand – David Copperfield creative this time. What this meant was, five of the six big wraps on the casino now were from Screaming Images. We had gained their trust very quickly. We also did six more "diamond walls" for them in the third quarter of 2014.

We also had three more tower banners for the Redskins, a ton of football stuff for Colorado Buffaloes, and the entire package for the Mayweather vs. Maida boxing fight, including the huge building wrap on the spine of MGM facing the Tropicana. New clients that quarter included Red Bull (direct), Polo clothing, iHeartRadio music festival, Conder (East Coast festival producer), and Route 91 music festival, which was in its first year at the original MGM Festival Grounds (which was also new).

Route 91 was a Live Nation festival. I made a note on my office desk to make five calls a day until I got the print work for this event. I called everyone I could find on Google searches, hit up all of my Live Nation and MGM contacts for introductions, but didn't make any progress. I was so determined on this one. Finally, out of desperation, I clicked the "Contact Us" link at the bottom of their website and sent a big, long message saying exactly why they should use us. Next day, I was called by Dennis, and he was laughing. The guy from the festival had called him and asked, "*Is this Swanson guy for real?!*" Dennis told him yep, so he called me, and introduced me to his coworker Marcy (super cool).

She started sending me specs to quote and introducing me to her team members. We were able to match all their usual pricing, and we ended up getting a majority of the work – and it was a lot. The actual festival wasn't until the first weekend of October, so I decided to take a little vacation.

My friends and I had been discussing for quite some time riding our Harleys out to Sturgis – and this year it would happen. We planned to leave the first week of August and be gone for eight days.

It would be the first time I'd ever let someone else handle my work. I planned to keep an eye on it, of course, but we would be on the bikes 10 plus hours a day. I left Lee in charge, and we headed out.

We left the morning of Aug. 2nd, 2014, way early. There were seven of us, all on Harleys. We had planned for that first day to take the scenic route through three national parks, and ended up in Moab, Utah that night. About 575 miles of riding.

The second day we cut out of Moab super early with a target destination of Fort Collins, Colorado. Our ride took us along the Continental Divide, through Rocky Mountain National Park, and then up and out of Estes Park.

It was dark when we arrived at our hotel – 14 hours and 560 miles later. That night an old friend I'd known since elementary school rode his Harley over and had dinner and beers with my buddies and me. You can't ride a Harley-Davidson through Colorado without stopping and paying respects to Gary Misenheimer.

The third day we rode from Fort Collins into Sturgis, South Dakota. Most of our route took us across the top of Wyoming. We had rented a house and wanted to get there in daylight. By this point there were hundreds of bikes on the road, all heading toward the Sturgis motorcycle rally. Right before we arrived at the South Dakota state line we, all seven of us, were pulled over by Wyoming State Troopers. They actually pulled out a little credit card machine and charged us $185 each for speeding. They gave us little dummy tickets, but said they wouldn't show up on our records. It was a total Sturgis shakedown. We rode 400 miles that day.

As we pulled into the outskirts of town, there were trailers pulled over on both sides of the highway with people rolling out sparkly clean motorcycles, wearing clean clothes, and freshly shaved. We had ridden 37 hours in the last three days. We had bugs all over our windshields and visors, three-day stubble, dirty clothes, and sunburns. We looked like a gang from Mad Max. I can speak for myself and all my friends: we would never tow our bikes anywhere.

We rented a super rad house in Sturgis. It had a garage big enough to fit all our bikes, with tools we were welcome to use. The first day in town we rode in and had breakfast at the local VFW. After that we decided to head out to Deadwood – a historic old town famous for being the hangout of Wild Bill Hickok in the 1870s. Killer old mining town. It started raining on our way back and we got stuck in a torrential downpour. We actually had to pull off the highway and take refuge for about an hour under the awning of some old, abandoned building. It suddenly cleared up, and we rode back into Sturgis to hit Main Street.

There were a bunch of famous saloons we wanted to check out, and we hit them all. We were at a place called One Eyed Jack's having a beer, and there was a sort of makeshift boxing ring in the center. It was like an old Clint Eastwood movie. There was a dude in the ring wearing jeans, boots, and no shirt, and he was beating up one guy after another – bare-knuckle. He'd knock one out, and then another guy would raise his hand up and yell out, take his shirt off, and get up there to fight. It was crazy. Total Wild, Wild West stuff.

That night we headed to a famous campground called Buffalo Chip. ZZ Top was playing. It was a big, huge field with a massive stage at the end, and the entire field was a mud bog from the rain earlier. We walked around in total sludge. There were hundreds of dudes that had brought their Harleys onto the field for the show, and in between songs instead of clapping or cheering they were revving their bike engines. It was crazy. And ZZ Top totally jammed.

While there, we went up to Mount Rushmore, out to Devil's Postpile, to Rapid City, and rode through the Black Hills and Spearfish Canyon. It was beautiful. I'm a total city slicker, and it was awesome to see how beautiful our country is.

The night before we left, we had a barbeque at the house. We all sat around the table at the end of the night and took a vote: home by scenic route, or fastest way. We were all beat up and voted unanimously for the fastest route. We left at 5 a.m. the next morning and it was freezing cold. We definitely hit all the elements on our trip. We arrived in Salt Lake City that night after 8 p.m. All told, 695 miles on the bikes that day.

The next morning, we were kickstands-up at 8 a.m. It was 435 miles to home, and to Scout and Ranger. I had missed them terribly. The guys crashed at my house in Henderson that night, and then headed home on their last leg back to Orange County, Calif. About 3,000 miles in the books, everyone home safe.

Everything at the shop had gone well. Lee did a fine job watching the fort. I was a bit beat up but was ready to get back to work.

* * *

We started work on Route 91 in September. We also had a bunch of work for UFC 178. We were still getting bombarded by MGM, Colorado Athletics, Anheuser-Busch, Corona, Big League Dreams – all the usuals. A new customer I picked up was the Sunset Galleria Mall in Henderson. I'd been cold-calling and sending messages through their website for months. One day I was in the mall, and I saw a blonde lady walking around wearing a mall employee badge, so I followed her. She walked through a hidden side door behind a retail store, and I followed her back. Once we got to the mall offices, I just introduced myself. She said, "Oh! I actually have a print job to bid on!" She gave me instructions to measure a big hallway at one of the entrances where they were going to build construction walls, so I went and did it immediately, and sent her a quote the same day. Her name was Heather, and she was the mall's director of marketing. I got the job, and started a business relationship with her that would last a decade.

Also in September, I was told by Marisa that she couldn't do my books any longer. She decided to step back into the corporate sector again. I was crushed. I immediately started a search for another outsourced bookkeeper, and found a guy named Aaron. I checked out his website to see the kind of folks he worked for, and how long he had been in business. He was a CPA, and I confirmed his license was current. So I hired him.

During the fourth quarter of 2014, we stayed super busy. I picked up a super cool job wrapping a helipad at Sunrise Hospital the first week of October, a huge job. We finished that hallway job at Galleria Mall, and Heather was giving us a ton of work. We did a big fabric stage backdrop for Wiz Khalifa which we shipped to Amsterdam, and also another 40-by-20-foot backdrop for Social Distortion. We got two more of the big building wraps at MGM Grand and had now put over 100,000 square feet of building wraps on their hotel. In the fourth quarter, I also picked up a few new accounts via cold calls and emails, including SLS (formerly Sahara Hotel and Casino), Marshall Retail Group (manager of retail stores in all the casinos), OutFront Media (formerly

CBS Outdoor), and Rock in Rio – who would be throwing the biggest music festival in the history of Las Vegas in May. We weren't awarded the entire festival yet, but it was a foot in the door. All I ever needed.

By the end of December, I knew we needed more printing firepower in the shop. This time I wasn't messing around with another 64-incher. I was looking at 10-foot-wide printers.

* * *

Back around the middle of December I had stopped by the local VFW (Veterans of Foreign Wars) on Lake Mead Parkway. They had a big marquee sign out in front of their building that I drove by a couple times a week. It was in bad shape and wasn't even readable anymore. I walked in and asked who to speak with about the sign. They said to talk to the "Commander." His name was Greaser. Greaser comes out and I say I'd like to fix your sign. He said they couldn't afford it, and I said it would be donated. He asked what I wanted, and I said, "Nothing." He asked if I wanted to put my name on it, and I said "No." I explained I owned a local printing company and that we were having some success and wanted to pay it back. And I told him about my breakfasts at the VFW in Sturgis. He seemed reluctant, but I got him to email me their logo.

I sent over the bucket truck, and we surveyed the sign. Lee came up with a killer design that they approved right away. We printed it on 3M cast/long term pressure-sensitive vinyl and mounted it to Dibond. Two pieces, both sides. Chris donated his time to install, using the bucket truck, and it came out killer. Good karma for us all.

About two weeks later Greaser called asking if I could come down right away. I thought, "Oh shit, did the sign come down or something?" I hopped on my Harley and headed over. When I pulled up, they were all standing out front, and Greaser was holding something in his hand. I got off my bike and walked over. Greaser walked up and gave me a huge hug. Then placed a killer custom wooden plaque in my hand that said, "Thank You Screaming

Images." I started crying. I wasn't expecting it at all. I told them all to never pay for a sign again – anything they ever needed, just come see me. They came to the shop about once a month, and we donated little signs to them as they needed them, and this relationship lasted through my sale of the company. Pay it forward, friends, there's no other feeling like it.

* * *

In the first week of January, I pulled the trigger on an HP LX-850 printer: 10-foot wide, latex ink. I bought it from our friends at Montroy. I was shitting my pants because the monthly payment on this printer was more than the mortgage on my house. I needed to keep this thing running, or I would be in big trouble.

First thing they said before delivering it was, I'd have to remove my punk rock wall for it to fit in the shop. No way, I said. I already had an area measured and taped off. We had to take the punk rock wall *down* to bring the printer in, but we put it right back up afterward. A little forethought and pre-planning is all it takes, friends. The culture of my shop was staying intact no matter what. It was our brand.

In the first quarter of 2015 we were averaging 90-plus jobs per month. Now with the 10-foot printer, we could do in-house much of the printing we'd been outsourcing to Chattanooga and Denver. Which meant we were even busier, so we added a couple more team members. We were at five now, including Chris the installer. We had very loyal customers sending us work almost daily: MGM, Corona, Anheuser-Busch, Colorado Buffaloes, Central Christian Church, Sunset Galleria, Sunrise Hospital, and Marshall Retail Group among them.

Some of the new customers picked up in first quarter were Source 1 Events (huge; they did every local event), Premiere Boxing (production and management of the majority of the boxing fights in Vegas), NASCAR (entry-level stuff, after cold-calling them for what seemed like forever), Findlay Toyota, UFC direct (another I'd been working on for years), and Circle

Productions who we met at Route 91, at the MGM festival grounds.

We also did some very cool stage backdrops for the Dead Kennedys, Joykiller, another one for Fu Manchu, another 40-by-20-footer for Social Distortion for their tour promoting the 25th anniversary of their self-titled album, a big fabric one for I Prevail, and then one I was super stoked about – a 30-by-20-foot fabric for Rancid. We were now able to print these backdrops directly to fabric in-house on our new LX-850 printer.

There were a couple of huge events in May we were working for. Floyd Mayweather and Manny Pacquiao would finally get in the ring together. We were doing all the fabrics for the press conferences and red carpet walks, which were in L.A. and New York City, promoting the fight. They loved us and I was pretty confident we had the entire graphics package for the event wrapped up. It would be the biggest fight in history. And then we were doing tons of promo work for the Rock in Rio music festival – but I knew I had to keep working hard to land that one. It would be the biggest music festival ever in Las Vegas, and they were building a huge outdoor festival space on the Strip at Sahara just for this show.

By this point I was having a field day with social media on both Facebook Business page and my personal page. LinkedIn existed, but it didn't have the timeline feature where you could post stuff yet (or at least, not that I was aware of). I was gathering connections on LinkedIn like crazy but was mainly using it to find and message people for cold calling. Still, I was having great success on Facebook, even to the point where I was buying ads, and getting a lot of attention for little S.I.

Beginning of April, I was called by my main Rock in Rio guy, Ricardo. He wanted to come in with one of his Brazilian teammates I hadn't met yet to check out the shop. It was set for the first Friday of April at 6 p.m. So we stayed late, cleaned up the shop, and I put together a little presentation and tour plan for their arrival. Two weeks earlier I had submitted my bid for the entire festival package, which was huge, and I had a feeling this tour would make or break us. They arrived right on time and were greeted by Scout and Ranger at the front door, which they loved. I walked them to the back, and before I could say anything, Ricardo walked back into the print department area, looked around, and then came back out. I hadn't even started talking yet. When he came back, he told us we got the job. He said the reason he wanted to come to the shop was to make sure we had a big printer (meaning the 10-footer). If I hadn't bought that printer back in January, we would not have gotten that contract. Another big risk paid off.

Now we were up against it. The Mayweather vs. Pacquiao fight was May 2nd, and Rock in Rio was for two weekends starting May 8th. Also, April 25th was my 50th birthday – a big one. I'd been making plans to bring in one of the bands we printed for to the shop to have a big bash, but had too much going on, so I just went to Lake Havasu with all my friends, which is what I usually did. The shop was stacked with print work for both events, and the guys were working the whole weekend at the shop. As soon as we arrived in Havasu on Friday night, the TV was on and all they showed was stuff about the boxing fight. The whole city was going crazy. It was the biggest fight in history. I was feeling super guilty about not being at the shop helping Lee and the guys. The next morning, I got up early, apologized to all my friends who'd come out from SoCal for my birthday, and told them I had to go home and get back to work. I didn't realize it at this exact time, but looking back at it now, it was pretty much the exact moment my personal life was over. I was busier than I'd ever been, and I could not just walk away from it.

On April 26th, I was called again by the *Las Vegas Business Press*. They wanted to visit the shop and interview me about the fight and the festival and take photos. They came the next day and stayed about six hours. It came out in the newspaper the next day, and my phone started blowing up. It was my first-ever official media coverage for S.I.

The fight, weigh-ins, and grand entrance were all at the MGM Grand Garden Arena, which at the time was still the premiere venue in Las Vegas with a capacity of around 18,000 for boxing fights. It was formally billed as the "Home of Floyd Mayweather." Starting with the grand entrance, Vegas was busier than I'd ever seen, including the NBA All-Star Game in 2007. By the time weigh-ins rolled around on Friday, MGM Grand was literally wall-to-wall people. We had wrapped every possible surface with branding for the fight.

It was kind of a rough crowd. MGM and I came up with a plan: take everything down during the fight, so that when everyone walked out when it was over, there was nothing to congregate around. The crew and I waited outside, and I got a text as soon as Floyd and Manny started doing the walk into the ring. Miraculously, we got everything down and out the doors before the fight ended, and the coast was clear.

The next morning, Sunday, May 3rd, we started installing for Rock in Rio at the new festival grounds. I'd made a couple new hires at this point. Anna, previously my client at Marshall Retail Group, came aboard on a temp basis to do project management and quality control for Rock in Rio. Working on the festival was all she did. I also hired my next-door neighbor, and his first official day was that Sunday morning helping hang banners on the stages.

It was a little rough going as all the art was coming from Brazil, and there also was a bit of a language barrier. But thank God for Anna – she really wrapped her arms around it and moved everything through production. The doors opened at noon May 8th, and we'd worked 18-hour days that whole week, and the last 24 hours straight before the gates opened. That week, I literally just went home to feed the dogs and shower. It was super nuts. They kept pouring on new sign package after new sign package. I wish I could say everything went perfectly, but I can't. There were a few signs we didn't get up before the first day – but we did go back and get them all up before the gates opened the second day. I was crushed. They weren't all that upset, and understood the last-minute rushes, but I felt I let them down. Big lesson learned; I would never let it happen again.

The Rock in Rio team was amazing the entire duration of the time we worked for them. We all were handed passes for both weekends of the show. I personally chose not to go. By that point I was seeing Rock in Rio in my sleep. We billed $250K overall for May 2015 – a quarter of a million dollars. It was unfathomable.

* * *

By this time, several people had approached me asking if I had any interest in selling the company. A couple were pretty serious. One was a printing company from Memphis, and another was a big group from England that was huge into the sports market. I was listening to both.

Third quarter of 2015, we stayed hot. In both July and August, we had 110-plus billable jobs. We had a big job for UFC 191, another fight for Premiere Boxing Champions, a couple big jobs from Kawasaki, the Redskins, and Mayweather Promotions. The City of Henderson now gave us the majority of their print work, and it was a lot. Life is Beautiful was back for their third year, and we got a good chunk of the signage package. We landed 225 more light-pole banners from R&R Partners, plus hardware and install. Floyd Mayweather fought Andre Berto in September, and we did another massive building wrap along with the entire branding package for the fight – including *the ring itself*. Route 91 festival was back for a second year, and we did all that.

New customers picked up in the third quarter were Fox Sports 1 (TV station), Bonanza Beverage (distributor for Coors Light and Miller Lite), Henderson Harley-Davidson (Red Rock Harley loved us, and hooked us up), iHeartRadio Music Festival (massive job, landed from cold calls), Impulso (marketing agency for Tecate; they did a ton whenever Canelo fought), and, finally, UNLV Football.

I had been chasing UNLV since I landed in Vegas. Only took me a decade! There was another local vendor with some family ties or something, and he did a good job blocking me out, but I was persistent and finally got in. We did the football field walls at Sam Boyd Stadium, print and install, including installing the exact same framing system we used for the field walls for the Pittsburgh Steelers. Sharing that system with them was how I actually broke the door down.

July, August, and September remained busy with stage backdrops for Corey Taylor (Slipknot), Trivium, Crow, Pennywise, Alkaline Trio, and Teenage Time Killers – which was an all-star band led by Dave Grohl from the Foo Fighters and Reed Mullin from Corrosion of Conformity. COC was one of my favorite bands, and when Reed called the first time and told me the name of the band, I said, "Oh, 'Rudimentary Peni.'" Teenage Time Killers was a lyric from one of their songs and he was blown away I knew it. "Rudimentary Peni" was a super old-school punk rock band from England. It gave me credibility in his eyes, and we had many good phone calls after that reminiscing about the old punk rock days. He even came out front to meet me and my buddy after a COC show at the Hard Rock. RIP, Reed Mullins.

In the third quarter we also had 10 diamond walls for MGM. There was a brief period where they issued an RFP for these walls and gave them to someone else. That lasted about a month, and they came back and offered me an exclusive contract. My first MGM contract.

Now that we had the LX-850 printer, we had cut the time printing diamond walls down to six hours each (compared with three days before). Lee and I had also learned a little trick. We could load up the 850 with a brand-new roll at night when we were leaving, and let it run. We had all three of our HP printers churning out prints at night after we left for the day. Saved a lot of print time during our normal hours which were 6 a.m. to 6 p.m.

Our profit margins were a little tighter on items for MGM. There were a lot of people going after that work, so we had to compete. But I was getting a *ton* of marketing mileage from it. I posted pictures on social media of just about every MGM job we did, and for every single diamond wall. It got us so much work from new customers, it was crazy. Another big piece was that Lee and I were becoming super-efficient with the printing. Almost zero waste, and no reprints.

Another massive one we started in the third quarter was Champion's Center on campus at University of Colorado. It was the new athletic center, an amazing structure. We worked with the architect, Populous, and the FF&E company, Maltbie, and did every single print in that killer building. To this day it's the nicest athletic facility I've ever seen. And we ended up getting the first of many articles about us in *Big Picture Magazine* once it was complete.

* * *

In October I heard from both the print company in Memphis and the sports group from England. They both arranged to visit the shop a second time. The guy from Memphis was kind of a hipster and took me and a few of my guys out to a fancy dinner to discuss his plan. I was fully transparent with my team about the whole thing. The guys from England were older gents and pretty formal. They just wanted to meet at the shop and chat, and I really enjoyed walking them through with Black Flag blaring through the speakers and then sitting down with them at a table in the Corona Bar with the top wrapped with a big picture of Lemmy from Motorhead.

* * *

We were busy at the shop. Fourth quarter of 2015 stayed the same and I was beginning to question how much longer we could sustain it. All four of the printers were running 20 hours a day. I was working just about every weekend. We now had a team of five, plus Chris the installer. I was still writing all the orders and managing all the workflow and scheduling, plus doing the invoicing. And, of course, the sales. By this point I was able to step back from running equipment except for weekends.

Something else happened that quarter that shocked me pretty big-time. Dennis informed me he was leaving MGM for a company I'd never heard of, Topgolf.

Anna had been a godsend, and we wouldn't have gotten through Rock in Rio without her, but I knew she was way too talented to stick with us. She was offered a killer job at UNLV, and we kept in touch. Plus, that meant more UNLV work for us. After she was gone, I realized we needed a full-time office person to help me with project management. I put an ad on Craigslist and received a ton of resumes. Even though most had project management experience, none of them seemed like a fit. There was one resume I got that didn't show experience, but for some reason I just had a positive vibe about. I replied and asked her to come in for a chat. She was super nice, very smart, and seemed to be incredibly organized. I offered Kelsey a job, and she accepted and joined the team.

This was all still super new to me, and every time I added another person or another piece of equipment, I thought I'd have a heart attack. And then, a couple weeks after doing it, I thought to myself, *"How the hell did I live without this for so long?"* Kelsey was one of those. She jumped right in and made a huge impact immediately. And everyone loved her.

* * *

So, at the beginning of 2016 we'd been in the shop three full years. Our team had grown, we added some pretty major equipment and had picked up a ton of new accounts. I had two groups pursuing a purchase of the company. I had a contract with MGM that was only for the diamond walls, but for nothing else. There was a ton of other work at all their properties, and we were getting a good chunk of it even though there was another vendor under contract. This did not make that other vendor happy, and I got my first taste of what the competition was willing to do. It was some pretty nasty stuff – but I'll take the high road here.

MGM had a main vendor contract that was awarded yearly. They invited me to bid on it in the beginning of 2016. Much like the Colorado contract when I was given the opportunity to bid, their material and specs sheets were very outdated. I offered to help, same as I had with Colorado Buffaloes. But all that did was make the guy handling the bid upset. I explained that I was only trying to help, but that didn't make things any better. I was not awarded the contract.

First quarter of 2016 stayed the same. Picked up some new accounts like Renaissance Fair (via cold calling), Summerlin Fest (same, cold calling), New Noise Festival (referral from Shamrock Fest), Pro Bull Riders (cold calling), William Hill Sportsbook (referral from Silver Sevens), Denver Airport (referral from Marshall Retail Group), Latin Grammys (via MGM), Westgate Hotel and Casino (intro from Dennis), the Las Vegas Monorail (via cold calling), and the Smith Center (cold calling, again). I was hustling, and it was paying off.

I was introduced to the owner of Frias Works by Cathy from Corona. We did a few small jobs for him at the casino, and then he hit me up on a huge job he was doing in Miami. It was a private concert by Kenny Chesney for the Corona folks in an old theater in Miami Beach called the Fillmore. I flew there for a walk-through and was tasked with making it look like the inside of Kenny's house. This meant covering up a lot of existing stuff and making sure whatever materials we used came off clean afterward. I spent a whole day measuring and surveying and came up with a plan they accepted. We pulled the job off, in a very short time frame, without a hitch.

We started doing work for Topgolf in January also, which would become one of our biggest and highest-profile clients. Dennis had come through once again. Construction was underway on the site that used to be MGM's backlot where the carpenters and engineers had their bungalows. When he had first mentioned the name to me, I had no idea who they were. I sure did now, and it was fucking awesome. I couldn't wait for that place to open, and I would be with them the whole way through the process.

* * *

By April 2016 I had informal offers to buy S.I. from both groups and was seriously considering them. As always, I sought advice from Chris, my best friend, who I'd known since little league, and who was a massively successful businessman. And who was also my shop's landlord. He'd been watching the trajectory of my business, and said I shouldn't sell. I should keep growing it. Problem was, we had no more room at 6504 Boulder Ranch. I would need a much bigger space, and more (and bigger) printers so I could bring everything in-house. I was totally self-funded, and that would be a huge undertaking. He offered to make an investment to help me get into a new shop. I crunched a bunch of numbers on what this would look like, and what I'd need to accomplish to pull it off. In 2015 we had $2 million in sales, and what it would take for me to be successful in a new and bigger shop, with a 16-foot-wide printer, was to double my sales the first year.

By the second quarter of 2016, Westgate, the Monorail, Topgolf, Frias Works, Pro Bull Riders, and UNLV were all turning into really big accounts. We continued to get solid work from Sunset Galleria, all the hospitals, MGM, Kawasaki, and LVAC. And we still got a ton of jobs from our long-time clients Colorado Buffaloes, Big League Dreams, the Redskins, and the Panthers.

We also picked up some rad new clients in the second quarter: Shoe Palace (170-plus stores in the United States), Envy Walls (modular wall systems used as construction barricades), Red Mercury (marketing company for bars and restaurants), and the Golden Nugget and the El Cortez historic hotel casinos in downtown Las Vegas. We did fabric stage backdrops for Plague Vendor, Agent Orange, Mac Miller, and Big K.R.I.T.

All this was giving me confidence. I ended up taking the offer from Chris and looked for a bigger space.

One thing I knew for sure was that we had to be closer to the Strip. I needed to get more visitors and potential customers into my shop. I also needed to make it an even bigger and badder punk rock playground, compared with the small shop. What I looked for was a big production space with not only plenty of room for the printers, but plenty of floor space for finishing on the big banners. At this point, for this, we borrowed a warehouse floor from a neighbor at Boulder Ranch. Another thing I needed was more help with operations. I needed to get that off my plate so I could focus on sales, or I wouldn't succeed.

Besides Circle Graphics in Denver, I still used the Chattanooga folks from National Posters Digital for the bigger outsourced stuff. They had a facility in Vegas simply called National that I also used from time to time. The entire group had been acquired a couple years prior by a company called Rock-Tenn, and they made a bunch of sweeping changes in Vegas, including letting the longtime president go. The new group had come in and raised all their prices and lowered the level of customer service pretty drastically. I saw opportunity there. National, for decades, had been the biggest grand-format printer in Vegas, and had all the biggest accounts. A lot of these accounts had been reaching out to me lately. I talked to the old president, who I knew pretty well, and asked if he wanted to join my team. I was planning a full sweep.

Doug agreed to come aboard, and he was instrumental in helping me find a facility and get new equipment ordered. We narrowed it down to two facilities – one on Polaris, near Russell, right across the street from a big dirt lot that would eventually become the home of the Raiders. The other was near Decatur and the 215 freeway. My first choice was the one on Polaris, so we applied there. Unfortunately, it was given to a company that maintained service vehicles or something (they didn't last a year, by the way). So, we applied at the Decatur building and were accepted.

6975 S. Decatur Boulevard was a 19,500-square-foot facility. The office with the break area was about 4,500 square feet, but most importantly the shop floor was 150-by-100 feet of complete open space. I hit the landlord up for a few buildout items, and they agreed. I planned on building a second personal office in the front area, a new separate room near the shop floor for prepress and fencing off an area in the back to create an enclosed yard. The office lobby space had a bunch of cubicles that we tore out immediately. No way I would make my teammates work in cubicles.

We signed the lease and started looking at equipment. I ended up buying a 16-foot-wide Vutek UV ink press, another new 10-foot-wide HP latex press (newer model than the LX850), and a 10-foot-wide UV ink flatbed press. In addition, we ordered a 29-foot Miller Weldmaster for finishing banners. All brand-new equipment. This facility and the new equipment would allow me to bring every single job in-house. No more outsourcing.

We would get the keys on June 1st, 2016. One big thing I needed to plan was the transition from the old shop. We were busy as hell and needed to keep printing. I could not let any of my customers down. Doug had some family matters to wrap up and wouldn't be able to start until Aug. 1st. I was on my own with the shop transition.

At this point, I wasn't sleeping well at night. It was a lot of stress. I went from $3,200 a month for shop rent to $13,000 monthly. And my equipment payments jumped from $2,600 a month to $24,000 per month. Oh shit. It was sink or swim.

First Job Direct
for MGM UFC Wall

Installing Mayweather Fight
Outfits Display at MGM

Huntridge
Theatre Before
Donated Banners

Huntridge Theatre After Donated Banners

Installing at
Chica Bonitas
Strip Club

English Buyers at the
Lemmy Table

Installing May vs Canelo
Building Wrap

Me and Greaser
Donated VFW Sign

Fabric Banners for
Mayweather vs Pacqiauo
Weigh Ins

Installing a Stage at
Rock in Rio 2015

Rock in Rio
Banner Tower at MGM

Red Rock Harley-Davidson Murals

CHAPTER 10
BIG SHOP ON DECATUR

"Values Here"

- *Dag Nasty*

Once again, I was risking everything with a big move. By the time we got to moving into the new shop, I already had my corporate vision and marketing plan solidified. I was going to be the industry leader in customer service levels. I was going to be loud, authentic, and make myself stand out. I was going to use the highest-quality materials for each individual application and base these decisions on the knowledge of 29 years in the printing industry, and 14 years being in business for myself with Screaming Images.

I would be a partner to every one of my customers – not just as a vendor. I would treat every customer, big or small, exactly the same – like a friend. I would provide fair-market pricing based on three decades working in many different markets and knowing the going rate per square foot of material nationally. I'd provide a soup-to-nuts service – one-stop shop – offering concept, design, print, and install. I would be flexible and start relationships that lasted forever. I would not let profit margins or burden rates dictate business. I would build relationships where the customers considered me a friend, with trust in me completely, and where they knew they were getting the best products, service, and price.

Maybe most important, I would stay within my personality, and if that meant wearing Vans sneakers and baseball caps to meetings with CEOs, so be it.

I never went to business school, didn't have a college degree. I just used common sense and logic. And, treated people like I myself wanted to be treated. I was a customer, too. I had embraced my personality and appearance, and it was working. A lot of people were referring to me as the "punk rock guy," but to me, punk rock had died in 1985. I was just being me. I branded us as WC02. "Working Class Since 2002."

* * *

By June 15th, 2016, we had just about finished the warehouse décor, and my personal office. We brought over and set up the spray-painted corrugated metal walls, and I was pleased with how everything looked. The third week of June, the first new press was arriving – the FB250 flatbed. The new 10-foot HP 3100 and the Miller WeldMaster were both arriving the following week, and we had a goal of getting everything running by July 1st. The 16-foot EFI UV press wouldn't arrive until mid-July, and that was the biggest piece of the new capabilities.

The first priority was the customers, and everyone understood this. All four printers were still running at Boulder Ranch and would continue to until we had the first two new printers at Decatur up and running completely. Then, the printers at Boulder Ranch would be shut down, drained, cleaned, and brought over. We had six on our team at this point – and everyone wanted to be at the new shop, which was understandable. It just couldn't happen that way. There would be no stopping of the printing.

Kelsey and Matt were at the new shop, Lee and Keith at the old shop, I bounced back and forth. The other two, and the most important ones, Scout and Ranger, were of course at the new shop. And they were loving their new work home.

The first day after I signed the three-year lease on the Decatur shop, I visited to start laying out blue tape on the floors to determine where to put things – presses, finishing equipment, desks, walls. I was using the best and worst examples from the other shops I'd worked at, and with, to make the best plan. I started from the shipping and receiving roll-up door. I planned it so materials arrived, went to the right side of the shop to where the presses were; off the printers to the open floors, for trimming off the rolls; then down the left side where the finishing equipment, welders, and tables were located;

back to the roll-up door where everything could be packed and labeled for installs, deliveries, and shipping.

This new shop was huge. I planned to put in a little boxing gym, and either a quarter- or half-pipe for skating. Maybe a basketball hoop. I thought we'd never grow out of it. Boy, was I wrong.

Another first order of business was adding new team members. We needed another press operator to run the 16-footer, and another prepress operator. Lee would pull double-duty doing prepress and running the smaller printers, and Matt had rejoined the team in a new role as manager of the press department. Plus, Kelsey would need some help up front with project management.

As mentioned previously, this was a huge financial step up. I went from $5,800 a month in overhead to $37,000 a month (not including payroll). I had to at the very least double my sales in the first 12 months to pull this off. Chris's investment was only designed to give me a little comfort and cover my new/additional expenses for the first six months. It was likely I'd lose a bit of money that first year or maybe break-even – I had a lot of hard work ahead. The only way I would pull this off was to completely step out of running the presses, doing finishing, writing orders, and doing paperwork. I had to focus solely on sales.

I saw several ways to increase revenue: bringing in new customers via cold calling, tapping into additional work and referrals from existing clients, and stepping up my social media efforts to attract more attention and get more referrals. Everyone kept telling me to start paying for search engine optimization (SEO) to bring in work, but I didn't see it as viable. I was going after big clients. And people like the NFL, NBA, NHL, major casinos, music festivals, and other major events didn't need to use Google searches to find vendors. They took hundreds of cold calls from potential vendors every week. I just needed to figure out more ways to make myself stand out and get their attention.

The first 90 days in the Decatur shop were a learning experience. Getting proficient with the new equipment, welcoming new teammates, and trying to get production running smoothly so I could focus on cold-calling and marketing. We brought in about $400,000 total those three months, which was way below the target I needed to hit. One advantage we did have at this point was we did everything in-house. I even brought a full-time designer aboard. We'd get there.

The next 120 days, through the end of the year, were a different story. We racked up $1.1 million in sales, thanks to some big months from University of Colorado Athletics, Topgolf, Westgate, MGM, and UNLV Athletics. I added new casinos in the Golden Nugget, Downtown Grand, and the El Cortez. There was a new venue and attraction called Speed Vegas I picked up, and we finally got our foot in the door with Levy (stadium concessionaire), Zappos, Back Bar, and Egan Productions (Fright Dome).

Somewhere around 100 days in, we had a shop meeting on the production floor, and I was totally tripped out that we were now totaling 15 on our team. And were discussing adding a second shift. This was something I'd never have even dreamed of as little as one year before. The work was pouring in, and I needed to ensure customers were being taken care of – especially MGM.

In October 2016, I wrangled a big one – the presidential debate at Thomas & Mack Center between Donald Trump and Hillary Clinton. It had been on my radar since they announced it and I was calling everyone I knew, contacting people I didn't know, stopping by the venue, trying to get in... Finally, I was called for a quote, and it was actually from an event company we'd done some work for the previous year. We bid, got the job, and it was a hell of an experience. We produced a massive amount of fabric banners and vinyl wraps, and every single box of printed material we brought in was inspected by bomb-sniffing dogs. It was a super-fun job. Something that makes you feel like all the hard work you put in is worth it.

* * *

Around this time, I'd had a friend called Seth for about four years. I met him through his girlfriend, who I had met at Punk Rock Bowling. She started bringing him to the shop parties at Boulder Ranch and we hit it off as we had the punk rock and combat sports stuff in common.

The girlfriend moved on, but Seth and I stayed friends. We went to shows, out on the lake, to fights, etc.

One thing I really enjoyed about Seth was introducing him to my friends. He was co-owner of a production/film company called WoodRocket. I always introduced him like this: "This my buddy Seth, he's a pornographer." We always joked around that he'd get me into one of his films as an extra someday.

One night we were out at the boxing fights at The Cosmopolitan, and we'd had a few beers. He was telling me about his latest production, "Riverdale." It was a porno/satire of the old comic book *Archie*. He said he had a speaking role for me. I think I shocked him when I said, "I'm in." The role was 'Pop Tate' who was the owner of the malt shop that Archie, Jughead and the gang hung out at.

Two weeks later I got the script. I had a handful of lines in a scene where it was just me and Jughead in the malt shop, and I was giving him a pep-talk right before he banged Veronica. I had done some research and gone back and watched some of the old cartoons so I could give a good representation of Pop Tate, haha. I nailed my scene in one take, and the guy playing Jughead, who was some sort of famous porn actor, told me he was impressed with how I'd done my first time acting. I said thanks and got out of there before the real action started. Big thanks to my buddies Seth and Corey – I don't think too many print company owners can say they guest-starred in a porno.

**

As 2017 started, we had a lot of work to do, not the least of which was to have a proper grand opening party and get folks into our new shop so they could see all the equipment and huge space we now enjoyed. I wanted it to be kick-ass, super fun for everyone. I wanted to have a killer band play – and I had someone in mind.

By this point I'd been working for Social Distortion for 16 years, and I knew their manager pretty well. I called him and told him about the party and asked him if he thought Mike Ness would do a solo set. He laughed and said no, so then I asked, "How about Jonny?" He said he'd ask. He called me the next day with a yes, and we finalized the deal to have Jonny Two Bags, guitarist for Social Distortion, who had also just released a solo album, play my grand opening party. I knew they'd say no to Mike – it was Jonny I wanted all along.

To prepare for the party I enlisted a bunch of my talented friends and customers. I got Corona to be the presenting sponsor of the party in exchange for 50 cases of beer. I got my next-door (shop) neighbor who did furniture rental to lend us a bunch of highchairs and tables. I got my next-door neighbor at the old shop, Larsen's Restaurants, to give me a killer deal on catering, and got my awesome client and partner Circle to donate some truss and lighting for the photo ops. I got my amazing friends at Source 1 Events to lend me some space heaters; Golden Nugget and Topgolf to donate some giveaways; and Smash Magazine to donate the biggest piece – their mobile stage, which we pulled right into the shop. In exchange for all these items I made big 2-by-6-foot standups that I posted all over the party, wrapped the tops of all of the high tables, and plastered their logos on all these items, as well as on the official invites, which were sent to over a thousand people – all from big companies in Vegas.

The party was Jan. 21st, 2017, and people started arriving early. It would be a packed house. I had two big 10-by-10-foot photo op areas built out of truss with lights and step and repeat patterns – one for S.I./Corona, and one for S.I./Jonny Two Bags. Larsen's was serving food by 7 p.m., with Jonny scheduled to start by 8:30 p.m. I also had two local bands playing after Jonny, and a punk rock DJ to bring it all home at the end.

The line to the open bar was literally 25 deep. We had trash cans full of beer all over the shop with Coronas and an assortment of their sister beverages – Modelo, Modelo Negro, and Victoria to name a few. Every single high-top table was taken, and in front of the stage it was packed. We had all the print equipment stanchioned off, with sponsor boards in front. I gave tours of the shop and equipment to customers that had never been there. It couldn't have been going any better. I got up and announced Jonny at exactly 8:30 p.m. to roaring applause, and he delivered the goods – a killer set.

I'd estimate at the party's peak we had 500 people there. After the bands and DJ finished, and most of the people left, I turned into the DJ and by the end of the night there were about five of us left in my office playing George Jones songs and trying to "Out George Jones" each other. Party guest of the night went to my buddy Tinkler's friend from Apple in San Francisco: Tinkler texted him a video of Jonny during soundcheck at the shop around 4 p.m., and the guy got up from behind his desk and took the next flight out to Vegas. He arrived around 7:30 p.m., just in time, and was one of the last of the five of us in my office after hours. He slept on the couch at my house that night, in his clothes, and got up in the morning and I took him to the airport – no toothbrush or hairbrush, same clothes, just flew back to San Francisco, back behind his desk at Apple by 11 a.m. Legend.

* * *

After the grand opening party's success, I was back on my sales mission, and MGM was top of my wish list. They'd already been giving us a ton of work, but the only contract we had was for the diamond walls. Their annual bulk contract RFP had gone out, and I filled it out and returned it in late February. I was as thorough as possible, even adding additional unrequested info about staff, managers, production processes – and I sharpened my pencil on the pricing.

These contracts up until now had been one-year deals – but this was going to be the first for three years. Biggest challenge with that was the pricing – a lot could happen with material prices in three years. So I had to be careful. MGM was the biggest contract in Las Vegas, and every single printing company in town was in on the bidding. Even some from out of state – but I knew those guys had no chance. I was going to defend my little island for sure.

In February there was a huge new attraction opening up in town – Speed Vegas. I knew the incoming GM from his previous job, so it was a pretty easy win for us. The first job we had was wrapping three of their huge shuttle vans. Our regular installers were super buried, but someone referred me to this guy named Gabe. By the time I was leaving the shop at 4 p.m. on the day of the installation we'd already moved one van inside and it looked like he knew what he was doing, so I took off. I figured he'd get the first one done that night; maybe with a start on the second one. But when I got to the shop the next morning at 6 a.m., he was finishing the third van! I inspected them, and they were all beautiful! Absolutely flawless installs. I was in shock over this kid – and knew I had to bring him aboard. It took me a few weeks, but we finally struck a deal. He was the best installer I'd ever seen. And ended up the best hire I ever made.

Another event happening in March was VIVA, the annual Las Vegas rockabilly festival and car show. I'd been after this one for years, and had done some small stuff in past years, but got the whole shebang in 2017.

* * *

An area I was continuing to develop was our corporate philanthropy. I focused on the organizations and things that meant the most to me, so it was youth sports, animal shelters, and places like Boys & Girls Clubs topping my list. Also, anything to do with music, especially punk rock, because it played such a big role in the development of my personality and the way I ran my business. There was an old legendary punk rock band from Oxnard called Agression that was a big influence. They were down to one surviving member, and he was a good dude, getting older, and struggling in his personal life. He started playing shows with other local musicians from Oxnard as a tribute to the band, and I helped out by donating a 15-by-10-foot fabric backdrop. I also printed him a bunch of free poster boards with one of their iconic logos and numbered them 1 to 100 on the bottoms so he could sell them for extra cash. He and his girlfriend always kept in touch and sent me old Agression swag whenever they came across it. I was always super stoked to get it, but was even more stoked to be helping him out. RIP, Big Bob.

I also tried to help local Vegas bands busting their asses to get places and make names for themselves. One night at a club called Beauty Bar downtown, I saw a local band, young guys, called Mercy Music. They were opening for Agent Orange. I thought they were great and wanted to help out. I searched for them online the day after the show and found nothing. I saw a few weeks later they were opening for Pennywise at House of Blues, and I was already going to that show. After their opening set I waited for the front man to come out so I could speak with him.

He finally did, and I walked up and told him I owned a local printing company, printed for the bands he had been opening for, and that I loved his band and wanted to print a backdrop for them. He looked at me like I was crazy and walked away. I was persistent and followed him and told him I loved his band and just wanted to help. He asked the same question they all did: "What do you want out of it?" And the answer was the same as always: I wanted nothing. Just to help. I loved paying it forward. He came around and I ended up donating two big fabric backdrops to Mercy Music, and I am still friends with those kids today – and they're kicking ass.

＊

On March 14th, 2017, I was driving back to the shop from a site survey and my cell rang with an MGM number. I answered, expecting one of my usual contacts with a quote request, but it was the procurement department. Congratulations, she told me, I was being awarded the MGM contract. I almost crashed my truck, I was so fucking excited! I couldn't wait to get back to the shop and tell the team. Huge moment for S.I. I was on my way to that goal of doubling sales in 12 months.

Something I started realizing was that whenever I could get someone to come in and check out the shop, I was getting their work. Almost a 100% success rate. The shop was fun, had a cool vibe, and was basically a walk-in business portfolio. Every square inch of walls was covered with art and prints of past jobs. Their heads always looked like they were on swivels.

And of course, everyone loved that they were greeted at the front door by Scout and Ranger.

There was a big UFC card coming up in April, and I decided it was already time to have another shop party. We called it "Team Appreciation Night," which it always was, but the real goal was to get more customers into the shop. I used to throw parties hoping just one particular client would come, and it worked most of the time. We fired up the taco truck and put the fight on all four TVs in the shop – including the "punk rock bar" which for this party was fully stocked. Cormier beat Anthony Johnson in their rematch in front of a huge crowd at S.I. Great party.

Whenever Social Distortion came to town it was a big deal. I've already said this, but printing backdrops for your all-time favorite band is pretty fucking cool. When they came in March, I got four tickets for both nights. I had a little trick I'd do at House of Blues – if I saw an empty table in the VIP area the night of the show, I'd offer $500 for it – the food and drink came out of this number. It was usually $750. I'd stoke out my friends and we would have many drinks during the show from the VIP section. The second night, after the show, we rolled out and heard a big commotion in the HOB restaurant. I popped my head in, and it was Punk Rock Karaoke. That was the official name for the band that comprised of several punk rock legends. They played old punk classics and invited people up to sing. I was pretty loaded and had no intention of singing, but wanted to see the stack of index cards on the stage to see the songs in their repertoire.

I was standing there flipping through them, when I landed on "Minor Threat" by Minor Threat. As I was holding it, Steve Soto looked down at me and said, "YOU'RE NEXT!" I put everything down and slunk to the bar in the back, but as soon as the song being played ended, Soto started yelling into the mic: "Where's the Minor Threat guy?!" That was me, and you don't say no to Steve Soto. I jumped up there, grabbed the mic, and belted it out. I heard a couple of kids in the front yelling, "He isn't even looking at the lyrics!" The song ended and I barreled off the stage completely soaked with adrenaline. I had just sung on stage with Soto (of the Adolescents), Greg Hetson (Circle Jerks), and Stan Lee (the Dickies). Unfortunately, Steve Soto passed away a little over a year later. (RIP, brother.) We did a tribute window for him at the shop.

On March 27th, 2017, the Oakland Raiders officially became the Las Vegas Raiders. But the talk about this began about a year earlier, in 2016, and even though it was kind of hard to believe, I started working the phones anyway. I put huge notes all over my desk at the shop to make five phone calls daily as motivation. I connected with every single person from the Raiders I could find on LinkedIn. I was a lifelong Raiders fan and would not let this one get away, but wasn't having any luck.

Once again it came from out of nowhere. I had met JR when he was working for Copperfield at MGM doing rigging. When he broke off to start his own company, Stagewise, he gave me a call and in hopes of creating a working relationship with him I donated some decals for the doors of his new shop, and a wrap for his small equipment trailer. Three months later, he called and asked if I wanted to print for the Raiders. He was doing the stage for their NFL Draft party April 27 to 29 at the *World-Famous Las Vegas* sign. He invited me to a meeting at the sign, introduced me to the Raiders advertising agency out of New York, and inadvertently, the creative director for the Raiders. We put together a quick bid on the printing and install, included a mock-up of the sign park/area, and told them we'd do the artwork for the banners for no charge, (it was just a Raiders logo against a black background) and we got the job. And that, my friends, is called what goes around comes around. Those little decals I donated to Stagewise got me in with the Las Vegas Raiders.

I was just about the happiest guy in Las Vegas seeing those printed Raiders shields laying all over the floor of my shop. I was still super far away from a Raiders contract, but I had my foot in the door. All I ever needed.

*　*　*

The summer before, at the Boulder Ranch shop, I had come up with an idea to make special Screaming Images T-shirts to give away to all the people who supported us on our social media accounts. I'd have contests on Facebook Business and give them away. Hats, too. The first batch of shirts we gave out Lee had designed to look like the walk-out gear for UFC fighter BJ Penn. They were a huge success. The first summer at the Decatur shop I decided to take it up a notch and call us "World Famous" for something cool that we didn't really do. It was just a marketing gimmick. Lee and I brainstormed and came up with: "Screaming Images World Famous Boxing Gym." The design incorporated some brass knuckles and had our motto on the bottom, "Fight Hard." They were a total hit, and I ended up having to order a second batch of 100 shirts to ensure everyone who asked got one (for free, of course). It was just a really good way of having fun, getting our name out there, and supporting the folks supporting us. We ended up sending T-shirts all over the country – even some to England, France, and Mexico.

*　*　*

April to June of 2017 the shop was buried. It tripped me out to walk around the shop and see four huge presses (plus two smaller ones) all running at the same time. We had picked up a huge building wrap job for The D hotel and casino downtown, had a couple of massive exterior building banners for Downtown Grand, and we had picked up Insomniac (EDC music festival) and the Tropicana Hotel and Casino. Another huge win was picking up SWITCH, which was a massive company with multiple locations in not only the same parking lot we were in on Decatur, but also just about every adjacent parking lot on our block. At the end of June, we'd been in the new shop for 11½ months, and in that time, we amassed $3.9 million in sales. I had hit my target of doubling the sales in one year.

The D hotel and casino had huge building wraps on both sides that had been in horrible shape for 2-plus years. I had been chasing that one really hard, and continually sent pictures to them of the successful building wraps we'd been doing at MGM. I finally wrangled an introduction to the director of marketing, via the director of marketing from the Golden Nugget, and they were actually in the process of getting bids from the previous and one other local vendor. The third vendor was quickly eliminated, and it came down to S.I. and the vendor that did the work the two times previously. The old vendor had done their homework and learned the material we'd been using over at MGM – so we were bidding against each other not only using the same material but also the same installer. The previous vendor had not done a good job on the last wrap – and this was not just coming from me, but also from the property. The film had not been cut into the window frames – it had been "bridged" over them causing tenting which was the reason the wraps failed. It had been up for barely a year. We, of course, had a plan to fix that.

Another issue was, based on some preliminary measurements we took, the template The D provided wasn't anywhere near accurate. I mentioned earlier in the book that this was a trick competitors used to not only try to keep the work, but also to cause problems for the next vendor, which to me was just a shitty and dishonest way to do business. So I did what I always did and took a proper survey, created an exact to-scale template in Illustrator, and turned it over to The D, saying it was theirs to keep whether they used me or not. And once again, it got us the job.

Creating that template took a little outside-the-box thinking – it was a huge building. My goal was to not have any film seams on the windows. Me and one of the installers climbed up to an upper ledge of the building and took exact measurements of the widths of every window and frame. We then went to the very top of the building and dropped a huge, oversized cloth tape to get the exact height. Then, I hired a drone to fly up to the exact centers of the building, both sides, and take photographs from dead straight-on. Using Illustrator, and with the photos of the buildings and our measurements, we scaled it exactly. It all fit perfectly. And, just FYI, this building wrap lasted 5 years. We ended up re-doing it around the time I sold the company – without anyone bidding against us.

Let's back up here and get into the building wrap installers. We used a company called Hangtime, with a great guy named Matt. It might be confusing that I keep saying we did everything in-house at S.I. – design, print, and install. However, this is the second time I mentioned bidding on a building wrap with both companies using the same installer. My rule here was, on installs, that our in-house installers did everything where the lift went from the ground up, even as high as 180 feet. However, anything from top of a building down on ropes, or swing stages, was done by Matt.

No insurance companies liked the fact that we were hanging off the sides of buildings applying big stickers. Even though it was Hangtime installing these bigger building wraps, we had to have the proper insurance and licenses (including high-enough bid limits) to do the work. I can tell you that between all of my business licenses and insurance, it was costing me almost $150,000 a year. My insurance agent talked me into not bringing rope access and swing stages into our in-house scope, and I had enough stress as it was without that stuff, so I listened to her. Plus, Matt was a pro.

* * *

In May 2017, we got some super fun news. Big Picture Magazine was doing a feature article on me and the company, and we would be on the front cover of the biggest grand-format print industry publication in the country. The article was called *"How I got the Job: James Swanson – Screaming Images' principal on printing his passions, working in Sin City, and how his punk rock lifestyle taught him to stand out in the business world."* It was an amazing honor – and it's super easy to find the article online to see yourself.

Another big thing happened in June 2017: I made my first post on LinkedIn. I'd been collecting connections, looking people up, and sending out sales messages for several years – but this was the first time I made an actual post. Unsure how long they had that feature before I discovered it, but I was now using LinkedIn like I'd been using Facebook Business – and it had a huge impact on sales. That first post attracted over 20,000 impressions. I had so much success with it, I made another post about a week afterward for some building wraps for the Canelo vs. Chavez Jr. boxing fight. I was off to the races on LinkedIn.

* * *

On Oct. 1st, 2017, right before 11 p.m., my phone started blowing up. I always turned the ringer off when I went to bed, but the vibrations kept going off for what seemed like 10 minutes straight. When I finally picked it up, there were 25-plus texts and 20-plus Facebook messages asking if I was okay. I immediately turned on the news and learned about the horrific massacre at the Route 91 Festival in Las Vegas, and I was devastated. I not only knew everyone involved in the production of the show, and everyone working at the venue – I knew I had hundreds of personal friends there. It was hard to figure out exactly what was going on; the scene was absolute chaos on TV. I immediately went to the shop to prepare for anything S.I. could do to help. I stopped on the way and bought 10 cases of water and waited for calls. I was in constant contact with my friends, and they told me streets were closed and that they were at the hospital waiting for news. I was also able to immediately connect with my main customer that had been working onsite, and he said to start rallying people to head down to the Red Cross to donate blood. It's hard to describe everything I was thinking and feeling at these moments, it was all happening so fast.

I got the call that my best friend's wife for sure had been shot, but thank God, she had survived. I felt super-guilty because I was the one that had given them their passes. I headed to the blood donation center around 5 a.m. and the line was already a mile long. By the time I donated, it was after 8 a.m. and I headed back to the shop. I had three hours in line to think of ways we could help, and came to the conclusion that supporting the community was the best course for both S.I. and myself to take.

And there it was: #VegasStrong was the rally cry being thrown up around Las Vegas, so we dove right into it. To be clear, that idea was not mine, nor from our shop. We just immediately jumped in to support it. We all needed to help each other, and S.I. would ensure that happened.

Two actions were on my mind, and we implemented the first as soon as I returned to the shop. We had our two biggest and fastest printers making #vegasstrong stickers and banners to donate, and I put it out on social media the next morning that anyone was welcome to come to our shop and get some. Within an hour of the post our shop was flooded with supporters. The Facebook post had been shared 44-plus times, with the message that everyone was welcome at the shop. No one was leaving without a sticker or banner. We ended up, over the next two months, handing out 8,000-plus stickers and over 1,000 banners. Every car I saw on the freeway had one of our #vegasstrong decals displayed.

Phase two was to donate a massive #vegasstrong building wrap. I reached out to my two main contacts, they immediately ran me up the flagpole to executive staff, and within an hour we had two Vice Presidents at the shop. The idea was a collaboration between Matt from Hangtime and me. I then got our vendor Marty, who sold us the product we used for the building wraps, to donate most of the material. S.I. donated the rest of the material, the design and the printing, and Matt and his crew donated the labor and installation.

This may have been the hardest part of writing this book. We had been with Route 91 since its inception. I knew everyone who worked for the festival very, very well. I was on-site every day, standing up on that main stage, setting things up. I knew and loved every single person who worked at that festival grounds. I just can't find the words to express how horrific this was. And then, how proud I was of how everyone in the community, and the entire team at Screaming Images, came together to support our city.

* * *

The last quarter of 2017 was a whirlwind. We were at 25-plus employees and regular hours included two shifts plus a shift on Saturdays. MGM sent us a massive amount of work and we were only at the tip of the iceberg. We also picked up ESPN, SGE Worldwide (nationwide producer of music festivals), Live Nation, became the main vendor for Pro Bull Riders, and picked up a ton of work from IMG Live, on the heels of the successful work we did for the UFC International Fight week in July. To this day, Jason and Dan from IMG are friends and a couple of my favorite dudes ever to work with.

In 2017, we hitched a ride on the wild side. That calendar year we had $4.4 million in sales and were well on our way to taking over the entire city.

* * *

By the beginning of 2018 I was working my ass off. My normal routine was up at 2:30 a.m., work for an hour at home, to the gym by 4 a.m., leave gym at 5:15 a.m., home to shower, walk the pups around the block, and get to the shop at 6 a.m. Everyone questioned why I got up so early, but really there was no way around it. I absolutely needed to be by the shop at 6 a.m. because I wouldn't be able to get all my work done otherwise. Plus, I had clients on Eastern time. Additionally, I needed those two or three hours of quiet time in the shop in the morning before everyone arrived and my day went haywire. I didn't really mind working hard – I was doing something I loved and was truly having fun.

My routine when I arrived was to check the shop floor for all the jobs expected for completion by the second shift the night before. Then I would walk the prepress room and all the printers and check every job ticket in progress. I'd put the tickets in priority order at each station, and sometimes move them from one printer to another. At this point all the presses ran all day on first shift, so it had to be very organized. Something I really pushed to production was to try and do the shorter runs on first shift, to allow flexibility on the presses with rush jobs, which always happen when you work for casinos, venues and events. The second shift guys didn't have these kinds of interruptions, and the longer runs on press were okay.

The first quarter of 2018 we were buried. We did both the baseball and soccer fields, print and install, for the USC Trojans, the baseball stadium at UNLV, a bunch of work for the NBA All-Star Game in L.A., the Mint 400 off-road race, Rugby Sevens tourney at Sam Boyd Stadium, the VIVA Rockabilly Festival, and started picking up work from Caesars Harrah's. We had $1.3 million in sales the first quarter – which put us on track for $5 million-plus for the year, my goal.

A super cool job that first quarter was the brand-new Las Vegas Lights FC soccer team. They were playing in the United Soccer League, just one step down from Major League Soccer. About a year earlier they announced the team was coming, and I was on the phones trying to win the work from day one (I'm also a huge soccer fan – Go Chelsea!). There was a lot of competition, including from a couple of really big out-of-state companies that focused exclusively on soccer. The team also wanted a partnership, and I was willing to do that, so I was kind of being coached on where my prices needed to be. I can tell you; the other vendors were being super-competitive with their numbers.

The unique situation on this was they were playing their home games at Cashman Field, which was the home of the local minor league baseball team, the Las Vegas 51's. This required an affordable and efficient way to switch the graphics from baseball to soccer every time their schedules overlapped – which ended up being 14 times that first season. And there was only a day or two to complete the conversion. At the conclusion of the RFP, we had the best solution and won the contract. Huge win for the shop.

Another thing that started happening that first quarter of 2018 was – I had a lot of pissed-off competitors. You have to realize that any new account we'd pick up, unless it's someone totally new to town like the Raiders or the

Lights FC, we took away from someone else. And in the last three years I had plucked $4 million worth of business away from the Vegas market.

I was still just trying to win work and have fun. I had out-of-the-box marketing ideas, and one I had a lot of success with was the "tribute window." It was a big window right at the entrance to the shop, and every time someone significant, or who had influenced my life somehow, passed away, we would craft artwork to commemorate them, print and install it in the window, and pay our respects. I would post it on all of my socials along with a little story about why and how they influenced me. It attracted a lot of attention. It reached a point that whenever we lost someone famous, our supporters waited anxiously to see how we'd pay tribute. Consistent posting on the socials, especially LinkedIn, was getting us a pretty major national following.

Also in early 2018, we were still paying it forward and picked up more causes for donations. By this time, we had at least three sports leagues, three schools, and about 10 youth sports teams we sponsored. I got requests all the time via socials to purchase banners for people that had passed, fundraisers for cancer, etc., and we donated banners to those folks every time. We also made monthly donations to ASPCA, St. Jude's, Doctors Without Borders, and several others. It was extremely important to me to pay our success forward.

Second quarter of 2018 was more of the same – tons of work. One difference though was we were being way more efficient with our time and procedures. This was largely thanks to our press operators, especially Tom, and our banner finishers Francisco, Herbie, and Manny – who were the best in the city. I wasn't afraid to take on any scope of work with those dudes on my team.

* * *

The Raiders broke ground on Allegiant Stadium in November 2017, and by springtime 2018 they were ready to start putting up signs. We were still bidding on jobs against other local vendors but were winning most. My first-ever meeting at Allegiant I drove my truck onto the construction site in the dirt and down into a big hole right in the center that eventually became the event level of the stadium.

In Spring, we also got a ton from MGM, Zappos, and Westgate. We built some big frames on the back of the LED boards at Topgolf facing Harmon and hung big banners on them. We did the USC Trojans' entire football practice field; International Fight Week for UFC; and all the signage for our eighth year as a Punk Rock Bowling sponsor. We did six tower banners for the Washington Redskins, printed a huge fabric stage backdrop for the Stray Cats reunion, and picked up the Mob Museum as a new client via my social media efforts on LinkedIn. We also picked up a huge new client, The Aces – Las Vegas' new Women's National Basketball Association team.

A couple of huge things also happened in spring 2018. First, around March, I was approached by one of our top three clients, YESCO, with a question: "Do you think you can put a jersey on the Statue of Liberty at New York New York?" I immediately answered: "Of course I can." Mark from YESCO, said, "Great, we'll be in touch." I knew what it was for. The Vegas Golden Knights were about to make the playoffs in their inaugural season in the NHL.

As soon as Mark left, I walked out of my office and back into the shop and pulled together a few of the managers and production guys and said we need to figure out how to make a jersey that will fit on the Statue of Liberty on the Strip. My biggest concern was it would be a huge banner hanging on a statue right above not only a huge rollercoaster, but also the biggest intersection on the Strip – Tropicana Avenue and Las Vegas Boulevard. If something happened and it came down, my name was mud.

After some research, talking to YESCO, and NYNY Hotel & Casino engineering, we had a dimension. Just one. The circumference of her waist. Someone at the shop mentioned we should go pick up a miniature/model from a tourist store, so I ran out and grabbed one that ended up being 1/32 scale. Our designer and a couple other guys were trying to cut paper shapes that would fit the model like a jersey, but nothing was coming even close.

After about an hour and 10 unsuccessful tries, our production manager, Chris, walked over with a roll of gaffe tape. He wet it down and wrapped it around the replica tight as he could in the shape of a jersey. He handed it over to me and I cut a "seam" down the left side and behind the tablet she held with her left arm, and then peeled it off and laid it flat on the table. Bango, we had our shape.

Next, we sent it into design, crafted a template/shape to match the pictures we'd taken, and blew it up 3,200% (from the 1/32 scale model). We checked the newly created template against the one dimension we had, and it was pretty close. We called YESCO and let them know we were ready to go. Great job with the gaffe tape idea to Chris Horst.

This jersey was huge: six 16-foot-wide mesh panels. We used the special mesh we'd used for years for the Redskins' tower banners – it was thicker. We double-webbed every edge and double welded/taped every seam. We made adjustment rows of grommets in 5-foot-wide increments for adjustments on site during install. We did everything we could think of in advance.

The news press was all over this. I guess they found out from NYNY – I wasn't responsible for this one, haha. They came to the shop as we were printing and took pictures of it on the press. They came back when it was on the finishing floor being cut and put together, and they returned once more upon completion, and we laid it out flat in the parking lot behind the shop. It was 85 by 65 feet in dimension.

April 10th came, and it was installation time, as the playoffs started in two days. I was having a mini heart attack. The installation story was outlined in the "Introduction" chapter at the beginning of this book, in case you missed it. No need to double up on the story here – but it's definitely a must-read.

Also in spring 2018, Adrienne, the editor of *Big Picture Magazine*, approached me about being a speaker at their first-ever conference, called WFX, in Minneapolis in May. I said, of course I'd do it. She said since the cover article she did on me the year before, there was a lot of interest nationally on what S.I. was doing out in Vegas, and she wanted me to talk about us being a "One-Stop Shop" – meaning we did everything in-house, design, print, and install. My time slot would be 45 minutes talking. No prob.

I asked about a month out if she wanted me to clean it up a little. The baseball hat, the Converse sneakers, the vernacular. She said no! *We like that about you!* Cool, this would be fun. She also asked if I could show my time-lapse video of the Vegas Golden Knights jersey install before I came up to talk. Sure! Then she said I was now the keynote speaker, and that she wanted me to talk for 75 minutes. Shit!

I flew to Minneapolis the day I was scheduled to speak. I arrived at the hotel about two hours ahead of time, showered up, and headed to the conference. I was greeted with a big sign with my name on it out front that said, *"How a Punk Rocker from L.A. Became a One-Stop-Shop Rockstar in Vegas."* As soon as I sat down in the room I was speaking in, people started coming up to me and shaking my hand and saying, "You must be the guy from Vegas..." I sat and watched the two guys who spoke ahead of me, and I have to say these dudes were super-polished speakers. Seriously impressive. Suits, rehearsed dialogue, choreographed moves – the folks in that room had no idea what was about to hit next.

I had taken my little time-lapse video and added a Lars Frederickson and the Bastards song, "To Have and to Have Not," (a Billy Bragg cover) which I used in a lot of my marketing videos. When it was my turn to speak, I went up into the wing of the stage behind the curtain, they turned the lights off and started my video. The room was completely packed. The song was about two minutes long, and they had the sound up way louder than I expected. As soon as the video ended, they turned on the lights, and I walked out to the podium. I didn't have anything choreographed, but I did have a little slide show I figured I could drag out for 75 minutes. As soon as I started talking, the crowd started throwing questions at me – these were all people in the same industry, and they were super curious about not just me, but also Vegas. They had a cool little gimmick where there was a big fuzzy square block, 12 inches or so, that was a microphone. One person would use it to ask me a question, and then throw it to the next person. It was kind of fun, and that little fuzzy square block was flying all over the room. I didn't even get to go through my slide show at all. Toward the end, the question most asked was, "Where can I get one of those hats?" (I wore an S.I. logo hat). I had a line of people waiting to speak with me when I stepped off-stage after I finished.

Another thing about that crowd. I'd been leveraging my popularity on social media and in magazines with my vendors. They always asked me to mention them in my posts and interviews, I asked them for considerations on product in return – and they always agreed. I had two guys that were bigwigs from one of my vendors in that crowd at WFX, and we had a deal. Despite all the questions I was peppered with, I did manage to work in during my speech that I was using their equipment, and we got a ton of donated product in return.

* * *

I was always pushing Screaming Images via super simple marketing. Easy little things that, to me, were making a huge impact. For example – I started having the press guys run S.I. stickers in the waste – an area on the roll of film that would have been left unprinted if we didn't do anything with it. I came up with a simple design to catch people's attention – black sticker with white skull and crossbones with our name in bold letters on the bottom. These 6-by-6-inch stickers would go on every single box, all four sides, that left the shop. So when the drivers were out delivering to, say, MGM, as they were carrying the boxes through the casino the stickers were very easy for people to spot because of the bold skulls. They saw our name, and in their minds, they immediately affiliated us with the property. Once the boxes were delivered to the marketing (or whichever) department back-of-house, the boxes would be laying around with our name on them, very easy to spot. There are dozens of people ordering print from every big-name customer you have – maybe someone who doesn't use us sees the box and thinks, "Oh, so and so is using them, I should too." New employees (which happens routinely in casinos) see our name from the very first day they start, and automatically start using us. Or maybe they don't. But what did it cost us? We ran the stickers in the waste. Pretty simple. No risk, all gain.

Another thing I made a big deal of was that all installers wore T-shirts with S.I. on the back. These T-shirts (unlike the special summer tees) were not designed to look cool – they were designed so the name on the back was as easy to read as possible. Anyone who saw them installing at a casino, or a stadium or a festival, knew who was doing the job. Maybe it was a big company involved with the event – like ESPN, or Fox Sports, or a marketing agency (pick any one of a thousand). They would think, "Oh, that's who the venue uses locally, maybe I'll call them next time I have an event in town."

Another big one was our vehicles. They're like rolling billboards for advertising. I always made designs for them to make them stand out. Skulls will make things stand out. We crafted designs to make them look like old WWII airplanes – camouflage (in blue and gray, the colors of our brand), with the little bullets on the front, the Spitfire eyes on the front, bullet holes – they looked really cool. Especially the bucket truck – which looked like a tank from an Arnold Schwarzenegger movie or something. Rolling advertisements for Screaming Images. They couldn't drive by without you looking. I even did a few social media campaigns where I posted that if you saw one of our trucks out and about, stop the driver and they'll give you a free shirt or stickers.

A fun story about the bucket truck. One day one of the guys who drove it a lot approached me and said, "Hey, we need new mudflaps for the bucket." I said, "Okay, order them," and he asked, "What kind?" I responded, "Naked lady mud flaps, of course." And they were ordered and installed.

Needless to say, our competitors didn't think this was as funny as I did. Nor did they think the skulls and crossbones, or army/military designs, were as cool as I did. They were all vanilla, not making themselves stand out.

They were getting dressed up for meetings, talking like salespeople, and not making any extra efforts to get their name out there. They didn't like the way I marketed, they didn't like me, and I didn't care.

* * *

Third quarter of 2018, the shop was still slammed. We picked up cool jobs from Audi Field (Washington, D.C., via LinkedIn), Orange County FC (soccer team via cold calls), and Phoenix Motor Speedway (via third party through social media). We did a huge job for Corona at Petco Park in San Diego, stage backdrops for Agent Orange, the Adolescents (Steve Soto tribute), the Mighty Mighty Bosstones, and the Vandals. We did a huge SGE festival called Surf City Blitz in Huntington Beach, iHeart Radio Festival at the new Las Vegas Festival Grounds, we started working for NHRA (via past relationship), did a bunch of cool stuff for the L.A. Rams (via third party), and a 200-foot-high Barry Manilow wrap for Westgate. We landed another big job for the Canelo vs. Golovkin fight.

Whenever Canelo fought, we got a huge job, six figures, across multiple properties, including building wraps. The agency that handled most of his content was Impulso, an amazing company to work with. Their owner Jorge is one of the best dudes I ever worked with.

We continued to get work from the Raiders – a lot of it from the general contractor. It just so happened I used to see their project director at the gym every morning at 5 a.m. Construction was in full swing, and we were awarded the fence banners for the perimeter of the whole site, the wraps on the faces of the construction trailers that faced the 15 freeway, and we even put Raiders shields on the top of the trailers so people in planes could see them as they flew over.

It seemed like everyone in town was partnering with the Raiders for related ancillary events, and a lot of them were already our customers. This was working out really well for us, as I was leveraging our relationships for every single event to ensure we got at least some of the work. One such event was a huge watch party at the Downtown Las Vegas Event Center, which was run by a guy named Bud who I'd been working with for a long time and consider a friend. It was sponsored by FOX 5 News, who we also knew and worked with. So we ended up getting the entire branding package, which was pretty substantial. It was the usual – wraps, big vinyl banners, big mesh banners, rigid signs – but they came at me with one odd request. They were putting in a faux football field and wanted to paint the end zones with Raiders and Fox 5 logos. Could we make the stencils for them to use for the paint? Of course we could! We had never done anything like that before, but figured it out pretty quickly, and everything went perfectly.

After this amazing event, Bud and I met for lunch, and coincidentally had the same thing on our minds: a partnership. The venue would continue to purchase all the event-branded print and install with us, push every event/company that came in toward us for their print and install, and we would then immediately supply them with a bunch of venue-branded items such as barricade banners, bar signage, and box office and cabana graphics. In exchange, S.I. would get one of their coveted cabanas to whichever events I wanted to attend, and I could have 25 guests who would get a full VIP experience. Done deal. The profit on the event graphics sent our way more than covered the cost of the venue materials we provided, and I was able to treat my friends and customers to a ton of killer shows.

We also still received a lot of attention on the socials, especially LinkedIn. I was getting requests for visits all the time, and of course I always obliged. In August we got a big one: our first international visitor! We were super stoked to have Mark from Monster Mesh in the UK, another grand format printer, come by the shop.

At the end of summer, we also released our newest S.I. summer shirts: "World Famous Tattooers." I had to re-order three times, and we sent out 200-plus T-shirts to our friends and supporters all over the country.

Going into the fourth quarter of 2018, I started to notice we were getting pigeonholed as only doing big stuff. People would send me messages that ended in, "But that's probably too small for you ..." And *absolutely it wasn't too small.* As I said several times already, I treated every customer the same, big or small. It's super important.

We picked up some new customers at the end of 2018: Sahara Hotel & Casino (cold calls), Ariat (Western wear, referred by PRB), Ad Art and 5B Artist Management, U.S. Men's National Ski Team, Stratosphere, and Red Bull Miami. Big work continued to roll in from MGM, Colorado, and Topgolf.

Topgolf was getting really fun. They were all settled in, having a ton of success, and were starting to let us get creative. I recommended wrapping the front stairs as an entry statement for some of their bigger events, and they loved it. I was actually getting okay at swinging a golf club, too. You'd still never catch me on a golf course, though. Way too slow for me. Topgolf only.

Also in the last quarter, we had several huge jobs. Beyond Wonderland Festival for Insomniac in San Bernardino, Calif., massive banners for the College Football Playoff, and the Las Vegas Bowl football game at Sam Boyd Stadium (via our friends at ESPN). We did a ton of work for the Khabib vs. McGregor fight at T-Mobile Arena – which ended up being the highest-grossing UFC fight of all time (and still holds the record).

Also, at T-Mobile Arena, we did the Pro Bull Riders National Finals. Funny about T-Mobile, I was only allowed to work outside. Another vendor had the inside locked up, and despite some Herculean efforts on my part, I couldn't shake them. Almost everyone that came to town tried to get me in there, but I would literally be stopped at the door before I walked in. Not sure what exactly was going on there, but good for that vendor. I protected my shit, too.

Another partnership paid off in the fourth quarter, too – the one with Bud at DLVEC. As an avid Harley rider, and through working for all three local dealerships, I'd been chasing the Las Vegas Bike Week committee around for years. Once they booked their event at Bud's venue, he gave me a hard intro, and we got the entire signage package. Afterward they said they wished they had known me before – and I told them I'd been trying for years (haha). We worked for them every year up until I sold the company. Those little investments/donations pay off, friends. I wasn't worried about hitting set profit margins on every single job. I played the long game.

As we finished the year, we ended up putting the Golden Knights jersey back up on the Statue of Liberty for the beginning of hockey season. She was a little beat up, but we fixed her up real nice. We also added some new folks to our corporate philanthropy/donations: We wrapped a van for ASPCA's "Rescue Unit," donated some basketball court graphics to several local Boys & Girls Clubs, sent 100 fleece blankets to the Henderson Animal Shelter, banners to Susan Komen Foundation, and bunch of bikes, skateboards, footballs, basketballs, and soccer balls to Toys for Tots' Christmas Drive.

I closed out the year with a trip to Atlanta to meet with the NFL, and a fun trip to Oklahoma City where my super awesome client Brooke took me to an OKC Thunder game. It had been a hell of a year. In 2018 we had $5.1 million in sales – a 16% increase over the previous year.

***

For 2019, I was super focused on staying diversified. I'd learned some big lessons in 2008-09 when the market crashed and tried really hard not to rely on one customer, one market, or one type of application. We were always looking to do and try new things, and one area I saw where we could make some headway was by using our Multi-Cam router, which we picked up in the last quarter of 2017, more efficiently. It had a 5-by-10-foot bed and was a pretty versatile piece of equipment. I had some slick sheets made for dimensional letters and started offering it to all existing clients, and of course Colorado Buffaloes were the first to take us up on it. I truly loved those guys!

There was no way I could find to keep track, but if I would have had to tell you which material we used the most, I couldn't do it. We were pretty evenly split between mesh banners, vinyl banners, pressure-sensitive vinyl, and rigid. And that was a good thing. We had been printing fabric direct on our UV ink 16-foot and 10-foot presses, but I knew it was time to step up to dye-sub. Tradeshow was a huge market, but I was so busy with everything else I hadn't had time to tap into it yet.

I can tell you, though, our biggest customer was 11% of our overall business, and if we were to lose them, we wouldn't have been significantly affected. It would have sucked, but we could carry on. You'd be surprised by how many printing companies can't say that about losing their biggest customer.

As we moved into 2019, I focused on tightening some things up. Accounting, administration, and human resources mainly. We'd been growing at lightning speed, and time was flying by. It was kind of like a snowball going downhill getting bigger and bigger and all you could do was just ride it out. In the last 30 months our sales grew 225%. We had gone from six employees to 32.

Work-wise, in the first quarter of 2019 we were rolling right along. We did the entire graphics packages for both the Pacquaio vs. Broner and Canelo vs. Jacob fights; we did both basketball and men's golf for USC; a job for the NFL for the Super Bowl in Atlanta; the Academy of Country Music Awards Show (new, via cold calling); the new U.S. Polo store on the Strip (via cold calls); a couple of trailers for Henderson Harley-Davidson; the Rugby Sevens tourney at Sam Boyd Stadium; UFC 235 at T-Mobile Arena (for IMG); a bunch of huge seat cover banners for the OKC Dodgers (minor league baseball); the VIVA rockabilly festival; and stage backdrops for the Old Firm Casuals and 88 Fingers Louie.

In February we had a massive job for the NBA All-Star Game in Charlotte, working for a combo of the NBA and Wasserman Group. Working for Team Wass was new to us (referral by the NBA) and was an amazing experience. I'd been trying to get in with them for years. I was in North Carolina for a full week – and was so happy to get back home to Scout and Ranger after everything was done and successful.

In February the Raiders had a huge event in the SkyFall Lounge at the Delano hotel. We did print and install for the entire event. A couple of really cool things came out of it: I was finally able to meet the Raiders' amazing creative director in person, and I wrangled an invitation to the event. I also was able to meet and shake hands with Jerry Jones from the Dallas Cowboys.

* * *

I was still hitting LinkedIn hard. Every time we did anything cool, I made a post, and we'd get tens of thousands of impressions. People used the platform's direct messaging to reach out for quotes. I had just about completely abandoned Facebook Business.

A brief update on how I was doing personally here. I was completely overwhelmed. I was getting 500 emails a day and responding to every one in a timely manner. When I was in the field, I was responding to emails at red lights and stop signs. I'll estimate 99% of the emails weren't just people reaching out to say hello. They were people asking me to do things. If it wasn't something I could do right away, I would respond and say, "Got it, give me a bit." I would at least let them know I received their email, and in turn, that they were important to me. I also tried to instill this ethic into all my team-mates who were customer-facing. Customers were the most important thing. Without them we wouldn't have a shop.

This meant I spent all my waking hours battling my inbox. I had a system where I would leave the email in my inbox until the task requested was completed, and once completed it was archived into dedicated folders. As you could imagine, after 18 years in business I had quite an archive. I was always in battle with my IT folks over the mailboxes/storage. They would say I had to delete some; and I wouldn't let them. They were telling me in 2019 that I had over a million emails archived. I kept them because that way I could always look back at them – what I did for them, what I said, what I charged, what material I used, who I spoke with, and who was copied. It was important. At least five times a year something would come up where I had to go 10 years back on emails. My customers stayed with me that long.

One thing I never did was leave a customer hanging. There was no "after hours." If I was awake, I was responding. This meant if someone had an issue that started as they were leaving work at 7 p.m., and they emailed or texted me, I personally was in contact with them until their problem was resolved. Even if that meant keeping me up until 11 p.m. And I'd still get up at 2:30a.m. I was fucking tired, man, for reals.

I always did my best to maximize my time. I'd spend an hour and a half every morning right after I woke and fed the pups and before heading to the gym, responding to emails that arrived while I slept. I would go through emails from the day before and make a task list, and plan routes for where I needed to go that day, so no time wasted. I literally wrote this stuff out on a piece of notebook paper. Every day.

Once I was at the shop by 6 a.m., I'd do the same as things came up. I wouldn't leave my office to go out in the shop until I had several things I needed to do. And I'd plan them out by the shortest route, whichever way would get me back to my office the fastest. For breakfast, every morning I'd cook it in the microwave and put it on the table in my office and just take bites whenever I walked by. Same for lunch. I was that busy. It was overwhelming.

Every morning there would be curveballs that would throw me off schedule. Anything added in just tacked on time at the end of my day. When I was at the shop, my door was always open, and anyone could come talk with me any time. Most times this threw my schedule off. I tried my hardest to be accommodating, especially when it was something important to them, whether for work, or for personal matters. If they sat in my office for 10 minutes, I'd get 10 emails while they sat there. It was hard.

I tried my best to keep everyone at the shop happy. At that point we had 35 or so of us, and it wasn't easy. Everyone had their own personalities, their own agendas, their own goals. Some worked well together, some didn't.

Some hustled, some did not. Still, they were all good people at the end of the day with families to support and personal lives to live. We gave them a team lunch every Friday, gave them $100 Rockstar awards every week, and had shop parties all the time. There were televisions everywhere, so they never missed March Madness, World Cup, Olympics, whatever it was at any moment. I personally went out and bought fresh fruit every morning; and they even had gym memberships available to them if they wanted. I really tried my best.

A lot of them were working *really* hard. They got time-and-a-half pay for everything over 40 hours a week, and a lot of them worked 50 to 60 hours weekly. Mostly press operators and banner finishers. I always tried my best to give them something extra in these situations. Whenever they had to work weekends (besides the Saturday shift guys) I always went in to show support. In 2019, I had to ask a couple of press operators and all the banner finishers to work on Mother's Day weekend. We had a huge job with a tight deadline. They could have refused, but none did. I was there with them the whole weekend and even made personalized gift baskets for, and wrote personal notes to, each of their wives, apologizing for keeping them away for part of their special day.

In 2019, I went into the shop most weekends. Catching up on paper-work, making collection calls, trying to keep up with my inbox, supporting the team – you name it. I was an owner-operator. I would never make the people I was calling and asking for work talk to someone else. I'd built myself into a trap.

* * *

Right around halfway through 2019, I had had a couple of competitors express interest in buying me out. Both of them were from out of state, and one even sent one of his executives to talk with me personally. So I hired a business broker to start putting together an evaluation on my company. This had always been my plan – and I was at my breaking point.

Second quarter of 2019 was more of the same. MGM continued to be huge, and to grow exponentially. There are so many people and so many departments and I was finally getting a good handle on all the different folks I needed to reach out to in order to maximize our contract with them. I was getting millions of miles from them in marketing value. And I kept reaching out and picking up work from ancillary folks working on the same events we were. MGM was our biggest asset by far.

We also had a ton of work from Insomniac (EDC), IMG Live (UFC), Frias (Corona activations), Topgolf, and three festivals from SGE. We did a ton of work for the NFL Draft (via third party), the Mint 400 off-road race (full graphics package), a 40-by-20-foot stage backdrop for the Stray Cats, a 30-by-20-foot fabric stage backdrop for Rancid, a 30-by-20-foot outdoor stage backdrop for the Interrupters, a big NFL event at Caesars convention space (direct), Disrupt Festival, Punk in Drublic Festival, a huge job for the NHL Awards, and four new tower banners for the Redskins.

The Raiders had broken ground on their headquarters in Henderson, and I worked my way into that one by asking for referrals. We were also helping them, via Legends, with sales pitches for the naming rights for the stadium – which was an amazing experience. I actually sat through a couple of practice sales pitches while we were installing graphics and can say those Legends sales guys were total badasses. I learned a lot.

Jemaa was a new dayclub/pool at Park MGM. It was part of the transition from Monte Carlo and was about halfway up the hotel, out on a huge deck. To promote it, MGM operations asked if we could wrap part of the lower rooftop so people in the towers could see it (and hopefully join the party). As I was never someone to say no, I said yes and then started the process of figuring it out. There are a couple of big challenges on an application like this. First, the obvious one: it lays flat and takes a direct hit from the sun, in the desert. Second, the roof was made of some sort of polyurethane product, and we had to figure out how to make it stick. We worked closely with 3M, came up with a bulletproof plan, and it worked perfectly.

We also donated a scoreboard graphic to the baseball field at Cimarron

High School, and had FOX 5 News broadcast live from the shop for the first time.

* * *

As we headed into the second half of 2019, I had another thing weighing heavily on my mind: Scout was getting old. I knew the day would come, maybe soon, and it scared me to death. I couldn't imagine my life without her. She was always by my side – at home, and at the shop every day. She still greeted everyone who came to the door at the shop at Decatur and was the total Screaming Images ambassador. She had arthritis pretty bad in her back legs but could still swim like a fish. I got her in the water as much as I could. I loved her so much.

* * *

In mid-June we did one of my favorite things in the 20-year history of S.I. We gave a field trip to and hosted the Nevada Blind Children's Foundation. Their school was right around the corner from my house and every day when I drove by, I noticed that they had a big monument sign and a banner frame that was empty in the front. So one day I stopped by, introduced myself, and offered to donate the signs. They were super excited, and I ended up hanging out there for an hour. By the time I left I had offered, and they agreed to, a field trip for all their kids to S.I. in two weeks.

My entire team was pumped. We had the shop all set up to safely navigate 22 blind kids through on a tour. We had games and activities arranged, and a sandwich bar ready for lunch break.

When they arrived, they were all greeted by Scout and Ranger at the door, which they loved. We did an introduction of the staff in the front office area, where my entire team described their job at S.I. I then took our special visitors through the shop. We walked by all the equipment, and I would pull a couple of them out, hold their hand and walk them the length of the printers counting the steps, so they could see how big they were. We had cut sections of just about every material we used and laid them out on a table and let the kids feel them while we described what we used them for. Then we had some huge puzzles we created on the floor which they played with for a while, including a model of Allegiant Stadium, and then we did hand and finger painting of their names on a huge banner for their school.

We all then headed to the break room and had custom sandwiches and chips. I sat at a table with about 10 of them – they were so excited to be at the shop, tell stories, eat food, and it was an amazing experience for me. They were so full of life.

After lunch we went back out to the front office, where we had an awards ceremony planned. We'd made little trophies for each of them, with their names written in braille. Once we were all out there, I announced to them that they all had been total badasses, and we had no choice but to give each one of them a "Rockstar Award." I had my entire team in the room, and as I called each one of their names, they got a standing ovation and thunderous applause as they walked up to accept their trophies – accompanied by Scout, of course. After every kid got their trophy, we went outside and took a group photo, then we all hugged each one of them as they got on the buses to head back to school. It was one of the best days of my life.

* * *

The usual folks were coming through big-time, led by MGM and YESCO. Shoe Palace was a new one we'd been working with for a couple years, and the hard work was paying off in spades – they were our third-biggest customer in 2019. We also did the WNBA All-Star Game at Mandalay Bay.

We had several big festivals – including Las Rageous at DLVEC, Life is Beautiful (full package), Day N' Vegas (first job directly for Goldenvoice), Psychofest, Ohana Festival in south Orange County (had been chasing that one for years; finally landed via cold calls), a huge one for Microsoft at the new Las Vegas Festival Grounds (featuring a performance by Queen), and for the third year in a row, iHeart Music Festival (also at LVFG).

A crazy one was iHeart. As we were going, the original scope kept getting bigger and bigger. Toward the end someone from their marketing company, Revolution, asked if we could turn their Ferris Wheel pink (for T-Mobile) – "Of course we can!" We did and ended up winning a Best of Wide Format award for it.

Our relationship with the Las Vegas Lights FC was also going really well. We were working our asses off on the conversions from baseball to soccer at the stadium, especially in the heat. Part of our deal was that I got to throw a party at the shop, and they would bring all their other partners so I could try to get print work from them. Steve, their V.P., and I came up with a plan to host a party around a USA Women's World Cup game, to make it attractive for them all to come.

The United States played Sweden at the end of June, and we had a huge party planned. Every single one of the Lights FC partners was coming. I hired the taco bar, had the punk rock bar all decked out for soccer, and had all four shop TVs firing. We set up some games out on the shop floor for kicking soccer balls at targets – it was looking like a fun day. The game started at 11 a.m.

They surprised me a little when they said their beverage partners were bringing alcohol, haha. It was a Thursday! But we had production shut down for the day, so I told my team I didn't mind them having a couple of cold ones as long as they had a safe ride home. Absolutely no drinking and driving home afterward.

So, everyone did day drinking at S.I. Especially the folks the Lights FC had brought with them. The taco bar was completely wiped out, and after the USA won, 2-0, we all headed back to the shop to kick some balls. A cool thing was, USA men's soccer legend Eric Wynalda was the head coach of the Lights at that time and was at the party. One of the games we set up was kicking the ball at a big banner we had printed and hung on a frame. The banner had holes as targets to kick at, and the smaller holes in the corners were worth more points. Everyone was having a great time, and it was super loud and rowdy in the shop. Everyone had a go. At the end it was me and Wynalda out there for the final kick off. He went first, going after the top right corner for 100 points, and just missed. I went up there to go after the win. I could have gone after a bigger, easier target, but went top left for 150 – and nailed it! It was total luck, but I'll take it! What a fun day. A memory I'll never forget.

We picked up some new clients in the second half of 2019 – Circa Hotel and Resort (brand new casino downtown, picked up via cold calls), University of Nevada-Reno athletics (old customer moved up there), Coca-Cola (years of effort), the Hard Rock in Sacramento, to name a few. All of this, of course, was well reported on LinkedIn and socials.

We did a job at the Diablo's restaurant at the Mirage in the third quarter that seemed like a regular job at first but ended up getting us a lot of attention. It was the entire inside of their new restaurant, and they wanted it "super matte." I recommended wall covering instead of 3M vinyl wraps. The difference is we had to install it with paste – it's like wallpaper. The artwork they provided was sort of Mexican folk art, with super vibrant colors. We dialed in a graphics profile specifically for it and printed it on our 10-foot UV press so it would have a very matte finish. The prints looked great, and Gabe did an amazing job on the install – it came out killer. I immediately made a LinkedIn post, and it went viral. We ended up getting a bunch of calls about it, and there ended up being an article on us about the job in a magazine called *Global Trade Press. Bango* – the power of social media.

In the second quarter we had a request to wrap two bass guitars for Gene Simmons of KISS. As you might imagine, 12-year-old James was thrilled. I guess we'd done a good job, because in the third quarter we got another call from his manager asking if we could wrap 30 more. Yes, please! Super fun job. And speaking of favorite bands, we also did another huge stage backdrop for Social Distortion for their 40th anniversary tour. At this point I had lost track of how many backdrops we'd done for them. And how lucky was I? Printing my fave band's stage backdrops for 20 years.

* * *

I was constantly trying to find new things for us to do. I was always looking at what other people in the media industry were doing, especially on LinkedIn. I kept seeing all the digital and LED boards that were replacing traditional print stuff, especially in the concert and festival industries, and I wanted in. In the fourth quarter of 2019 I made a big plunge and purchased some digital boards from Asia. The plan was to start another division of S.I. called Screaming Media.

We continued to gain the Raiders' trust. We were doing a ton of work at the new stadium, and a ton of work up in Henderson at the new HQ. They'd also already announced ASM Global as operators of the new stadium, and I reached out to as many people on that side as I could find as well. And I was having good luck. In August 2019, they announced a naming rights deal had been struck and the Raiders' stadium would be called Allegiant Stadium. Also, in August the general contractor folks invited me for a walk-through of the stadium, at this point still just steel girders, no roof. It was amazing. Hard work really does pay off.

At the end of 2019 also, Shoe Palace was turning into a really big account. My contact Lacey was one of my favorite people to work with. They had 167 stores in the United States, and we would get super valuable experience with retail and kit-packing, which was definitely another direction I wanted to head into. It sounded scary, but once we started doing it, it was actually really easy. Their flagship store was in Hollywood on Melrose, and this is something else that made me pretty happy. We wrapped the exterior of their store several times a year, and I always showed up to the installs on that one, so I could walk my old stomping grounds. Plus, to make sure I had good pictures for LinkedIn.

In early November I got some news I thought would be unbeatable. After wrapping MGM buildings for the last six years, I was finally getting my first building wrap on the Luxor. There had been a lot of politics involved with that property, and I had been patient and played the long game, and finally got it. But that thrill was very soon surpassed when on Nov. 18, 2019, we were awarded the print and install contract for the Raiders and Allegiant Stadium. I was now the official vendor for my lifelong favorite team. The long hours and hard work were definitely paying off.

We'd had another great year. The first half began slower than expected, but we pulled in $3.1 million in sales in the second six months to finish off at $5.6 million for 2019.

I wanted to do something killer for the team for our 2019 Christmas party, so as a group we decided to have it at Topgolf. We had a whole block of bays reserved specifically for us, catered food, and an open bar. After the golfing competition we had a white elephant party in the Topgolf clubhouse, and Gabe stole the show by pinkling everyone's killer gifts as soon as they got them (haha). I gave Uber vouchers to everyone who was drinking to ensure everyone got home safe.

Also at the end of 2019, the valuation for my company came back in from the brokers, and it was acceptable to me. I would put Screaming Images up for sale in 2020.

Blind Children

First Raiders Job

Grand Opening Party
at Decatur Shop

Henderson Harley Trailer

Jonny 2 Bags from Social Distortion
Playing at S.I.

Lars from Rancid hanging out at S.I.

Lights Party

Naked Lady Mudflaps

MERCY MUSIC
Donated Backdrops

Printing Vegas Strong Banners

Tribute Window Steve Soto

Tribute Window ZZ Top

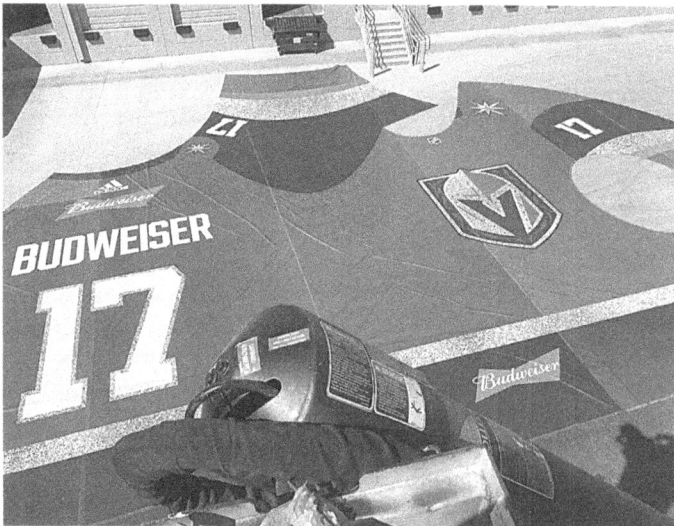

VGK Jersey Outside Shop

CHAPTER 11
SOCIAL MEDIA

"Media Blitz"

- *Germs*

My first venture into social media was in 1998 on a website called *high-schoolreunion.com*. Can't remember how I found it; I didn't know much about the internet back then. I was still in Simi Valley, and my buddy Wolfie was the only person I knew who had it at his house. We'd hang out at his pad on Lucas Court in the driveway listening to tunes, watching sports, riding skateboards, and drinking – then we'd go inside and play around on the World Wide Web.

It was also in 1998 that I transitioned from the first printing industry job I ever had at Jordan & Horn/Techtron to a full-time sales gig at Imagic in Hollywood. I had no idea how to use a computer outside of designing graphics. Even email was new to me. But I thought the internet was pretty cool.

I liked going on the high school reunion site because I could reconnect with people I hadn't seen or talked with in decades. Old friends, guys I used to play baseball with, girls I used to go out with... I always liked staying connected, still true to this day.

In 1998 less than 25% of homes had internet. When I moved from Simi Valley to Long Beach in early 2001, the first thing I did was get internet service. By this time, I think the stats indicated about half of all homes had online access. I'd have parties at my house, playing killer tunes, with a bunch of girls around; but as soon as someone saw my computer they'd ask, "Do you have internet?!" and then jump on it. It was totally new, and a big deal. And they would rather do that than party.

I had a girlfriend in early 2003 spending a lot of time on something called MySpace. She was obsessed. I'd ask her what it was, and she'd try to explain: "It's like having your own little website." I still didn't get it. Also, since at the end of 2002 I had started Screaming Images, both the girlfriend and any type of social media had gone out the window. Her because she didn't like my new schedule, and social media because I had gone back to what I knew: cold calls, on the phone.

In early-2004, having gotten S.I. off the ground and still being single, I started looking into social media again. I joined some new internet website called *match.com*. Back in those days doing something like that was a pretty big secret – you didn't want your buddies to know you were resorting to the interweb to get chicks. The Match website led me back to MySpace in mid-2004, and I finally got it – and it *was* pretty cool. You could build a profile, add pictures, and even put your own music there. I can clearly remember the first "profile song" I added there, "Preppy" by JFA. Haha. No idea why I chose that one.

What I realized was that on MySpace, you could not only search for old friends, but it would also recommend you to people that your friends were friends with. For me, it ended up that a lot of those were good-looking girls. It was a lot like Facebook (which wasn't around yet). You send a request, and they accept or deny it. Except everyone was accepting. I'd post songs and pictures, send out requests, and was all of a sudden connecting with a lot of people I hadn't spoken with in ages, and a lot of people who would have never been in my orbit otherwise. I loved connecting with people and seeing what they were up to. And I was also meeting a lot of girls – MySpace had replaced *match.com*.

I moved to Las Vegas in September 2005, and by then I was huge into MySpace. It seemed like any time I met someone new my first question was, "Do you have MySpace?" It was a good way to check them out. See what kind of pics they posted, what they were into, what kind of music they liked. It was huge. Another thing I started doing, besides connecting with old friends and trying to meet new girls, was posting pictures of my work on the platform.

I got a lot of miles out of MySpace, for sure. At some point in 2007 I asked a friend from London named Tinkler if he was on MySpace and he said, "Everyone is on Facebook at the moment." The next morning at the gym I asked my trainer Noelle if she was on MySpace, and she said the same thing. So, I went home that day, signed up, and created a Facebook profile.

At this point social media was just getting bigger and bigger, and I had access to a ton more people. I started posting pictures of my S.I. jobs on my Facebook feed right away and had pretty good reactions. Facebook seemed a little more formal than MySpace, so I laid off contacting new girls, and went back to *match.com*.

I guess the point here is, I was already using social media as a means to an end. Partially meeting girls, but mainly promoting my business. It was free, and from what I could tell, limitless. In 2007, my main concern overall was getting attention for Screaming Images, and Facebook was helping do that.

With all the success I'd had with social media, when I first saw LinkedIn and learned it was specifically for business, I was all-in. I signed up and created a profile on Jan. 29, 2008. It didn't seem to have many functions then, so I just started collecting connections, and using it to find people for sales calls. I was happy with that at the time, it was a good resource – kind of like an online business almanac.

In late 2008, I discovered you could create a separate "business" page on Facebook, so I did it. I had a ton of jobs pics to post and didn't want to bombard my personal profile every day. So, I'd post on the personal page with a link to the business page, in hopes of getting people to follow me there. I'd also have contests to give away S.I. hats, T-shirts, stickers, etc. I'd post on my personal page to let people know the contest started in an hour, or whatever, on the business page so they'd visit there if they wanted a chance for some free swag. It was working really well and was also a lot of fun.

Facebook Business was still new to me, so I wasn't exactly sure how it went. I did see I was getting *Likes* and impressions from people I didn't know, so I figured Facebook was sending it out in the algorithms to a targeted audience. Another thing I could do was copy the link to the business page and email it to prospective customers, so they could see a collection of work-related images with descriptions, as opposed to writing a big, long email with a ton of pictures and a lot of megabytes attached. Anyone could look at it, as a public page. They didn't have to follow or connect or anything. I was using it as a sales tool, multi-platform.

After a while I began taking advantage of another function it offered – buying ads. You could choose how many people you wanted to reach, and how long the advertisement would run, and it didn't really cost much. Maybe $50 for a week, targeting 10,000 additional people. All Facebook was doing was adding you into their algorithms to a wider audience. It didn't say "Sponsored" or "Ad" or anything like it does today. It just looked like a normal post. I got a lot of impressions from this, and a lot of people reached out for quotes or to refer me to someone else who needed printing. Screaming Images was a pretty easy name to remember, so they also tagged me on other people's posts who were asking for stage backdrops, vehicle wraps, or whatever. It was worth the money.

After a few years, another purpose Facebook Business served was as a picture archive. They were taking my photos and sizing them down for me, which made them emailable. Any time I was cold-calling someone about stadium graphics, windows wraps, whatever – I could just go to the business profile, pluck out 10 pictures, and put them all in an email. "Ever thought of something like this?" I would say. It worked pretty well.

Meanwhile, on LinkedIn, I was steadily increasing my connections base. It wasn't really a platform to share my work yet, but by this time you could find just about anyone on there and send them messages if you were already connected.

My first Instagram post was in June 2013. I guess I was a little late to this one, but that was okay, I was having success on other platforms. And all I was doing was ganging posts up with the personal Facebook anyway. But because of Instagram, I had a chance to discover hashtags. Here is how hashtags work (if you don't already know): Say I made a post about work stuff and added #screamingimages. If someone saw that hashtag and wanted to see more about what Screaming Images was doing, they'd click on the hashtag and every single post that has that same hashtag will show up. You would sometimes also find posts and pictures of people actually screaming, haha, but 99% of what came up would be things I posted. So, same way, if I added #stadiumgraphics to a post, and someone clicked it, they would see other posts with the same hashtag, of which some would be by competitors (if they were using socials). It may seem disadvantageous; why would I do it, right? Well, there was also a hashtag search function that people could use to search that hashtag if they were, say, looking for stadium graphics. Then I would come up for sure, and maybe get a chance to bid on their project. So, I always tried to come up with unique hashtags that people might search for if they searched for items I might be able to provide. Hashtags like #buildingwraps, #festivalgraphics, #fleetwraps, #exteriorbanners – you get the drift.

Another thing I did was search hashtags for myself. Say an event happened that we did printing for, but it was on the other side of the country, and I didn't have any good pictures. I could search hashtags on Instagram to find photos of my work. So, say we did the stage banners for a festival, I would just search their hashtags – something like #rollingloud – and I'd always find a killer shot to download, then share to my own social media platforms.

Here's a real example. Social Distortion was going on tour to support their 40th anniversary, and we printed a 40-by-20-foot fabric backdrop for them. I got a super good picture of the backdrop laid out on the shop floor before we sent it out; but it wasn't cool to post until after their first show with it, to keep it a surprise for fans. I waited until the morning after the first show of the tour, which happened to be in Irving, Texas. I opened Instagram, and searched hashtags for #socialdistortion. Bango – about a hundred killer pictures of the backdrop, at the show, showed up, and I picked a favorite. And that day I made a post on all my social media platforms with both the picture I found on hashtags, and the one I took of it laying on the shop floor.

Another way to get pictures for socials: in 2016 we did three fabric stage backdrops for Pennywise. They were playing three nights at the Hollywood Palladium and playing a classic album in its entirety each night. We made a backdrop for each album. I (unfortunately) was unable to make those shows and needed to get pictures of each night for the backdrop. So I created a contest on my socials. I had some custom S.I. T-shirts made with the PW logo on the front pocket and Screaming Images "Hollywood" on the back – they were rad shirts. I posted that whoever sent the best picture from each night of the show, that person would win one of these custom shirts. And it worked! I got at least 10 killer pictures from each night. And the winner of the contest? It was my old buddy Hutch, formerly of KROQ. He went all three nights (of course) and sent me *killer* photos.

On a Monday morning in May 2017, I opened LinkedIn to make some connections and look up someone's contact info and saw something new – a feed for posts! By this time, I was pretty good at making posts that would catch people's attention from MySpace, Facebook, Facebook Business, and Instagram. Fortunately, I'd taken a rad picture the day prior intended for use on Facebook. However, right at that moment I decided to post on LinkedIn instead. We were preparing to do the signage package for Punk Rock Bowling at the Downtown Las Vegas Events Center. I was standing inside the venue, under the LED entry arch to the venue that was all logo'd out with PRB content, and the background of the shot was the huge building wrap on The D we just finished a few days before. It was a double-whammy shot – a double-double, haha. I wrote we'd just finished the building wrap install on the west side of The D and were prepping to start on the east side. I hashtagged #buildingwraps, #downtownlasvegas #DLVEC, #festivalsignage, and #screamingimages – and got a huge response. It was 62 Likes and five comments. But even bigger, it attracted 20,000 impressions. Twenty thousand people had seen my first LinkedIn post. I was off to the races.

Here's the thing about me posting on any kind of socials – I could care less about Likes. Comments are good, because it's interaction and allows you to reply. But what I looked for was Impressions. How many people actually saw the post. That was what mattered.

I had so much fun with that first L.I. post that I made another a couple of days later – a building wrap at MGM Grand for the Canelo vs. Chavez Jr. fight. It got around 50 likes – but more importantly, about 8,000 impressions.

After these first LinkedIn posts, I was bombarded with connection requests, and I accepted every single one. I was getting about 50 a day. Back then I wasn't as worried about scammers as I am now. Nowadays, anyone wishing to connect who seems like they have a lot of connections, and have put some effort into networking on the site, are accepted. My position here is that everyone has something to say, and I'm willing to hear them out.

As far as LinkedIn messages go, anyone who puts time and effort into sending me a personally written message, and not some copy-paste deal (it's easy to tell), gets a response. It's the polite thing to do. They're just trying to make sales and connections, same as me. I'll support them when I can. It's good karma.

For a while I posted on both LinkedIn and Facebook Business – same exact content.

Different audiences, I figured. But after about six months or so the only reason I was posting on Facebook biz was for my picture archive. I wasn't getting any action from it, especially compared with LinkedIn. I posted just about every job we did that I thought was noteworthy – including big as well as small jobs. Sometimes the small ones, even though they were less-dollar jobs, were just as important. I had some rules: only positive posts, never more than once a day, and never anything that showed a mess in the background.

Another less stringent rule I had was on *when* I posted. Always in the morning – you could catch someone having morning coffee, or someone who just got to the office. And, almost never on a Friday. The only thing on most minds on Fridays is how to get work done and get out the door for the weekend. Sometimes a good time to post was on Sunday evenings. I felt like some people might be winding down their weekend, and maybe peek at socials during that down time. Everyone does it differently.

One of the most important aspects to a quality post is the picture. I would always take them at an angle to give perspective on size and scope; have a background that also grabbed attention; and showed where the photo was taken. Maybe something ended up in the background that was cool, but not our work. Oh well. I never intimated that we did it, and if I was asked, I would say, no, we didn't do that. It was all about perception. I was trying to get the attention of viewers. If the photo was taken at the shop, on the floor, I would always make sure the shop was clean and organized and had key elements as a background. This could mean a piece of equipment, or some of the décor (of other S.I.) jobs on the walls, or maybe a teammate wearing a Screaming Images T-shirt (logo always prominently displayed). Also, especially when it was a big banner or wrap laying on the floor, I'd get a 12-foot ladder and take the shot from the top of it. And I'd put one of my teammates on the floor next to it to give perspective of its big size.

Perspective. It's important. I always tried hard to ensure when people saw a picture, they understood how big it or the job was. Or maybe even to try and make it seem a little bigger than it was. Many times, when people came to the shop they'd say, "It looks bigger in the pictures." Oh well. The shop was 20,000 square feet!

I'm not sure what qualifies as a viral post. I had at least five posts that generated 500-plus likes, and a couple that got 700-plus. As stated earlier, those numbers aren't as important as impressions. And several times my post had over 100,000 impressions. Pretty good for a free website. One post that might have qualified as viral was the first post I ever made about a print-and-install job for the Raiders. Actually, every time I ever did a Raiders post it got a lot of attention – but this particular one had over 3,000 likes when they asked me to take it down, which I did immediately. The Raiders were very, very good to me, and I always did whatever they asked. I had posted pictures of some walls wraps I'd done at their temporary HQ over on Polaris. The day I posted was a Friday, and it did pretty well that day. But the next day, Saturday, it really took off. I was actually out in the middle of nowhere riding Harleys with executives from MGM and Topgolf. We were taking a water break in Nipton, Calif., and I was sitting at a table looking at the Linked app and the number of Likes was just rolling like a slot machine. It was a trip to watch; it was happening so fast. I think that's the only time I ever had a truly viral post on any of my social media platforms. I did take a screenshot of it before I deleted the post.

I was on LinkedIn for one reason, and one reason only: sales. Trying to bring print and install jobs into the shop, and also to sell my company.

Selling my business had been my plan from day one. Well, day one in Las Vegas. About a year into the LinkedIn news feed era, I was getting pretty good at it. There was a lot of information on people's personal profiles if you went looking. Often their email address was even included in their contact information. Another thing I always looked at was the link to their companies, where you could find even more stuff, like a link to a list of all their employees on LinkedIn.

With sales, I would get a target in mind. Maybe an event coming to town. I'd use Google to look for a point of entry – an initial contact. It depended on what the company was, but I'd usually start with a vice president of marketing, or operations. My line of thought was, if I initially contacted a V.P., they wouldn't be who I'd actually get work from. That it would be someone working for them. So, if I could get their attention, they'd probably hand it down to someone on their team, maybe a director or a manager. If that introduction or recommendation to the director or manager came from a V.P., they'd be more likely to reach back out than if I'd contacted them directly. It worked more often than you'd think.

Another thing I did sometimes to hedge my bets, and make sure I got the right person, was send several connection requests out. Say I found the V.P. of the company, found their profile, and sent a connection request. I'd then go onto the company's LinkedIn page and look for that "Other employees of this company" link. I'd scroll through that, select a few more people to connect with based on their position, and go from there. One of the big customers I landed with this method was Switch (in Las Vegas).

This one might seem a little weird, but another thing I'd do is look at their Facebook profile (if they had one). Maybe I'd see a picture of dogs, or them on a boat or motorcycle, or at a show – and then I could have something in my pocket to use to connect with them once we started talking. Everyone, including CEOs and VPs, have a personal life and things they like. I've ridden Harleys, had boat trips, and been to punk rock shows with some of the most buttoned-up corporate people you've ever seen or heard of.

When I made posts, I'd always stay within my personality. You're never going to sell someone something when you sound like a used car salesman. I'd use my slang-type of vernacular and try to be funny. And dramatic. I used a lot of exclamation points to make it seem exciting. I even used borderline cussing sometimes. I'd say things like "big-ass" this, and "Oh sh*t" that, and people responded in a likewise manner. I wanted to get people to notice my post, then I wanted them to read it and look at the pictures. Most of all I wanted them to interact with me in the comments section (and in my inbox).

I always, always, reacted and responded to comments on my posts. They took the time to interact, and I was going to acknowledge them for it. I also spent a lot of time scrolling through news feeds, reacting and commenting and supporting other people's posts. Between that, and all my posting, the chances were pretty good that when I reached out to someone, they already knew who I was and what I did.

Something else I started doing after a while was targeting. If I was after a particular job, event, or person, I would target them with a post. The pictures would be something I knew would interest them, the verbiage I added would be aimed at catching their attention, and I'd even look at their own, their company's, and their co-workers' profiles and posts and emulate their hashtags to help me get their attention. I'd then sit back and wait, keep an eye on my post analytics, and then bango – I'd see they looked at the post, looked at my profile, or they would just simply react to the post. I got 'em.

When I say post analytics, some of you may know this, some may not. But down on the right side of your post, right across from the impressions total, there's a link that says "View Analytics." You click and it takes to you a sub-menu with more information on your post – all good stuff like impressions, unique views, engagements – but on the bottom there's another section that says, "top demographics of unique views." From there you can toggle to categories – company size, job titles, locations, companies, and industries. These analytics actually tell you which companies have looked at your post, what cities they're in, what industry they're in, the position of the person looking, and the size of their company. It's pretty easy to deduce whether you've reached the people you're targeting with your post by looking at this information. And all of this, my friends, is free.

I spent quite a bit of time on LinkedIn. It was actually super fun, and I made a lot of friends from all over the world. Vegas is a big tourist town, and a big town for tradeshows and conferences, so everyone comes to Vegas sooner or later. I had people from all over the United States, and from at least seven countries, visit my shop for tours. England, Germany, Brazil, France, and Mexico to name a few. All printing industry folks, all cool dudes (or gals) just like me, hustling printing, in another country. They loved the vibe of the shop, all the history on the walls, the tunes, the pups being there, the cool employees. They all sent messages ahead of their Vegas trips asking if they could stop by. I said yes to every single one. Sometimes, if I had time, I'd even pick them up from the Strip and drive them back to the shop – enjoying punk rock tunes in my truck together (haha). They were all hustling, they all had a story, and I supported every single one of them. I was super stoked to know them.

Another thing I did with LinkedIn connections and friends around the country was making fun bets. For instance, when the Golden Knights were playing in the NHL playoffs, and I had a friend who lived in the city of the opposing team, we'd make a bet that the loser would post a picture of himself wearing the other team's hat. It was a lot of fun. I did it many times. Relationship builder.

I also got a lot of direct messages from people asking to have a chat. Most were smaller guys, just starting in the printing industry, asking how I did it. Some were bigger companies (competitors even) asking about materials and finishing procedures I used on certain jobs. I talked to every single person who asked for advice – kept in touch with them even, and was truthful about materials and procedures with everyone. Why would I share materials and procedures info with competitors? One of my big rules was to worry about what we were doing at Screaming Images, not what everyone else out there was doing. And I'm also a big believer in what goes around comes around. Maybe they'd help me one day. Plus, there's enough work out there for everyone, if you know how to go after it.

There was one thing on LinkedIn, interaction-wise, that I was always careful with: keeping my opinions to myself. As an owner of a business, I think that's super important. Republican or Democrat, gun control or not, immigration or not, vaccine or not – you get what I'm talking about. You never want to take the chance that someone you're doing business with, or are trying to do business with, has a different opinion. That matters to a lot of people and could influence their purchasing and relationship decisions. I have an opinion on everything, believe me, but I always kept them to myself. I do the same in my personal life.

Through the years I had a lot of folks reach out to me on LinkedIn. There were a couple of "social media experts" and a few "business consultants." One thing they always said was that I should be posting from a Screaming Images profile, and not my personal one. *Why?* It didn't make sense. I was posting from a personal point of view. I was being authentic and sharing my personal industry knowledge. I was engaging with others and building relationships that not only brought business into the shop, but also built friendships that would last forever. I was staying within my personality, which is what I set out to do from the very beginning. And it was working.

James Swanson · You
Principal/Founder, Factor Media/Screaming Images
7yr · 🌐

Completed the north side of our building wrap for the D! We're on the south side today starting peel. And, oh yeah, we're also a sponsor of Punk Rock Bowling in three weeks,   ...see more

🔥 62   5 comments

First Ever Linked Post

James Swanson
Principal, Screaming Images
3w · Edited · 🌐

We're getting pretty familiar with this little lady. Mask produced by us and installed by our awesome friends at YESCO. Those guys on the ropes are studs! Prou ...see more

😊❤️😮 722   31 Comments · 60,167 Views

👍 Like   💬 Comment   ➦ Share

📈 60,167 views of your post

Mask on Statue of Liberty
During Pandemic

James Swanson · You
Principal/Founder, Factor Media/Screaming Images
5yr · Edited · 🌐

What a nice view from the 15 South
🚗 #raiders #buildingwraps

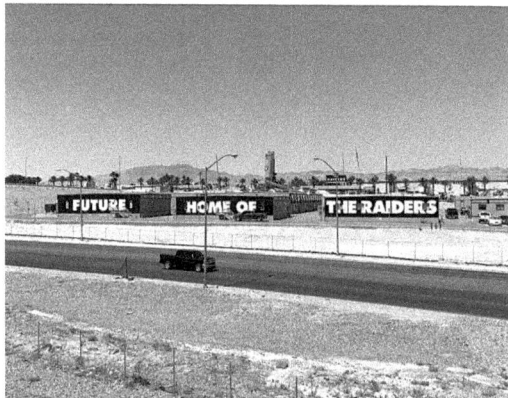

🔥 123   5 comments · 1 repost

Raiders Construction Trailers During Stadium Build

2nd Ever Linked Post

Aces WNBA Championship
Building Wrap

Aces Jersey on
Statue of Liberty

Donated Building Wrap
after Route 91

James Swanson · You
Principal/Founder, Factor Media/Screaming Images
5yr · 🌐

Rad view from the roof of the Tropicana of the huge wall murals we've been doing for MGM Grand for 4+ years!

🔥 100   7 comments · 1 repost

MGM Diamond Walls

James Swanson · You
Principal/Founder, Factor Media/Screaming Images
2yr · 🌐

"Put the logo on the building as big as you can", they said.

Done.

#mgmresorts #luxor #betmgm #buildingwraps #vegas #screamingimages

Luxor Building Wrap

👍 551   41 comments · 6 reposts

320

CHAPTER 12
2020 PANDEMIC

"The World's a Mess; It's in My Kiss"

- *X*

The year 2020 started like shit. On Jan. 4th, I had to send my beautiful companion Scout to heaven. She was 14 years old.

She'd always hated going to the vet, so I set an appointment to send her to heaven from the comfort of the only home she'd ever known. Setting that up with the doctor was the hardest thing I'd ever done – I couldn't stop crying. But Scout was pretty sensitive to my emotions, so I tried my hardest to be strong for her. We arranged it for 2:30 p.m., on a Saturday. We woke up early that morning and started a little trip out to her favorite places. The first place was Lake Mead – her favorite place in the world. I found a quiet beach, put down a blanket, and we just sat there for an hour. We left there and drove over to the ramp we had launched our boat from for the last 14 years – probably 200-plus times.

I picked her up and carried her out to the end of the dock and stood there with her in my arms for as long as I could hold her. We then went to the park where we'd been playing ball her entire life. I set up the blanket, and we just sat and for an hour watched all the pups playing. Then we went back home, and I set up a chair in the front yard and laid her down next to me. She always loved sitting in the front yard, saying hi to all her neighbors and friends. The next was the hardest.

I carried her to the backyard and set her on the deck of our boat, which I'd always kept in the RV parking on the side of our home. I got up there with her, picked her up, and we went and sat on the back bench of our boat for an hour. I was trying to be strong for her, but tears were gushing down my face. I'm pretty sure she knew what was going on. After that we had about 30 minutes until the doctor arrived. We went into the front room of the house, and I set up her favorite bed and blanket, and laid her down. She ate her last meal from my hand. After that I just laid next to her and brushed her hair for 20 minutes until the doctor arrived. She was so calm. She went to heaven at 2:45 p.m., in my arms, and the last thing I ever said to my Scout was, "Thank you for letting me be your Poppy."

***

I had pretty lofty goals for building sales for S.I. in 2020, but this definitely threw me for a loop. I never hurt so bad in my life – she was my whole world. So I did the only thing I really knew how to do. I buried myself in work.

A beautiful thing came from all this, though. On Jan. 17th, Scout directed us to a good boy-blonde Labrador named Charlie in Utah who needed a home. We rescued him, and Ranger and I welcomed Charlie to our little family. He was four, almost five, and was a big handsome boy. Almost 100 lbs., tall and skinny. Really big for a Lab.

The backstory I heard was, he had two previous owners and they both let him go. I met one of them, a middle-aged lady. She lived in Salt Lake City, and we agreed to meet halfway in Cedar City, Utah. I met her in the parking lot of a Walmart right off the highway. She already had Charlie out of the car, and his bag sitting beside him. She asked me, "Do you want him?" I replied: "You don't?" She said she was moving and couldn't keep him. I said get in the truck, Charlie, and home we went. Scout was already watching over us.

***

Our sales totaled $5.4 million in 2019. I figured it'd be a good opportunity to grow that number in 2020, as the Raiders' new stadium was under construction, and we had the contract and a title of "Proud Partner" with both the Raiders and Allegiant Stadium.

The first quarter every year was historically slower for us. January began about as usual with about $350,000 in sales. In February, things actually picked up and we did close to $475,000 – which was a lot higher than usual for that month, if you figure $441K was the average sales per month the previous year.

* * *

Around the end of 2019 I'd heard stories out of China about a virus they were calling Corona, causing a big ruckus there. I really didn't think too much about it. Then in early 2020, I heard it was coming into the United States via tourists coming from Asia and Europe. I still didn't think much about it because I remembered the SARS and MERS epidemics and heard (or maybe read) about swine flu, Asian flu, and Spanish flu over the years. Plus, every year seemed to have a flu season with people saying you should get flu shots, etc. It never much affected me personally, and I didn't remember ever hearing about it disrupting economies. So, it honestly wasn't on my radar besides hearing the news mentions.

March started out gangbusters. In 10 days, we were over-capacity busy, and it looked like we would break a sales record for a month that was historically dead slow. We had the entire graphics package for a music festival in California from Insomniac, a big boxing fight for the promoter Top Rank, then 200 light pole banners – print, hardware, installs and permits – for the Las Vegas Golden Knights hockey team. We did a refresh of the 210 "Welcome to Las Vegas" light pole banners for R&R Partners, a building wrap and a stack of events work orders from MGM, and a couple of large orders from the Raiders for events at the end of the month – along with other smaller projects from everyone else. About the 15th of the month, rumors surfaced around town about the "corona virus" spreading in Las Vegas, and that public businesses were being closed down. Then there were rumors the governor of Nevada would shut down the casinos. All this had never happened, at least not in my lifetime. It was all pretty unbelievable.

Then March 17th, all these nightmares came true when Steve Sisolak, then governor, announced he was closing down all casinos in Las Vegas. It was immediately confirmed by our clients at MGM, who then reached out for us to print a big package of "Casino Closed" signage. Sisolak also announced closure of all Las Vegas businesses unless they were categorized as *essential*.

Also at the beginning of March, we had a huge job for the NFL for an in-house conference at Green Valley Ranch. We had deployed a couple of our brand new digital/LED posters to their conference, and they loved them. We set them up and showed how to load content onto their phones so they could switch the creatives themselves, which they loved. Two days before the governor closed the casinos, the NFL shut down their conference and that was the only chance I ever got to rent out those LED posters.

The day after the forced closures, every single job we had in house was canceled, and we went from being over-capacity busy to having nothing. And I mean zero jobs. I had 38 employees at the time, and six grand format printing machines all with lease payments. The rent on my 20,000-square-foot facility was $13,000 a month. Nothing like this had ever happened before and I still didn't really understand what it meant to me and my crew. It was absolutely crazy. In this kind of situation there weren't really any precedents telling a guy like me what to do. I just knew I had to take care of my team.

I waited it out a couple of days to see what would happen and had everyone do a spring clean and shop re-organization. I thought for sure everything would open back up and the work would come back any day. But it didn't. And the situation just seemed to get worse and worse. Las Vegas was like a ghost town. The strip was completely deserted and looked like a scene from a futuristic horror movie. It was unbelievable. Very clearly the situation with S.I. wasn't going to fix itself. I had to do something.

I'd heard a lot of businesses were requesting rent abatement, and that it was supported by the local government. So I called the landlord and requested it. The landlord immediately rejected me without even considering it. They even went as far to say, on that *first phone call*, that if I didn't pay the rent, they'd evict me. It was shocking because I'd had a really good relationship with them the entire time there on Decatur. They loved how I made our shop such a creative space, and routinely asked if they could bring in current and potential renters to see our facility. I never said no. As a matter of fact, I gave them all the grand tour every time they brought people in. I silently decided to abate the rent on my own and see if they would really come after me. My teammates would be paid before the landlord for sure.

Next thing on my to-do list was to call the folks holding leases on the printers. Specifically, HP and EFI (there were also other leases for the router, welder, etc.). My overall thought was, if I could get grace periods on the rent and printers, it would amount to about $50K a month, and I might be able to avoid laying off some of my team. Both HP and EFI initially rejected the request. I countered that if they didn't give me some sort of abatement, I would sell their printers and buy other brands as soon as this pandemic cleared, and the work resumed. I knew we had some leverage because they were getting some marketing mileage out of the fact that I was posting pictures of their printers in action on my shop floor on LinkedIn, and the fact that everyone saw I was using their equipment. After a bunch more back-and-forth, they agreed on a 90-day grace period. One step down. And one thing to keep in mind here: again, there was no precedent; and I truly thought there was no way it could last more than six weeks.

After a week of this we still had zero work. Not one job. I sat with my accounting team and my outsourced CFO (one of my best friends, Kevin) and came up with what my monthly nut was, considering I now had 90 days abatement with printers. I should also mention I struck a deal with my material suppliers to put my statements/accounts on payments hold. They readily agreed as they were great partners. I was their biggest local account, and they knew I'd be the first in town back up and running. I will give them shout-outs here: Montroy and Laird. Once we arrived at the total amount of money that had to go out monthly to keep S.I. in business, I had to make the hardest decision of my life with my staff. I decided that instead of straight laying some off, I'd furlough them, which meant I would still pay for their medical insurance, with every intention of bringing them back as soon as it turned around.

On March 24th, around noon, I called a meeting in the break room to inform all my teammates. I was super emotional. These were all super good people who trusted me with their livelihoods. There'd been some conversations with them, and everyone pretty much knew what I was going to say, they just didn't know the details. It was a super hard time for them, and I felt absolutely horrible. I had meetings with a few of the managers and created a plan to keep 10 people going and furlough the rest. This was based purely on what we needed to have on hand in case some work did come in. It wasn't based on salaries, tenure, or personalities. It was based on who we needed there to help get to my goal which was to bring everyone back to work as soon as possible. At the time of this meeting there were 38 of us. We kept a project manager, a prepress operator, a press operator, an installer, a finisher, a production manager, a bookkeeper, and the designer. Plus, myself.

I want to give a shout out to Victoria here, who volunteered 100% on her own volition to keep working, even though she wouldn't be paid, in exchange for accruing hours of PTO against time she worked. She was the person in the shop who did all the invoicing. I didn't really need to explain the situation to the team. They knew the shop was completely dead work-wise and saw what was happening in the world around them.

I explained the plan to keep 10, and that the rest of them would be furloughed. I told them I would still pay for their health insurance. I promised I would work harder than ever to pivot to something to get us all back to work as soon as possible. I said for the rest of the day I would call them in one by one and talk to each one personally. My voice was breaking when I said all this – a position I never wanted to show in front of my teammates. When finally done, I went into my office and cried my eyes out.

The one-on-one meetings went way better than I thought. Almost every teammate understood the situation, and said they trusted me to turn things around. This meant the world to me and gave me even more resolve to figure this out for them. The furlough would start the following day which was a Wednesday. Rumors were circulating about a government stimulus package to help people during the crisis. My outsourced CFO and I put together an information sheet on how the furloughed team members could apply and informed them they were eligible for unemployment benefits even though it was a furlough, and how to apply. The stimulus ended up coming through quicker than anyone expected, and they started getting checks around April 11th.

At this point the local government was saying the only businesses allowed to operate were those deemed *essential* – or that the city couldn't continue without. Were we essential? Probably not. Was I going to close down because they said that? *Hell no.* I had teammates to bring back. There also were rules for places that remained open, like everyone remaining six feet apart, and to wear surgical masks. Of the 10 of us remaining, only three were coming into the shop; and the other two (besides me) were rotating. Everyone else was working remotely (which was a new concept at that time). Allegiant Stadium was still under construction, and they were fighting like hell to stay open. The first bit of print work came from them in the form of safety signage geared toward workers following rules set by the governor, and about abiding to avoid shutdown. That signage came via the general contractor building the stadium, Mortenson-McCarthy, and they were well-known for their safety protocols. They were always awesome to us, by the way. Every print and signage competitor in town besides us closed their shops with the government restrictions.

Rumor was that city workers were driving around and knocking on the doors of businesses that looked open, to check if they were essential or not. We kept about a hundred printed safety signs saying things like, "Please wear a mask" and "Please stay six feet apart" laying around on the presses in case they visited to see what we were doing. *We were essential as f*ck. No one was shutting me down.*

* * *

I was the only staffer who went in every day, and I kept the same schedule as usual, arriving at 6 a.m. and staying until 4 p.m. I usually went to the gym before going to the shop, but all gyms in Nevada were shut down by the governor. I spent all day in the shop reading news reports, scouring LinkedIn and other socials, trying to come up with some pivot to get my team back to work. One of the areas getting hammered by the restrictions were restaurants. Some were allowed to stay open by saying things like "curbside pickup," so I jumped on that. Raising Cane's (the chicken finger place) was a very new customer from late in 2019, so I called Kylie, one of their local directors (and who I had worked with during her time at UNLV), and asked what they were doing. She was already all over the curbside pickup thing and loved the idea of some directional signage in the parking lots for her restaurants. So we started printing for them. Still, it wasn't enough to sustain a 20,000-square-foot shop with 38 employees, so I kept hustling. Next on my list was floor and carpet decals – the businesses allowed to be open could be interested in putting reminders on their floors for people to stay six feet apart. We picked up some of that stuff. Still not enough though.

* * *

When Scout went to heaven I was crushed. Charlie boy was definitely helping with our grief (he loved coming to the shop every day), but my heart was still broken over losing such an amazing companion. I was determined to pay tribute to her, and came up with an idea in early January, before all the coronavirus stuff. I had really nice gold coins made with Scout's picture, and started a nonprofit called Scout's Honor, which I would use to exchange these coins for donations and use 100% of the money to help pets and their owners in need of food, medicine, and surgeries. I was excited to get going on this – but the coins didn't arrive until mid-April and by then the world was in a pandemic and economic crisis. Not a good time to ask people for donations.

On April 17th, I got up in the morning, put one of Scout's coins in my front pocket for good luck (for the first time), and headed to the shop at 5:45 a.m. Upon arrival I went through my usual routine of walking the shop and checking job tickets, and then having breakfast. I was the only one there. My plan for the day was to reach out to all my furloughed teammates to see how they were doing and give them an update, and then continue working on ways to turn the shop around. A couple weeks earlier on LinkedIn I had seen a post from an East Coast company that was pitching acrylic dividers for slot machines. Great idea, I thought. I hadn't gotten anyone to bite yet until I reached out to a longtime friend and customer, Adam, who was at the time assistant general manager of the El Cortez Hotel and Casino in downtown Las Vegas. And by the way, the El Cortez is the second-oldest casino in Las Vegas, opening in November 1941. I asked if he had considered plastic partitions to help the casino reopen. He replied that, funnily enough, he'd been sitting at his desk that morning doing some drawings on this exact thing – and asked if I could come down right away to go over it. I said, "Hell, yes!" My Scout coin lucky charm was already working on its first day in my pocket.

It took about 15 mins to get there, and Adam was waiting as planned. Keep in mind that security for the closed casinos was super heavy then. He walked me in, past a few more guards, to the completely empty floor. What a trip. Again, it was like some apocalypse movie. We exchanged pleasantries while walking through the empty casino. He and I had a lot in common. He also once upon a time was a printing company owner, selling his company several years earlier. One of the smartest and nicest guys in Las Vegas. I had my crude drawings for slot machine dividers in hand, and he had some drawings he made as well. We discussed logistics of material, sizes, weight, application, etc., on the dividers. Then he said, "I don't really make a lot of money off slot machines. Where I make my money is at the blackjack tables..." Let's go look at them, I said.

We walked across the casino floor to one of the pits where the table games were located. Keep in mind, this was something totally new to me, even though I'd always been really good at figuring out ways to do things. I said we could take three 4-by-8-foot sheets of quarter-inch acrylic, and cut notches at the table height so we could slide them into the tables. These would separate players and allow him to get four people at a table. Then, I said, we could cut slits in the top of each 4-by-8-foot sheet to place a bendable 1/16th-inch piece of acrylic into the slots horizontally, to protect dealers from players. We'd leave a 6-inch opening on the bottom for chips and cards to be shared. He loved it. All we needed was to get an official set of measurements and determine how we would attach it all to the table so it would stay up safely. We were both super excited and agreed I would come back the following Monday with a couple of teammates to survey.

Over the weekend, I reached out to a news reporter, Mick from the *Las Vegas Review Journal*, who I'd spoken with after a few of our higher-profile local installs. I said I might be onto something big and asked if he was interested in going to El Cortez with me Monday to observe a meeting I was having about solutions for re-opening casinos. He replied immediately that he was all-in. I also called our local vendor that supplied us with the acrylics we used for printing on a pretty regular basis, and he also readily agreed to join us. This was Jeremy from Laird Plastics. From my S.I. team, I looped in our designer, an installer, and a sales guy, Scott. I got them all approved to go into the casino by Adam, and our meeting was set.

Since we had a bigger crew this time, it took us a while to get vetted by casino security. Once in, we went directly to the pit, and I explained what I envisioned for the blackjack table dividers. Our designer and installer quickly did a field survey on the table and made some adjustments on what I envisioned – in particular, the vertical shields dividing the players would not go all the way to the floor. They would be cut up higher and stay in place via custom attachment hardware, and this would give players more leg room and cut down on material and weight. Perfect, we all loved the idea. They also came up with a way to make the attachment hardware without having to tap or screw anything into the actual table, which was super important to Adam. Once we all agreed on the plan for moving forward, we also agreed to return to the shop, cut the first prototype set, and be back tomorrow to install it. I could see by the look in the reporter's eyes: we were onto something big.

We caravanned back to the shop to get the ball rolling on this prototype. I was in a hurry to get this one done – I had furloughed teammates in mind. I was pretty confident we were way ahead of the rest of the country on this, but you never know. This amount of this material wasn't something we normally kept on the shop floor, but we were lucky that we had Jeremy from Laird with us as he called ahead to his warehouse and had material delivered to our shop. By the end of the day, we had the first prototype designed and cut, and we were ready to install in the morning.

At 10 a.m. the next day, we reconvened at El Cortez to install the first prototype of our new invention and see how it fit and looked on a table. Same crew as the day before. It took about an hour to install, because it was the first time, and totally new. Our plan was to make them so they could be installed in 15 minutes or less per table. Overall, it looked really good and seemed functional. There were a few size adjustments and a couple modifications that Adam requested, so we marked it up, removed it, and headed back to the shop to make a second prototype.

We were ready to install the second prototype the next morning. This was Wednesday, April 22nd. We went there late morning, checked through security, and this time it took just 40 minutes to install. The size was totally dialed in this time. We still had one more adjustment – the size of the divider between the dealer and the players – and we also needed to do some tightening up with the attachment hardware. We returned the next morning with those modifications and got a sign-off from Adam. He then informed us there was still one more step: Security had to sign off. They had to check it through the cameras to ensure everything was visible, and that all transactions could be monitored via security camera feeds. So we left it up and got out of there. Mick from the newspaper was there every second of every meeting and took a ton of notes.

I was called by Adam the next day, a Friday, that security was close to signing off, but had some questions. Could we return Monday morning? We set it up for 10 a.m.

The entire team headed there Monday morning, and we were introduced to the El Cortez security team. It seemed the shields/dividers had passed the test – but they had questions about cleaning them. Would it affect the sheen on the acrylic? Because that could affect the camera feeds. How often would they need to be cleaned? How easy would it be for people to knock them down? Or take them apart? We answered all questions to their satisfaction, and they gave Adam the green light. The reporter took a bunch of pictures of the final product, and we were out the door to wait to hear back from Adam on orders – which depended a lot on what the Nevada Gaming Commission would say.

On April 28th, the *Las Vegas Review Journal* published an article titled: "Las Vegas Firm Creates Safety Shields for Use at Casino Tables," and my phone and email immediately started blowing up.

* * *

Calls and emails came from multiple news outlets. First, TV news stations. They wanted to visit and interview me. Calls also came from Indian casinos, who for the most part are not regulated by their states and wanted to know how much we charged per set. We hadn't even thought about this yet! Also, a bunch of calls came in from companies that supply equipment and services to the casino industry. They too wanted to know how much – but also wanted to know how fast we could get some out the door.

One of my big concerns was – if we started producing a ton of these table game shield sets – what would happen to all the poly-carbonate material after all this ended? We still didn't know how long it would last. We found a company that not only recycled this stuff, but also picked it up. And we made a plan for that.

Next was pricing. We knew it took three 4-by-8-foot sheets to cut one set of shields for a blackjack table, and that material cost was around $160. We put a price tag of $999 per table, and drew up an instructions sheet for install that was very similar to something you'd get from IKEA. Our big thing here was to make them modular, easy to set up by their own staff, and recyclable. One smart thing I did from the get-go was get my guy from Laird involved, and for him to come with us to all the meetings. This would come in handy big time a little farther down the line when everyone was fighting for the material, when it started to get as scarce as toilet paper. He was squarely on our side.

On May 1st, a Friday, we started bringing back some staff. I was so F-ing happy. We had sheets in production on the router by Monday and were shipping table sets out by Wednesday. People were ordering 20 units at a time. To be clear here, we were using equipment we already had and material we already used. We had just pivoted and were using them for different purposes. We were back in business.

We had orders and requests for information coming in from all over the country. Local people couldn't just pop over to the shop because of the social distancing rules, and people from out of state (and country) couldn't either, obviously. I devised a plan for that. I found a local prop business that sold used gaming tables, so I went there and bought a blackjack and a poker table. Brought them back to the shop, we cut shields sets, and I set them up right in the middle of the shop floor. We put barriers up on three sides with backgrounds that had the ShareShield logo on them, which is what we were calling this product, and also one that said Keep Vegas Clean which was another initiative we pushed. We added a casino-like carpet underneath, and we had a casino floor right in our shop. Now what we could do was have a FaceTime call with anyone who wanted to see what they looked like and how they functioned. It also worked well for news crews and magazines.

This period was super crazy. Everyone in the country wanted to talk with us. The easiest way to put this in perspective is with a timeline of people who visited us and interviewed me:

4/29/20 – Channel 13 News (CBS affiliate), broadcast live from the shop, interviewed me

4/29/20 – Getty Images, interviewed me and took pictures of equipment-cutting shields

4/30/20 – *Washington Post*, reporter flew out with a cameraman, interview with me

5/2/20 – Univision, interviewed me at El Cortez for live broadcast

5/5/20 – Channel 3 News (NBC affiliate), broadcast live from the shop, interviewed me

5/7/20 – Fox 5 News (local), broadcast live from the shop, interviewed me

5/7/20 – *New York Times*, Zoom call with me for newspaper and online article

5/14/20 – *Sports Illustrated* magazine, Zoom call with me and online article

5/16/20 – *Forbes* magazine, phone call with me and online article

We also had articles on us in *Travel & Leisure, Business Times, Vegas Inc, Slate* magazine, *Atlantic City Weekly, Daily Mail* (UK), and a bunch more. We also had calls from 60 Minutes-like TV shows from France (Envoye Special) and Brazil to set up interviews in our shop at the end of May for shows in those countries. And the local broadcasts from FOX 5 and NBC were picked up by their national affiliates, and my interviews were broadcast in 27 states.

But the best thing happened on May 19th. I was able to bring every single one of my teammates back to work.

There were a couple of exceptions. Two asked to "come back in a couple months," which meant after their stimulus checks expired. We politely declined and turned their furloughs into layoffs. Pretty remarkable here is that of 28 furloughed employees, all but two returned to work instead of taking the easy way out. I had a solid team.

At this point I also needed to add support – we were completely buried. My old buddy Dennis mentioned he had a couple of good people he had to lay off. He was over at Topgolf by then, and they were 100% closed. He asked if I could use their help. I was super stoked to bring Mary aboard to help with sales, and marketing and managing shields orders, and Ken to help with creative/design. I was lucky to have those two during the pandemic year.

By now we were also having a handful of visitors back to the shop. Everyone had different levels of comfort with all this, between masks, social distancing, vaccinations, etc. – so right at the front door we put a big 2-by-6-foot vertical board with a table in front of it with red, yellow, and green rubber wristbands. The board instructed them to choose a color wristband that conveyed their comfort level, and put it on before walking in. Green meant "I am good, let's hug it out." Yellow meant "I am cautious – let's not overdo it with the hugs, handshakes and stuff." Red meant "stay six feet away, I am just here for business." Personally, I wore green and wanted to hug every single person who walked in the door, because I was so fucking happy to see them.

* * *

Charlie was finally settling in. He'd had a rough first couple of months – I think he was heartbroken. Two sets of people he loved, and they both let him down. I was going to make him feel loved again. He had his forever home now.

* * *

By mid-May, and as busy as we were, none of the gaming table shield sets we made were being purchased by local casinos. We were invited to participate in a contest of sorts at Bellagio. It ended up we were competing for the blackjack table shields business with six other local companies. Everyone had jumped on the bandwagon once I started getting all the press – which was cool with me. Everyone was trying to get by. There were cabinetry companies, set designers, exhibit builders – all there. These were all super high-end shield sets. Ours was built to be inexpensive, modular, and easy to set up – that wouldn't fly at Bellagio. It was okay, though, we were already beyond buried with the Indian casinos and their suppliers. Plus, there was another little problem starting to develop: the polycarbonate and acrylic materials became very scarce. But remember, I had included Laird Plastics in all the original meetings at El Cortez. That decision paid off in spades – every time a truck of material came in it was offered to me first. I had to make decisions on the spot when these calls came in. Everything was really fluid; we took orders and shipped them out in three to five days. Making big purchases of material was risky, because I didn't yet have orders. But I kept rolling the dice and buying the whole truckload – $60,000 per pop. I hoped the orders would keep coming.

MGM reopened its casinos June 4th. We did zero tables for them. Again, it was okay. We were still their go-to for printing and installation. There was plenty of that type of work to go around, and we were getting most of it.

Also in June, the construction of Allegiant Stadium, new home of the Raiders, was coming close to completion. Their first home game in the new stadium would be played with no fans in attendance because of the virus. In April I came up with the idea of using big banners to cover up seats with logos of their sponsors since there were no fans. I waited patiently for the Premier League (English soccer) to start. I was a fan first off, but I also wanted to see what they would do with the seats without fans. They were the first league to restart. They suspended their season in March but were able to restart on June 17th. I already had mockups of stadiums with seats covered with banners made, and had sent them to the Raiders, Redskins, Panthers, and to the NFL, but no one was really hearing it. I was up early and anxious to see what the EPL would do. Games showed on TV, and sure as shit they had the entire bottom sections of the seats, closest to the field, covered with banners. I was taking pictures of my TV and sending them to everyone saying, "I told you so!" Major League Baseball started back up in late July, and they also had seats covered. They were done very poorly though. The NHL reopened in July also, but they did it differently. They picked two hub cities, and everyone played there. When they started their season, I was anxiously watching to see what they'd do. Yep, seat covers. But theirs were different. I had been working for the NHL for a long time, and they are perfectionists with branding and signage for their events, which I loved. True to form, they'd built frames underneath the banners and around the seats so all the banners were squared off, taut, and looked perfect. I took more pictures off my TV.

I had a meeting with the Raiders mid-August to discuss seat covers for their upcoming season. I had 10 or so folks from both the Raiders and Allegiant Stadium there. We were in the stands, by a specific seat section, to discuss it. The first 20 rows covered is what was mandated by the NFL. I pulled out photos from a couple Major League Baseball stadium seat covers to show them. I said, "You can do it like this," then, showing them the picture of NHL seat covers, I said, "Or, you can do them like this." Hands down they all wanted the seat covers framed out. I said it would cost a lot more, and they said provide a quote.

The quote was super high, as I knew it would be. I gave it to them, and they fell out of their chairs, and asked for a quote the other way, without the frames. So I quoted them that way. Didn't hear back for a week and we were starting to run out of time. Finally, they approved the version with the frames – but now we only had two weeks to get the job done. It was a lot of work. Shit.

An issue we covered with the frames was that our setup wouldn't need to tap or screw into any of the seats, which were all brand new. We had a pretty brilliant system planned by my installer and buddy, Matt. We got a deposit and bought all the metal sticks we needed to build the frames. It was a lot of work just getting them into the stadium and up into the seats, let alone building and installing them. For the sizes of the banners to be exact, we had to wait for the frame to be completed so we could measure. They weren't perfect squares or rectangles; all were different sizes and shapes. Matt had a crew of about 15 working 18 hours a day to get done in time. Another big part of this was, the Raiders wanted their luxury end zone club completely covered with a banner, because they didn't want anyone to see it on TV until fans were allowed in the stadium. It also had an odd shape, had to be installed without drilling or tapping any holes in a brand-new stadium, and it had to be super tight. It required us to make a banner that was 75 feet high and 225 feet wide in one piece. I worried about this one. But the install crew came through, and that sucker fit perfectly and was tight enough to ride a skateboard on.

We literally finished the seat covers job the day of the first game. I walked out of the stadium at 2:30 p.m., and the game started at 5:15. The feedback from the Raiders and the stadium folks was phenomenal. And once it was on TV that night my phone started blowing up again. Everyone I spoke with from around the country and in my industry said the Raiders had the best seat covers in the NFL.

* * *

Another big project we had for the Raiders in September was right across the street from the stadium – the Teammates HQ warehouse. We wrapped every square inch of the inside walls with Raiders branding – it was a lot. About 20,000 square feet. I had Gabe install this one all by himself. About halfway through, everyone from the Raiders operations teams said, "Damn! Gabe is a beast!" Yeah, I already knew that.

* * *

Charlie had come a long way in the last nine months. He was happy and feeling loved. He was always so excited in the mornings when I got home from the gym because he knew he was going for a walk and then going to work. He loved going to the shop every day. My teammates in the front office showered him with affection, and I think he felt like he finally had a home. He was the sweetest boy – my gentle giant.

In October I made another huge decision: we would add to our family again. I wanted to have another puppy to raise from a baby. I found a breeder of Red Fox Labradors in Reno, Nevada, and secured the first female of a litter. She was due to be born at the end of November, and we would call her Finch.

* * *

So now we headed into the year's final quarter. We'd been consistently busy since the newspaper article in April. The shields business was still going but slowed some. By this time of the year everyone in the country was doing it, which is what I expected. I saw some hard times coming.

I told everyone at the shop that we just had to work harder than everyone else to keep that kind of business. It had morphed out – and besides table game shields we also started doing dividers for offices, shields for countertops, shields for inside cars – just about every kind of divider you could think of.

But I knew that as the year wound down, we would get slow again. A second wave of the coronavirus was coming, masks were being mandated again, and there was a super crazy presidential election.

We'd had record sales numbers all through summer. Our best month was September, when we had $900,000 in sales, an all-time S.I. record. Morale in the shop was super high. We had pulled a rabbit out of a hat during a worldwide pandemic. October slowed down a bit, and I was still sensing some more pain coming our way. November our sales dropped to $400K; and at that point our overhead and payroll was really high, so we lost money again that month. December sales went back up to $570K, for the most part due to a big seat covers job we did for the NBA's Oklahoma City Thunder. But the country was back to being in a crisis.

A huge piece of news came on Dec. 11th, though. We were awarded the exclusive print-install contract with Resorts World – the Las Vegas Strip's huge new hotel and casino.

Wow, 2020 was a hell of a ride. I lost $320,000 in March and April, but then turned it around. We had record sales numbers all through summer, shipped thousands of blackjack table sets to Indian casinos all over the country, and helped the Raiders open a new stadium. Total sales figures for 2020 totaled $6.3 million – a 15% increase from the year prior. During a worldwide pandemic. I turned a $270K loss the first four months of the year into a profitable year. If I hadn't called Mick from the *Review Journal* to join us for all our shield meetings at El Cortez in April, after 18 successful years I would have gone out of business in 2020.

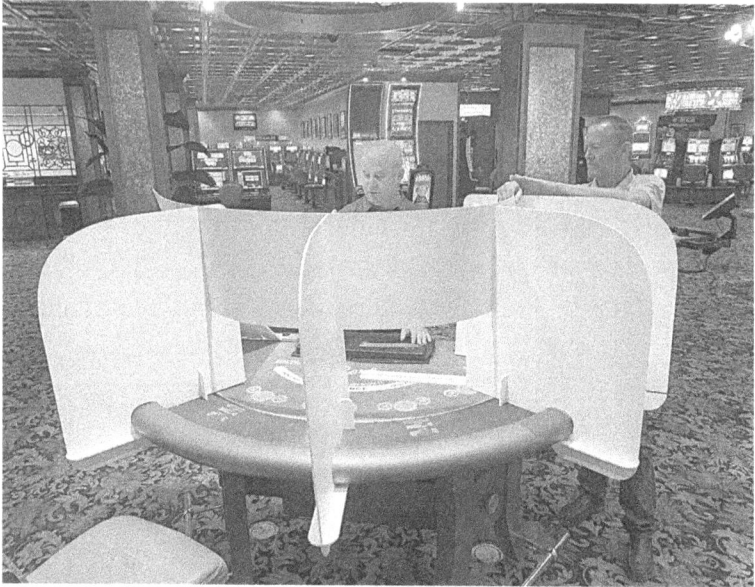

Blackjack Table Shields El Cortez Hotel

Las Vegas Raiders seat and End Zone Covers 2020 Season

CHAPTER 13
2021: END GAME

"Great Rock n Roll Swindle"

- *Sex Pistols*

The year 2021 started just like 12 months prior: dead. A second wave of Covid hit in Winter 2020, there was a crazy presidential election, and even more craziness from the White House on Jan. 6th. We had ridden our wave of blackjack table dividers and other plexiglass products as far as we could. We started in April 2020, and literally were among the first businesses in the country, if not *the* first, to make dividers for gaming tables. I'd played it super smart and manipulated the news and social media to get us attention all over the country, and it had worked. The problem was, everyone saw what we did and emulated our products. That, combined with the fact that most places needing dividers now already had them, made that line run its course. I saw that coming and tried to be as frugal as possible. Hard times would return for a while.

Another thing in late 2020 had been the brief return of events. Every host of big events, all over the country, charged out the gate hard after the first round of Covid wound down. I knew it wasn't stable. It all would slow down again. Call it owner's intuition. A lot of companies in the markets we served just didn't have money to spend. As a result, we had a really bad first quarter and lost a lot of the money we had earned back after losing revenue in the first quarter the previous year. If you can follow that. Basically, in the first quarter of 2021 we were right back in a pandemic crisis. But again, with owner's intuition, I saw better times coming in 2021.

* * *

I knew the entire country was still in economic hard times. I had these Scout's Honor Foundation coins I'd sat on for almost a year, and I knew if I didn't start putting them up for donations it might never happen. Around mid-January, I got together with Mary, and we created a PayPal link to collect donations. I posted about the foundation on Facebook, Instagram, and LinkedIn. Everyone following me on social media knew all about Scout, how much I loved her, and what a special girl she was. I explained in the posts that 100% of donated money would go to help dogs get food and needed medicine and surgeries.

In exchange for a $50 donation, I would send them a gold "Scout's Honor" Coin with her picture engraved on it. I would pay for all postage and send monthly updates on the pups we helped. The coins were really nice, and super well-made. I had no idea what the reaction would be – but the response was immediate and overwhelming. We received probably 50 donations that first day – Mary and Angelica started helping me get coins out the door immediately. The donations continued to pour in, and we still get some to this day. I am super stoked to say Scout's Honor has raised over $10,000 to date and helped hundreds of pups. Scout was still making a difference in people's lives from heaven.

* * *

My plan for the last decade had been to build the company and sell it. I was killing myself with stress and the hours I put in. It had destroyed all of my social skills. For the last five years of Screaming Images, I pretty much had no personal life.

When you move to sell your company, you go through a process called a valuation. A business brokerage is hired, which goes through all your financials, your inventory and equipment, your employees – what they do and how much they're paid, your current client list and how valuable that is, how scalable your business is based on the markets you're in, what city you're based in, the industry you're in, and how many competitors you have in your local market. They take all this and come up with a multiple to add to your assets. That's how they come up with the value (there's a lot more to it, this is just in layman's terms). I had gone through all this in the middle of 2019, and the brokerage came back with a number I was pretty happy with. Before we could put it to market, 2020 happened and it all went out the window.

After the first quarter 2020, I wasn't even sure I would still have a business. I literally went from a valuation in the millions to the possibility I could lose it all and have nothing for 18 years of hard work. I didn't have a big corporation behind me, any investors, or some big family business to bail me out when the world went south. Still, by summer I had turned it all back around with the blackjack table dividers. I had pivoted, adapted, and pulled through. So in Summer 2020, I went back to the brokerage, asked if we could put it back on the market, and was informed we'd have to go through the whole valuation process again. So we did, and the end number ended up being pretty close to the first.

By the time the valuation was complete we were into January, ready to start sending it out. I met with the broker offsite one morning in mid-January and he asked what I wanted to do, and I told him I still wanted to put it out. I saw a few more weeks of hard times, but a ton of work coming after that. In the end I was right.

A reason I had that ol' owner's intuition that it would turn back around was, we'd been the only grand format print company in Vegas that stayed open the entire pandemic. We were there for not just our customers locally, but everyone else locally, too. That also included people from out of town coming in for events. Plus, we had the Raiders contract, and I knew all that would pay off.

With all this stressful stuff going on, I had an amazing thing coming up that was keeping me rolling forward and working hard. Finch was coming home on Jan. 22nd, and Charlie, Ranger, and I couldn't wait for her to join our family.

For anyone wondering where I came up with my pup's names: My favorite book of all time is "To Kill a Mockingbird." If you're unaware, the main character was a little tomboy named Scout. She was tough and feisty, and that was exactly how I wanted my Scout to be.

For Ranger, she had had a super hard beginning of her life before she came to us, and was super scared and cautious, and only crawled on her belly for the first month she was with us, so I wanted to toughen her up. I thought Ranger would be fitting. Charlie came with his name, but I gave him the middle name "Jem" when he came to us. Jem was the name of Scout's older brother in "To Kill a Mockingbird." And Finch was, in the book, the family's surname. The little tomboy girl, the main character, her full name was Scout Finch. There you go.

* * *

The valuation was officially ready to send out in the third week of March. The broker had a list of thousands of potential buyers they mass send a generic sell sheet to, but I told them they didn't need to do that. I gave him the names of 10 printing companies from around the country and told him that's all he needed – one of them would buy S.I. The way it goes is, they send a generic sheet stating type of printing, sales revenues, the region we were located, and a few other generic details. If the company was interested, they would need to sign and send back a very formal non-disclosure agreement, and then they would get the full package.

Two days after the generic package was sent, we had nine signed NDAs. The process usually was that the buyers were supposed to go through the broker with questions and for more details, but every single one of them didn't want to do that. They wanted to talk directly to me. Every one of the potential buyers knew exactly who I was from social media, industry magazines, and plain-ol' word-of-mouth. So, I had seven Zoom calls set up that week. The majority of them said to me in the first minute of the conversation, "I was hoping it was you." After the calls, and within three days, we had five letters of intent – basically an offer. I did have two favorites I really hoped for.

* * *

So, like I predicted, the first quarter wasn't good. We had sales of $274K in January and $292K in February which are disaster months considering our monthly average in 2020 was $520,000. Things started ticking up in March and we had $473K in sales, led by a lot of small-to-medium jobs from MGM. We also got a ton of work for the new Virgin Hotel, which I picked up from months of hard cold calling. Virgin bought the old Hard Rock Hotel on Paradise, went under renovations for over a year, with an opening date of March 21st. We also got a bunch of work from the Raiders, and even picked up $18K in work from ShareShield, our plexi/divider products.

April was about the same, with a really nice job from Kawasaki. May jumped way bigger though, with $575K in sales, led by Jimmy Jazz, a shoe retailer with 170 stores in the United States. Retail and shoe stores were a big market I was hot to get into; and that we were well-equipped to handle. We'd been doing all the Shoe Palace stores for several years and had recently finished a good-sized job from Adidas. We also got good jobs from Insomniac (music festivals), the Las Vegas Aces (WNBA), and the Las Vegas Lights (Vegas' professional soccer team). It was about to hit hard; I could feel it.

* * *

At the end of May, I signed a letter of intent to start exclusive negotiations to sell Screaming Images, the company I had started 19½ years earlier and built from the ground up, to a company in the Midwest. At this point we would start a process called "due diligence," which in layman's terms is where the buyer requests detailed information and we provide it. I wasn't really looking forward to it, as this type of stuff wasn't my strong point. And I had a couple good friends that recently sold their companies, and I heard horror stories. Plus, I was busier than hell at the shop, just trying to print stuff and get it out the door.

June was gangbusters with $709K in sales. To be clear here, that means selling $700K-plus worth of *banners and stickers*. It was almost $200K over the monthly average from the previous year. This was all led by a six-figure job from our brand-new customer, Resorts World, who were opening June 21st. I'd won the contract via a full year of cold calling. We also had a big job from the Raiders, a huge exterior banners job for Yaham, and I picked up another new client, Caesars/Harrah's.

The Resorts World job was a beast. They wanted to wrap 29 huge construction walls in the seven days leading up to their grand opening. It was practically impossible – but I had my secret weapon – Gabe. He took the job on his own, no helpers, and finished in time. He worked 20 hours a day seven days in a row. He'd leave to go home, take a nap and shower, then go right back. I'd never seen anything like this kid. I wouldn't have had the success I did if he wasn't on my team, that's for sure. Hardest worker and most honest guy I'd ever met.

Finch was six months old by now and was making me super happy. She was defiant and rambunctious as hell, but also super loving and sweet. She loved her toys and playing fetch – things I really missed about Scout. She also absolutely loved coming with me and her brother and sister to the shop every day. She would be completely wiped out when we got home.

***

Due diligence with the buyer trucked right along. I sat through Zoom calls just about every other morning listening to lawyers and CFOs, and not understanding anything they said. Thank God I had my buddy (outsourced CFO) Kevin on my team to translate everything after calls. We were eyeing a close of the sale in October. Between all this, and how busy we were at the shop, all I was doing was working and sleeping. And even that was only 5½ hours a night.

July was another big month with $650K-plus in sales. We had more banner work for Yaham. We were covering a building at Resorts World that was only framed, with exterior mesh banners to make it appear like a completed building. We called it *urban camouflage*. We had two big building wraps at MGM Grand – one for the Fury vs. Wilder boxing fight, and one for

Hakkasan nightclub. Insomniac was back with a vengeance after missing their biggest festival, EDC, in 2020 due to the pandemic. We were just starting on that one. We also had big jobs from the Raiders, Colorado Buffaloes football, and a super fun one for our friends at Impulso marketing agency that was across multiple MGM properties for the Fury-Wilder fight.

All my hard work with the casinos the past 10 years was paying off big time. Anyone can print stuff – but the key to winning, maintaining, and keeping customers is customer service and communication. I always answered my phone. I responded to emails within 15 minutes. I could be onsite at properties and venues within an hour. I was always a presence at job sites during install – I was an owner-operator. I also recognized the massive marketing opportunities I was on social media posting content of big jobs we did continuously for massive names in Vegas.

I wasn't trying to make as much profit as possible off of every single job, which was a huge mistake all my competitors kept making. Profit-wise I would win most, break even on a few, but I *always* ended up with new customers due to this stance. I played the long game and won big at it. My customers never left me. They were so comfortable with us; they didn't even bid their big projects out. They just gave them to us. By this time Screaming Images was the go-to for anyone coming into Las Vegas with an event. We were referred by everyone in town, and we were plastered all over LinkedIn.

Besides all this craziness at the shop, I still had the due diligence proceeding for the business sale. It was a lot of work. The buyer asked for things I hadn't heard of or seen for almost 20 years. Things I didn't know where to find. They were searching on the internet and finding things that were either long taken care of, or simply weren't accurate. I then had to prove it. Everything they asked for was eventually found and uploaded to a secure Dropbox that we called Scout's Project (it had been a year and a half since she went to heaven, and I was still broken-hearted and missing her every day). The lawyers from both sides were going back and forth about tax issues, accounting procedures, equipment leases, expenses, write-offs, add-backs... It was exhausting.

∗ ∗ ∗

Finch was growing up very quickly, a huge force in the shop every day. Customers loved her and would sometimes stop by just to visit with her. During this time, she and Charlie built a huge bond. My heart was full in that area for sure. My pups, as always, were getting me through difficult times. Twice a day I'd break from all the madness and walk them around the entire complex on Decatur. They loved going on walks.

∗ ∗ ∗

We continued breaking sales records in August with $740K-plus. We had a huge month with MGM. They converted a section of the Luxor parking lot into a tailgate arena for football games and other events at Allegiant Stadium, and we did all the branding – print and install. It was all designed and led by Daren Libonati, of course, the most badass events and venues guy ever in the history of Las Vegas. The dude was an inspiration.

We continued with the graphics package for EDC/Insomniac's event set for October – rather than its usual end of May. We were working this early on tent walls for all their vendor booths and concession stands. Tons and tons of printed and finished vinyl walls. We also landed one I was super stoked about – working for TGI on the Gold Cup Final soccer game at Allegiant Stadium. I literally had been cold calling these dudes for five years. Persistence pays off, folks. On this one we also were the first to ever wrap the massive lanai windows at the stadium. You could see this wrap up the 15 freeway from the Flamingo exit, five miles away. We also had big jobs from Topgolf, the Redskins, we got the entire Life is Beautiful music festival signage package, and I picked up another one I'd worked on for years, WWE. World Wrestling Entertainment. They planned a huge event at Allegiant Stadium. My partnership with the Raiders was paying off in spades.

Come September we weren't close to finishing the due diligence, and the anticipated October closing date was looking unobtainable. The lawyers kept going back and forth on what seemed to me the same issues. We would take something out of the sales agreement, and they would put it back in. Then it would be taken back out. It was overwhelming, and I was seriously treading water on trying to keep up on all of this while the shop was busier than ever. Plus, I didn't fully understand most of it. But Ranger, Charlie, and Finch were all super happy, which kept me going.

The sales record streak continued in September with $795K-plus in sales. Once again led by MGM, with the addition of wrapping the suites at the Luxor tailgate area, a massive building wrap on Luxor facing the Strip for "America's Got Talent," and three more diamond walls. But the biggest one (marketing-wise) from MGM was a collaboration with the Raiders. We put a Raiders eye patch on the Luxor Sphinx, which would once again get us national attention, and with the local news as well. And also, another Best of Wide Format award from *Big Picture* magazine. This looked like a tough job but was actually super easy. We rented a lift to survey, and I asked the installers to get me two dimensions – ear to ear and the height of the eyeball. From there we took a straight-on picture, mocked it up in Adobe Illustrator, scaled it to the two dimensions we took, and produced it. It was actually printed and finished on one shift the night before we installed. We'd done this type of thing so many times by now it was second nature. As was the risk always associated with this type of work. I had one of MGM's highest executives, and one of my biggest allies, standing next to me during the install. She was stressing. I wasn't worried.

Besides MGM work we also did a ton more for Insomniac as they prepared for the return of EDC, more from the Raiders as they prepared for their season opener, a big building wrap for Westgate, a bunch of work from Revolution marketing for iHeartRadio music festival, floors for MLB broadcast booths from TNT Sports, and a big job from our friends at 160over90 for the UFC Fan Experience.

For October, we did $701,000. Everyone at the shop was beat, but we couldn't take a break yet. Insomniac was ready to turn in the exterior fence banners for the festival, which was usually the last item, and the biggest part of the job for EDC every year. Because this was the first year back after missing a year, there were more fences needed than previously. I expected it to be a lot – but not as much as what came in. It was 165,000 square feet of printed fence banners. And we had about 30 days to do it. Luckily part of my crew consisted of the three best banner finishers in the country – and also the three of the hardest working guys. Manny, Francisco, and Herbie were badasses. I had a meeting with them when the banners went on press and I gave them some incentives. They said of course they were up for it. We agreed they'd go on 12-hour shifts every day until the job was done. I told them if we got ahead, I'd do my best to get them days off. Besides the incentives, they were also getting overtime and double-time working those hours. I asked them the hours they preferred, and they said 4 a.m. to 4 p.m. Though they did end up working past 4 p.m. most days. For support, I took off mornings at the gym so I could arrive every day at 4 a.m. with them. Every morning when I got there, I'd go to the back and give each of them a big hug. Being there that early also gave me good quiet time to sort through all the due diligence requests. It went right down to the wire, but those dudes finished the job. It was an amazing feat. I will never forget those homeboys.

That month we also had a huge job for YESCO, doing the fence banners for the Fontainebleau (which was the newest Vegas casino) construction site. Luckily it was late October, and I was able to give Manny, Francisco, and Herbie a few days off before they tackled that one. They were simply the best.

At this point in the deal's due diligence, we hit some pretty major snags. I wasn't sure the deal would go through, and to be completely honest I wasn't sure if I even still wanted to do it.

My little business I started in my underpants in Belmont Shores, Long Beach, Calif. had become the biggest grand format printing company in what was perhaps the biggest print city in the country. I had no personal life, was majorly lacking in sleep, had a through-the-roof stress level – but I started thinking to myself that maybe I could do it a couple more years. If I could make it that far alive. The only personal things I still did was walking the pups and going to the gym. I wasn't even reading books anymore. But I had *so many* opportunities on the horizon, especially through my partnership with the Raiders and Allegiant Stadium.

November was the mother of all months: $830K in sales. We were at our max with two shifts going. The only way I could continue to scale the business was by adding a third shift, and somehow incorporating a Sunday shift into that. The setup at that time was working really well – I had the second shift working Tuesday to Saturday. There were a few reasons for that. Number one, working with the Raiders and MGM, we always had jobs sent in on Saturdays. Especially when the Raiders had a home game that week. If we didn't have a Saturday crew, I'd have to ask people to come in on the weekends. They'd get paid overtime, but most of them still didn't want to do it. A built-in Saturday shift was perfect, and the guys on that shift actually liked having Mondays off.

Being short a crew on Mondays after 5 p.m. was a little tough, but my thought process was that on Saturdays the second shift guys wouldn't have the hour-to-hour interruptions of rush jobs, customers coming in, and production schedule changes. They could focus on the jobs due that day, and then ensure they cleared out every single other job on the racks, no matter when they were due, so the first shift guys came in on Monday mornings with an absolutely clean plate. It worked really well.

* * *

Remember Heather from the PAC-12? The one I gave that free poster board to back in 2010? She continued to pay me back in November by giving us the graphics package to the PAC-12 Football Championship Game which was scheduled for the first time at Allegiant Stadium, the first week of December. At the beginning of summer, we had started building a branding opportunities deck for Allegiant Stadium for anyone planning events there. We walked the stadium with Raiders and Allegiant folks, identified areas we could brand, took pictures, and then went back and measured all those areas afterward. We put together a comprehensive deck that had pictures, descriptions, sizes, materials, prices, and even artwork templates. We got it approved by the stadium; and Heather was the first one we sent it to (in an official manner). The deck was 126 pages long, and I was expecting she'd have it for a week and select a handful of areas. Nope. I got it back about an hour later and she said, "Okay, let's do it." Which ones, I asked? "All of it," she said. Whoa! Wasn't expecting that at all – it would be a massive job. I loved Heather, she did not fuck around.

This job would be a tight turnaround. We were doing just about every brandable surface in the stadium, and 75% of the designs/graphics were going to include the two teams competing for the PAC-12 Championship. The races in both divisions were super tight with no clear leaders. We were able to get going on the generic PAC-12 branded items, but we'd have to wait until the division winners were settled to begin printing stuff with team logos.

Some of the items we were doing for the game were fabric banners on the field walls, locker rooms completely wrapped, exterior stairs and windows wrapped, clubs and suites wrapped – it was pretty crazy. Plus, we only had a five-day window to install it. We had to wait on the sidelines for when the game ended to begin removing everything we had installed. The reason is, Allegiant Stadium was the premier venue in the country, and their event schedule was packed with events right before and after the PAC-12 game.

The races to win the PAC-12 divisions came down to the very last week. The PAC-12 had a rad designer, and he had designs prepared for the top six teams in advance. The game ended up pitting Utah against Oregon, and once announced, we were off to the races. We had all eight of our in-house installers on this one, and we started installing on Monday, Nov. 29th for the game on that Friday night, Dec. 3rd. Everyone at S.I. was pulling days of 12 hours-plus – the production team at the shop, and installers at the stadium. I was driving back and forth from the shop to the stadium to deliver more printed items several times a day, into the evenings. That week might have been the hardest we ever worked at S.I. Most of the installers worked from 6 a.m. to 11 p.m. every day.

To step back a bit, let's look at one of the biggest lessons I ever learned on installations, and it came from my old friend Patrick from the NBA at the All-Star Game in Phoenix in 2009. When you have a big install, you also have a customer responsible to his or her superiors for this install. Your top priority is ensuring the customer feels comfortable that the install is being handled and is on schedule. What prompted him to tell me this was, in Phoenix we did a lot of the little things first. We were doing it this way because either those graphics were in the top box, or maybe the first thing unloaded, or maybe just because the installer thought it was easiest. After the first two days in Phoenix, we were on track and had a ton of the little stuff installed, stuff that wasn't highly visible. But there were six big, huge towers and three big-ass stages that were the most visible items, and they didn't have anything on them yet. So even though Patrick is on the ground and knows we're on track, to his bosses across the street, or driving by or looking down on the job from the roof of the arena, it looked like nothing much had been completed. This causes stress for the boss, which causes stress for Patrick, which causes stress for me. The customer is the most important thing, folks. Without the customer you don't have the work, which means you don't have a business. By putting the big things up first, the customers and their bosses see the progress, remain calm, and your job is easier. If you cause the customer stress and pain on the install, they will remember next time they award a big job. It might be doing things backward, or out of order, but *so what?* You must make the customer happy. Put those big, visible things up first. Let your customer be calm and happy. This is important. It will get you their next job every time. This coming from a guy with the title of Senior Director of Events and Attractions for the NBA.

With this in mind, I asked the production team for some of the bigger items first at Allegiant. The big stairs wraps in the front because they were highly visible from the front gate. The big windows on the sides of the stadium because they were highly visible from the 15 freeway on the east side and the main parking lot on the west side. And most importantly, the fabric sideline walls. These would be highly visible to the PAC-12 staff and indicate we were on track, so they needn't worry. We also had to keep things in mind like the players' arrivals, media days, etc. We had to have the locker rooms done before the players came to the stadium for the first time for their walkthroughs. We had to have certain clubs and press rooms done for the media and events. It was a lot.

We pulled it all off on time, of course. We had no choice – a nationally televised football game at the raddest new stadium in the whole country. There was no such thing as failing. We were told we had to be finished by noon on game day, and we were there until the last hour. The last things up were the fabric corners on the field walls. Super stressful job, but so worth how it makes you feel at the end when you watch all your hard work on TV, knowing millions of people see it. Even better knowing you have a super-stoked customer.

* * *

I mentioned earlier the hours and hard work we were putting in. This was not just for the PAC-12, but across the board, and was pretty much Screaming Images' trademark for 20 years. We had ten capable local competitors but got these big jobs every time because of our accomplishments, reputation and record. Every potential teammate who visited to interview for a position with S.I. was informed of this. They would have to work hard. I'd even gotten to where to get this point across to them before they'd sign on, I'd try to scare them with it. We were the best grand format printing company in town because we worked harder than everyone else. This was our reputation. Simple as that.

* * *

Now we're into December and trying to close the sale of my company before the end of the year. A few issues remained, and overall, I wasn't feeling warm and fuzzy. My biggest issues were ensuring my customers would be cared for. And that my teammates' futures would be secure. There were also a few business details left to sort out that I won't mention because of legality issues. This entire process had been brutal.

We had two big jobs left this year, a job for Oklahoma City Thunder doing thousands of seat covers for their basketball arena, and the Las Vegas Bowl football game, hosted for the first time at Allegiant Stadium.

Here, near the end of the S.I. story, I'll reiterate some of the actions and ideals that put me in the position I was in at that moment – selling the company I built from scratch for multi-million dollars. I did things differently. It was plain to see, and it was no secret. I was very clear with everyone about the methods I used. I was doing things differently than everyone else. There were no sets or standards in the printing industry, or any other industry for that matter, that I was bound to. I was not dependent upon profit margins, burden rates, or private equity.

I self-funded the entire journey with no business loans, lines of credit, or other type of financial assistance. I had disrupted the printing industry, and the city of Las Vegas. I took risk after risk and blazed new trails. I did it all while maintaining all required licenses, including contractor's licenses, and insurance levels that met the requirements of not only MGM, but also the NBA, NFL, NHL, and the NCAA. Everything I did was above board, and I was extremely proud of that. I had marketed myself and my company in a way no one else had previously. I made myself stand out in a crowd. I out-worked and out-hustled every other grand format printing company in Vegas. Screaming Images was a brand that was not just known nationally, but all over the world.

***

The 2021 SRS Distribution Las Vegas Bowl game was set for Dec. 30th at Allegiant Stadium. Much like the PAC-12 Championship game three weeks prior, we would only have a short time window to install everything. Unlike the PAC-12 game, we already knew the teams playing, three weeks prior. It was Arizona State from the PAC-12 versus Wisconsin from the Big Ten, so we got the artwork earlier. The scope wasn't as big as the PAC-12 game, but we still had a ton to do, and the biggest piece was the fabric field wall banners. Two nationally televised football games in a three-week period – we were on a roll.

We were having our best year ever, even with the horrible first quarter. We would surpass $7.2 million in sales, up from $6.3 million the year before. A pretty big piece of my mind was telling myself I could handle this stress level for a few more years. I kept going back and forth and wasn't sleeping a hell of a lot.

I did my best to keep the company sale negotiations a secret. I confided in only one person working for me, and that person was helping me funnel details and info to the buyers so we could complete due diligence. Of course, there had been rumors the last 90 days that I was selling to this one company in the Southwest, and that company had actually been in the mix for a while but was eliminated in May when I signed the LOI from the Midwest company. Unfortunately, the rumors originated from one of my vendors and circulated through my employees. None of what was being said was accurate. I chose the buyer based not only on the financial offer, but also for what I thought at the time would be best for my customers and my teammates.

Game week came for the bowl game, and we were ready. I had known the executive director for the game for several years. It used to be played at Sam Boyd Stadium, over by my old shop on Boulder Ranch, and we'd done the graphics for the game several times. But moving it to the country's premier football stadium put the game on a whole different level. We blasted through all the printing on schedule, our installers put things up at an expedited clip, and everything looked amazing. Every time I walked by an ESPN person on the field, they told me what a great job we were doing.

I walked the playing field at Allegiant Stadium during this install knowing this would be my last job owning Screaming Images. We finished on the morning of Dec. 30th. I went back to the shop, hugged Charlie, Ranger, and Finch, worked at the shop until 4 p.m., packed up the pups and headed home.

I had decided the night before we finished the bowl game that I was killing myself. All I was doing was working and it wasn't fair to me, but even more importantly it wasn't fair to my pups. I wanted to return to having a normal life, and the deal I made with the buyer from the Midwest was supposed to help me get there. I didn't want a lot, really. I wanted to be able to go to the gym and walk the pups in the morning without having to look at my watch. I wanted to be able to have a social life again. I didn't want to have to go to bed by 8 p.m. so I could wake up at 2:30 a.m. I wanted a vacation once a year. I wanted Finch to be able to grow up on our boat like Scout had. All pretty normal things I hadn't had for a very long time.

I arrived at the shop at 6975 S. Decatur on Dec. 31st, at 6 a.m., as usual, with the pups. The final sale documents were all in my inbox waiting. The lawyers and accountants had signed off on everything. It was a slow day at the shop, being the last day of the year, and a Friday. I spoke with all the shop guys, and pretended like it was a normal day, even though it wasn't. The guys from the Midwest were coming to the shop on Tuesday, Jan. 4th, and that was the day I would announce everything to my team. Right around 11 a.m. I went into my office, called in the pups, and shut the door. I went through and signed all the electronic documents that would sell my life's work. I immediately was emailed from the other team's lawyers stating the documents were received and in order. I made a cup of tea and sat in my office quietly for about an hour before I received another notice via email from the other side. The money had been transferred. I opened my online account to check, and sure as shit, there it was. I was no longer the owner of Screaming Images. Unknowingly to me, things would get even crazier from here. But maybe that's another book.

Boulder Ranch Shop —
Working Class Since 2002

Boulder Ranch Shop —
Front Office

Boulder Ranch Shop

Boulder Ranch Shop —
First 10' Printer

Boulder Ranch Shop —
Punk Rock Wall

Boulder Ranch Shop

Decatur Shop —
Local News Interview

Decatur Shop —
Live on Fox 5 News

Decatur shop —
Ronda Rousey UFC

Decatur Shop — Tribute Window

Decatur Shop — Breakroom

Decatur Shop —
Sublime Stage Backdrop

Decatur Shop —
Scout and Ranger
Poppy's Office

Decatur Shop —
Charlie Front Office

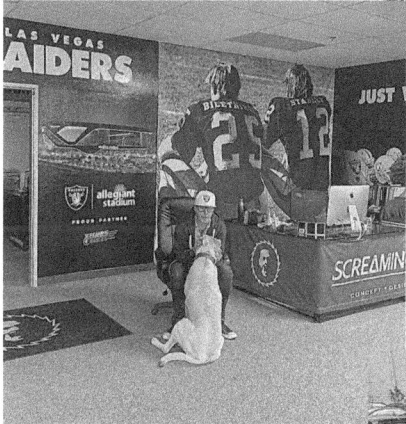

Decatur Shop —
Poppy and Charlie

Decatur Shop —
Delivery Truck

S.I. Branded Bucket Truck
at Mandalay Bay

Decatur Shop —
Rugby Sevens Banners

Decatur Shop —
Gene Simmons Bass

Decatur Shop —
Scout in Her Poppy's Office

EPILOGUE

"Crown of Thorns"
- *Social Distortion*

Cheers to all the risk takers. If it was easy everyone would do it.

I remember one night in the late 1990s, at a bar with my teammates after a softball game in Simi Valley. The team was Rotten's Row. We all were discussing what we would do for a living if we had our choice. Three of the four guys I was with said professional golfer. I thought, *What?* Boring. My choice was rock star. Without even thinking.

I'm a very lucky guy. I worked for, and became friends with, people in bands that I loved when I was a kid (and still love). Members of some killer bands even visited my shop. Mike and Ron from T.S.O.L., Lars from Rancid, Jonny from Social D, the Interrupters, Tony from Ill Repute, Big Bob from Agression. Lars even came to a Raiders game and sat with us in our company/season seats.

I walked through sports stadiums and facilities that I'd seen on TV since I was a kid. I did projects for the World Series, NBA All-Star Game, NBA Finals, NHL All-Star Game, NHL Awards Show, NHL Finals, Super Bowl, Pro Bowl, and NFL Draft. I worked for six NFL teams directly – and even got to stand on the sidelines for NFL and NCAA games. Multiple times. And, most of all, I got to work for my all-time favorite team, the Raiders, and had a pretty big hand in their brand-new stadium and moving to Vegas. I was living the dream.

Everything I've done my entire life has been unconventional. It was never intentional; it's just the way I am. I always liked the deep track on albums over songs played on the radio. I always liked the items on the menu that were first to be eliminated. I always liked the jeans and shoes that would be discontinued. I liked the red Vans better than the blue Vans as a kid.

I built my business unconventionally, too. Most people acquire some capital, write a business plan, and hope they can pull it off. I started my company while in debt, with no capital, no college degree, and no business-type experience. All I had was industry knowledge. I did it for one reason: to take care of the customers better than the companies I had worked for. I had a dream, not a plan.

For the first 6 to 12 months I was self-employed, I was just waiting for it to collapse – but it didn't. I kept busting ass, kept taking risks, and it kept working out. I worked really, really hard, and believed in myself. The years prior to starting S.I., I drank too much, did too many drugs, had horrible credit, was irresponsible, got in trouble – the works. But slowly, once I started S.I., I began turning my personal life around.

I recognized after the first two years that if I wanted to keep this going, I needed to move away from the beach and grow up. I chose Las Vegas for three reasons. The airport there made it easier to travel; I wanted to buy a house; and I wanted to get a dog.

The first two didn't make me grow up. It was the third. Scout. I fell in love with her immediately. She'd look up at me with those big, beautiful eyes, tail wagging, and I just knew I would do whatever it took to give her the best life.

My plan moving to Vegas was to continue exactly what I had been doing – focusing on sports teams and stadiums. I never thought in my wildest dreams I'd work in the casinos; that I'd have a big shop and 50 employees; that I would pretty much take over the whole city, print-and-install-wise.

I wish I could say that it was all fun and games, and it was all easy – but it wasn't. It took a lot out of me. I gave up a lot of personal time and things to get the business to the level it ended up at. But looking back at it all now, it was worth it. I'm proud of everything I accomplished.

Anyhow… If this book inspires someone, or if something I did, or the way I did it influences even one person, I'd be super stoked. Anyone can do it if they're willing to put in the time and effort. That's the message here.

J.S. / S.I. Summer 2024

MENTORS AND THANK YOU'S

"Under Your Influence"

- *Dag Nasty*

I've had a lot of help along the way. From the early days when my bosses let me slide on my shenanigans because they saw something special in me and taught me the trade. To the people that gave me the first big jobs that helped me get S.I. started. To the people in Las Vegas who trusted me with their work, referred me to others, and spread the word about me being a good vendor. And especially to the people that worked with me at the two shops and helped me bust out all of that work.

HUGE THANKS TO ALL OF YOU. I COULDN'T HAVE DONE IT WITHOUT YOU.

Gene Mayer	Wayne Odekirk
Jim Pickert	Jeff Odekirk
John Mazeika	Drew Livingston
Tim Wild	Steve Hutchison
Tom Wilhelm	Robert Alvarado
Tim Horan	Patrick Mahoney
Keith Jajko	Heather Vaughan
Chris Coffey	Pat Carrigan
Kevin Holmes	Andy Garcia
Sean De La Cruz	Rutger Jansen
Scott McCormack	Cathy Gelpi Popick
Vic Maukauskas	Dennis Lafontaine
Gabe Chavez	Christa Meyrick
Chris Clark	Laura D'Amore
Adam Weisberg	Chloe Janfaza
Mick Akers	Chris Sotiropolous
Scott Paul	Shannon Miller
Chris Bloyer	Nick Gennarelli

Hatcher Parnell
Brent Depaepe
Jason Depaepe
Cory Hilliard
Steve Pizzi
Michelle Massaro
Dan McAllister
Jason Baker
Dan McGowan
Aimee Wenske
JR Leake
Daren Libonati
Eric Kovac
Bud Pico
Blake Victor
Todd McElyea
Branan Allison
Rob Cornelius
John Saccenti
Doug Henry
Chris Brull
Mark Stern
Shawn Stern
Todd Huber
Jack Grisham
Mike Roche
Ron Emory
Jonny 2 Bags
Shane Trulin
Mike Ness
Tony Cortez
John Gilhooley
Dan Hodge

Josh Sribour
Scotty Hayes
Matt Vanderpool
Paul Whitehead
Rich Purvis
Mark Pachowitz
Lacey Flynn
Jeremy Bowe
Jamie Gallegos
Rob Cardenas
Diana Meng
Ashley Craven
Danielle Culberson
Josh Nevels
Tim Nevels
Brian Carter
Fred Magenheimer
Jorge Cornejo
Ricardo Comprido
Nicole Craig
Denise LaForest
John Camp
Frank Whybourne
Wes Whybourne
Jerry Catania
Jason Allen
Steve Tinkler
Eric Devaney
Mike Turturro
Brian Saliba
Nick Stevens
Seth Fischer

MOST OF ALL:

SCOUT RANGER CHARLIE & FINCH

If I left someone important off this list – I am truly sorry.

www.ingramcontent.com/pod-product-compliance
Lightning Source LLC
Chambersburg PA
CBHW052014030426
42335CB00026B/3148